CLASSIC

TSUKEMEN

SAPPORO ICHIBAN

PRAISE FOR

HOMEMADE RAMEN

"*Homemade Ramen* is the most comprehensive breakdown of ramen I've ever seen—everything from how to achieve various clarities in the broth to what each chicken part contributes to your stock, and that's just the beginning. The use of tapioca starch in Sho Spaeth's ramen noodles is ingenious, but I wouldn't expect anything less from this ramen-savant. This book will make a ramen scholar out of you."
—SOHLA EL-WAYLLY, best-selling author of *Start Here*

"When I started my ramen journey there was nothing in English to read to guide me. If only a book like *Homemade Ramen* had been available. It demystifies everything!!"
—IVAN ORKIN, chef and owner of Ivan Ramen

"Sho Spaeth has crafted the ultimate guide to the world of ramen—an essential companion for every cook who cherishes the art of perfect noodles. . . . [A] must-have for ramen enthusiasts and culinary adventurers alike."
—NIK SHARMA, best-selling author of *The Flavor Equation* and *Veg-Table*

"Whether you're a ramen novice or a seasoned pro, you'll find something to savor in these pages. Sho Spaeth's expertise, combined with his infectious enthusiasm, will give you the tools, techniques, and knowledge to make incredible ramen at home, and have fun doing it. This isn't just a cookbook—it's an invitation into Sho's obsession. And trust me, you'll be glad you accepted."
—J. KENJI LÓPEZ-ALT, best-selling author of *The Food Lab* and *The Wok*

"Sho Spaeth is arguably one of the most fastidious, meticulous ramen makers in the United States, and this book is an obvious demonstration of his dedication to understanding ramen. I do not think there is a book that explores ramen in more depth in the English language. This book unquestionably pushes the craft of ramen forward, for both home cooks and professionals alike."
—MIKE SATINOVER, chef and owner of Akahoshi Ramen (aka Ramen Lord)

"Sho Spaeth does his homework. *Homemade Ramen* is the first ramen cookbook that genuinely supports a home cook's journey into this mystifying craft and introduces building a foundation for making "kodawari" ramen at home."
—KEIZO SHIMAMOTO, founder of Ramen Shack

“Despite the title, Sho Spaeth’s work on *Homemade Ramen* brings restaurant-level knowledge to anyone aspiring to dive into making ramen at home. Studded with recipes, but more importantly, packed with ideas, this book will prove invaluable for years to come.”
—**SCOTT LaCHAPELLE,** chef at Pickerel

“Sho Spaeth’s enthusiasm for ramen is the heartbeat of this cookbook. His boundless passion transforms every broth, hand-pulled noodle, and vibrant topping into a celebration of flavor and culture. His personal insights and infectious passion turn this cookbook into an inspiring manifesto—inviting you to reimagine your kitchen as a creative haven where every bowl of ramen celebrates warmth, innovation, and tradition.”
—**JONATHAN ZARAGOZA,** chef

“As with chess, ramen can be enjoyed at the most basic and accessible level while also having near-infinite depth beneath the surface. *Homemade Ramen* is the essential explorer’s guide to that universe. Take this book and graduate from your dorm-room instant ramen to the next plane of soupy enlightenment.”
—**ERIC HUANG,** chef and founder of Pecking House

“The amount of knowledge that Sho Spaeth has on the ‘science of ramen’ is vast, and being able to translate that knowledge into recipes for home cooks is extremely rare. I personally have never seen a ramen book this in-depth and accurate published in English.”
—**ERIK BENTZ,** chef and co-owner of Café Mochiko

“In this masterful collection of recipes, history, and vivid technical explainers, Sho Spaeth presents ramen not as an impossibly complex set of rules and ratios but as a matter of joyous tasks that any home cook with a bit of *oomph* can embrace one by one.”
—**ELAZAR SONTAG,** restaurant editor at *Bon Appetit*

“Beyond the fact that they both involve doughs, ramen is a lot like bread: many moving parts, but none all that complicated to pull off when considered in isolation. Sho Spaeth is a wise and knowing guide to the art and science of ramen making, and *Homemade Ramen* is the practical manual to ramen I did not know I’ve always wanted!”
—**ANDREW JANJIGIAN,** head baker at the *Wordloaf* newsletter, and author of *Breaducation*

HOMEMADE RAMEN

HOMEMADE RAMEN

SHO SPAETH

PHOTOGRAPHY BY LINDA XIAO

W. W. NORTON & COMPANY
Independent Publishers Since 1923

For Aya

CONTENTS

INTRODUCTION

I MUST have been about ten years old when I realized I was a ramen pedant.

My best friend, Nick, was visiting Japan for the first time. For years, I'd raved about the wonders of Yotsukura, the sleepy seaside town in Fukushima Prefecture where my extended family lives: the buzz-saw wall of sound of the cicadas in summer; the salted salmon we'd eat for breakfast; the futuristic arcade games; the vending machines that sold everything from ice cream to beer and cigarettes; and, of course, the ramen.

Nick knew ramen was my favorite food, but any attempt on my part to differentiate it from the instant Sapporo Ichiban we'd occasionally eat at my house in New Delhi, where we both lived, would run up against the limits of my vocabulary. Ramen—real ramen—was just different, I'd say; similar, of course, in almost every way—the clear broth, the saltiness, the springy noodles—but better, much better. I had no idea how ramen was made, so any description of the superiority of "real" ramen would end in exasperation. "You just have to try it," I'd say, although neither of us believed he'd ever get the opportunity.

And then, all of a sudden, he was sitting in my grandmother's house and my cousin Fumiko was generously offering to drive us over to Aizuppo, my favorite ramen spot. And for the first time in my life I felt the peculiar anxiety surrounding issues of taste and discernment: what if what I love isn't any good?

I ordered my usual for both of us: the standard chuka soba with extra menma, or seasoned bamboo shoots, and a side order of gyoza. When our ramen arrived, any worries I had about the quality of the food evaporated: it was just as good as I'd remembered it. I turned to Nick to ask him how he liked it but stopped midsentence when I saw him gingerly lowering a pile of noodles into his soup spoon with his chopsticks.

"What are you doing?" I hissed. I explained—in a whisper, trying to convey my embarrassment to Nick without drawing the attention of the servers or other customers—that the noodles were best enjoyed straight out of the soup; that the proper method for getting them into your mouth was less about shoveling than inhaling; that while a foreigner might be forgiven for suboptimal chopsticks skills, using the soupspoon for noodles wasn't done—that it was, probably, disrespectful.

In response, Nick pointed to Fumiko, who deftly placed a small coil of noodles in her soupspoon as we both watched, dipped it into the broth, and then tipped the contents into her mouth.

I think a lot about that moment, particularly now, since the primary focus of my work as a food writer is giving readers the proper context for the different foods people eat: why they're prepared the way they are, why they're eaten at certain occasions or times of day or seasons, how they're typically enjoyed. The main lessons I've drawn from that experience are ones of humility: enthusiasm, no matter how genuine, isn't a substitute for knowledge and understanding; a gentle suggestion works better than a harangue;

there's no one right way to eat any food, let alone ramen; and no one likes an asshole.

I tried to keep those lessons in mind as I wrote this cookbook, particularly because ramen isn't a singular dish. Like pizza, or hamburgers, or pho, or any food that achieves the kind of popularity that results in subcategories and styles, ramen is a bundle of traditions, conventions, cultural trends, proscriptions, and crazed opinions. What I hope to do here is offer insight into those traditions, elucidate core techniques, and demonstrate different general styles of ramen: light, clear soups or thick and creamy soups; ramen you dip into soup, like soba, known as tsukemen; and soup-less ramen, also known as mazemen and abura soba.

Above all, I want to show you that making great ramen at home isn't hard. If you've prepared instant ramen on a stovetop, you've already mastered the single most important technique behind making a bowl of noodle soup: bringing water to a boil.

That may sound a little reductive, and yet it's true. The primary differences between a bowl of instant ramen and a bowl of noodles at a ramen restaurant have to do with time and temperature. While the elements of a bowl of restaurant ramen—the broth, many of the toppings, the seasoning, the aromatic oils and fats—take far longer to make than a bowl of cupped noodles, they can all be prepared by bringing a pot of liquid to a boil. Further, each of those elements can be prepared *well* by maintaining the temperature of the liquid at just under a boil.

To put it another way, if you can boil water, you can make ramen. If you can simmer water, you can make great ramen.

I don't mean to denigrate the skills of cooks toiling away in ramen restaurants all over the world, and I'm not trying to say their long hours of labor can be reduced to a catchphrase, that they are merely "simmerers of liquids." The difference between making a couple of good bowls of ramen on a weekend and making a good bowl of ramen hundreds of times a day, every day, is so vast as to be incomprehensible.

However, I believe that the difference between good ramen and great ramen is one of degrees, both literal and figurative; that the difference between a cook who makes good ramen and one who makes great ramen is less about culinary technique than about culinary knowledge; and that someone who understands the physical and chemical consequences of cooking a range of things—meat, seafood, vegetables, stock—at 205°F (96°C) rather than 212°F (100°C) will make a superior bowl of noodles. Making great ramen is less about muscle memory and repetitive mastery than making great sushi or a stunning pâté en croûte, but it nevertheless requires the same attention to small details, the same reverence for fine distinctions.

"TO PUT IT ANOTHER WAY, IF YOU CAN BOIL WATER, YOU CAN MAKE RAMEN. IF YOU CAN SIMMER WATER, YOU CAN MAKE GREAT RAMEN."

The purpose of this book is to furnish home cooks of all proficiencies with the basic culinary knowledge required to appreciate all the small details that make a bowl of ramen amazing. I hope you come away from it knowing that the only obstacles between you and a stellar homemade bowl of ramen are the necessary will and inclination.

II

A VERY BRIEF HISTORY OF RAMEN;

OR, WHY RAMEN IS DESIGNED FOR THE HOME COOK

RAMEN is a thoroughly modern dish, one whose provenance can be traced through the great power conflicts of the early twentieth century, postindustrialization, and global trade.

Japanese cuisine can be split into three categories: Japanese food (washoku); food inspired by Chinese cuisine (chuka riori); and food inspired by Western cuisine (yoshoku). The fact that China and "the West" figure so largely in Japan's cuisine has to do with the country's unique history. From the seventeenth to the nineteenth century, Japan observed a strict policy of isolationism: Japanese were forbidden from leaving the island nation on pain of death, and international trade was severely restricted. The goal of this policy was to guard the islands against the incursion of colonial powers, specifically the Spanish and the Portuguese, and to safeguard the population against Christian missionaries, whose religion was seen as a threat to the established order.

However, Japan wasn't entirely cut off from the world. Chinese and Dutch merchants were allowed to operate at the port of Nagasaki, where most trade with the outside world took place, and the small communities that were established to offer these traders food, lodging, and entertainment are generally believed to be where Japanese cuisine was first infiltrated by foreign influences.* It was in Nagasaki and the surrounding area where Chinese noodle soups, with wheat noodles and broths made from animal bones, rather than dried fish, first started to gain popularity; this is also where cutlets—thin slabs of meat, battered and fried in vats of animal fat—were introduced, courtesy of the Dutch traders. These two dishes, originally foreign foods—ramen and katsu—would eventually become as representative of Japanese cuisine around the world as sushi, and their provenances are reflected in their borrowed names, transliterated as they are from Chinese and Dutch, respectively.

It wasn't until the beginning of the twentieth century that Chinese cuisine began to gain mainstream popularity in Japan. From 1906 to 1923, the number of restaurants serving Chinese food in Tokyo grew from two to fifteen hundred, and among them was the legendary ramen shop Rairaiken,† which opened in 1910 and was the first restaurant in the country to serve so-called "shina soba,"‡ or "Chinese noodles," consisting of wheat noodles in a meat-based broth. The growing interest in Chinese cuisine was due in part to the fact that the food had become more fashionable and viewed with less suspicion as the Japanese embraced their country's imperial ambitions and expansion into China. Chinese cuisine was everywhere, from cookery columns in popular women's

* Barak Kushner, *Slurp! A Social and Culinary History of Ramen-Japan's Favorite Noodle Soup* (Global Oriental, 2012), p. 59.

† Katarzyna J. Cwiertka, *Modern Japanese Cuisine: Food, Power, and National Identity* (Reaktion Books, 2006), p. 144.

‡ While you'll still see some ramen shops that refer to ramen as "shina soba," it is generally considered a pejorative term, since the kanji character for "shina" implies that China is a lesser country.

magazines to menus created by the Japanese military apparatus. Like early Meiji-era efforts to mimic Western diets high in meat and fat to make the population more robust, the Japanese government sought to encourage its people to incorporate elements of the Chinese diet, which was similarly high in meat and fat yet more approachable for the population because of the use of soy sauce as a primary seasoning ingredient. The diet's heavy reliance on wheat-based foods, like dumplings and noodles, also aligned with the rationing of rice so that troops were guaranteed relatively large rations of rice.*

That introduction to a mainstream diet of wheat-based foods set the stage for what would become a ramen boom in the postwar era. After Japan's defeat in World War II, food was scarce, and with the cheap wheat made available by the occupying American forces, the Japanese government encouraged the population to eat wheat-based foods—specifically, bread. The confluence of cheap wheat and famine inspired Momofuku Ando, an immigrant from Formosa (now Taiwan) to wonder why, as the Japanese were presumably more familiar with noodles than with bread, the government wasn't encouraging the population to eat wheat noodles instead. The response to his query from government officials was that there were no reliable producers of wheat noodles, which spurred Ando to start producing the noodles himself.

Ando would go on to develop the first instant noodle product, Cup Noodle, and with that, ramen became a bifurcated food. Japanese consumers could order ramen in restaurants—noodle soup made with meat broths and wheat-based alkaline noodles—or they could purchase instant ramen at the store—noodle soup made by adding boiling water to precooked mass-produced wheat alkaline noodles that contained a dehydrated meat-based broth base. But unlike other foreign dishes that entered the Japanese culinary lexicon, such as tonkatsu, croquettes, stir-fries, and dumplings, ramen didn't translate immediately to the home kitchen.

The lack of interest on the part of the Japanese home cook in preparing ramen at home can almost certainly be chalked up to ramen's ubiquity: if you want to eat ramen in Japan, you have any number of restaurants to choose from, and should you instead want to eat ramen at home, you can buy one of many excellent instant varieties that are made in a matter of minutes.

The belief that making ramen is an onerous task has been exacerbated in part by the rise of kodawari ramen shops in the 1990s. "Kodawari" can be translated (simply) as "the pursuit of perfection," and kodawari ramen shops were run by chefs who sought to refine the various elements that go into a bowl of ramen to an exaggerated degree, each individual component prepared to the best of their ability: the soup lovingly tended to, infused with the finest meats and dried seafood; the noodles—their geometry, the proportions of their ingredients, the character and strength of their bounce and spring—carefully matched to the soup; and the toppings, a variety of delectably prepared dishes in their own right, chosen to complement the seasonings in the soup and the texture of the noodles. Kodawari ramen was and is a movement that seeks to transform the prosaic activity of preparing noodle soup into a finely honed craft, like preparing sushi, and around it has sprung up a mythos of ramen-making as an abstruse practice almost unachievable by mere mortals.

However, the very qualities that make ramen well suited to fast-food restaurants and for instant packaged products, as well as the increasingly sophisticated kodawari ramen shops, are what make it well suited to the modern

---

* Cwiertka, *Modern Japanese Cuisine*, p. 122.

home kitchen. Both in restaurants and at instant noodle companies, the bowl of ramen has been broken down into its various components. There are the alkaline wheat noodles, the various toppings, and the soup itself, which in turn can be further broken down into broth, seasoning, and flavorful oil.

For a ramen shop, preparing each of these components separately offers three benefits: consistency, efficiency, and variety. With each of the components laid out in front of the cook, assembling a bowl of ramen is less a matter of creativity than of painting by numbers: every bowl receives a set quantity of noodles, cooked to order, a set amount of broth with a set amount of seasoning sauce and of flavorful fat, and a set amount of various toppings. Anyone in the kitchen can put together a bowl of ramen as long as they can follow instructions, and it should be just as good as if it were made by the chef or cook who came up with the recipes for every element in the bowl. The component nature of this approach also offers ramen shops the ability to mix and match various elements. For example, a shop can produce three different bowls of ramen from the same soup, noodles, and toppings if it has three different seasoning bases. Further, the number of different types of ramen increases multiplicatively with the addition of other component variations—add another broth, and you can make six different kinds of ramen; add another topping, like a cabbage and meat stir-fry, and you can produce twelve different types of ramen; and so on.

The instant noodle industry similarly takes advantage of this deconstructed approach,

Instant ramen packets and what's inside

which is evident in the way their products are packaged—sachets for seasoning and (sometimes multiple) flavorful oils, etc.—and by the fact that many instant noodle companies use the same brick of fried noodles across their entire range of instant noodle soups.

But in the end, homemade ramen can be as much a convenience food as ramen made from a packet or ordered at a shop; convenience is written into ramen's DNA.

HOW TO USE THIS BOOK

LET me walk you through the way I make a bowl of ramen for lunch.

It could be a Tuesday during a busy work week or a lazy Sunday morning. The day of the week doesn't matter. If I have two hours available for lunch or just thirty minutes, the process is the same.

First I put a pot of water on to boil. As the water heats up, I root around in my refrigerator and freezer for the basic components of the meal: a serving of noodles I've made myself or bought; a selection of deli containers with broth, tare, and one or two aromatic fats; an allium of some kind, usually a scallion or naga negi (Welsh onion); a slice or two of roasted or braised pork, or perhaps some poached chicken; and a green vegetable, whether left over from a previous meal or a leafy vegetable that I can quickly blanch in the boiling water before cooking the noodles. I put the broth in another pot to bring it to a simmer, then fill a serving bowl with tap water and stick it in the microwave, on high, for 3 minutes. I pull out two tablespoon measures, one for the tare and one for the fat(s), and then I make any further preparation the ingredients may require: slicing the onion, torching or broiling the pork slices. I also grab a bottle of rice vinegar and a grinder of white pepper from my pantry.

Once the water comes to a boil, I blanch the leafy greens, if necessary; if not, I wait until the microwave dings and the broth has come to a simmer, then I add the noodles to the boiling water and set the timer. The noodles cook quickly, so I move quickly too: I increase the heat under the simmering broth to high, dump out the warming water from the serving bowl and add the fat(s) and the tare to it, along with a little sliced onion, a grind or two of white pepper, and a little bit of vinegar. I ladle in the boiling broth and wait impatiently for the noodle timer. Then I drain the noodles thoroughly, shaking off as much of the cooking water as I can, add them to the bowl, and, using chopsticks, give them a little shake and a lift and a fold, the better to offer a platform for the toppings, which I then layer on—artfully arranged or just in a heap.

A complete bowl of ramen, with almost everything made from scratch, prepared in about 15 minutes.

While this book contains detailed recipes for composed bowls of ramen, the recipes aren't meant to be representative of specific established ramen styles—nor are they meant to be clones of bowls from famous ramen restaurants. If that is what you're interested in, there's a short list of resources in the back that can guide you on your way.

Instead, I am offering you the knowledge I've accumulated over almost two decades of making ramen at home, my understanding of the why's and wherefore's of various techniques. I offer this sheaf of recipes as a guide, as proofs of concepts that embody the principles I believe stand behind a well-made bowl of ramen, and if you follow them as written, you will make many good bowls of ramen. My hope is that this book will make you a better cook, and by that I mean a cook who is more technically proficient but also philosophically inclined to see the value in delayed gratification and the importance—the joy!—of preparation.

Let's return to that bowl of ramen I described making in just 15 minutes. Every element that went into the bowl took longer than that; in many cases, far longer. If you make the noodles from scratch, they will require at least an hour and a half of your time, and they're actually best when aged for several days. The broth, depending on the type, may take anywhere from 2 (made in a pressure cooker) to 12 (cooked in a pot on the stovetop) to 24 hours (for a dashi where the ingredients are soaked in water in the refrigerator overnight). The seasonings can similarly take anywhere from an hour to a day (and can also benefit from aging). My favorite chashu recipe here (see page 277) takes at least 5 days to make properly, 6 if you take into account the time it takes to chill it thoroughly to ensure presentable slices.

Yet despite the long hours required to make its component parts, ramen is fast food, and that describes both the way it's prepared and the way it's meant to be eaten. Anyone who has sat down at a ramen restaurant or made Shin Ramyun for lunch knows this, on both a practical and a psychological level: you order from the menu or open a packet, a bowl appears in front of you almost immediately, and you polish it off in minutes. But by undertaking to make ramen from scratch, you are choosing to participate in all the lengthy processes required for its preparation. This both obviates its convenience and changes the way you will experience it. If you spend all day making all of its components from scratch to end up with a bowl of noodles that takes ten minutes to eat and leaves you with two sinkfuls' worth of dirty dishes, you will not enjoy the process. In fact, you will likely think very hard before ever trying to make ramen from scratch again.

My solution is to do what ramen restaurants and instant ramen manufacturers do: separate the processes of production and service. That means preparing almost everything you need for a bowl of ramen well in advance. This approach offers a convenient method for producing excellent ramen at home *consistently*, with as many elements as you like made entirely from scratch. You could, for example, make the stock on a lazy Sunday, prepare the noodles the following weekend, and start making a tare after you put your kid to bed one night and complete it the next morning while you make your coffee. All of the elements you produce will keep in the fridge or freezer until needed. Working this way means it doesn't require much thought or time when you want to eat a bowl of ramen: it is, again,

"A COMPLETE BOWL OF RAMEN, WITH ALMOST EVERYTHING MADE FROM SCRATCH, PREPARED IN ABOUT 15 MINUTES."

about as simple and straightforward as bringing a pot of water to a boil. Very little mess, very little stress, and you can be assured that the bowl of ramen you make will be better than anything that comes out of a packet.

Since the focus of this approach is on advance preparation, some of the techniques, methods, and recipes I offer in this book are designed to ensure that the disparate elements of each bowl of ramen will be just as good, if not better, days or weeks after they are prepared, which inevitably leads to trade-offs and compromises. For example, I like to cure the meats I use as toppings—pork roasts, chicken breasts, etc.—or marinate them after cooking to increase their refrigerator storage life and prevent the off flavors and odors that may be produced as cooked meat oxidizes over time. Similarly, I prefer noodle recipes that have added starches and other gel stabilizers, like powdered egg white, because they stand up better to prolonged storage in the refrigerator or freezer. And I generally do not add dried seafood products to broths that I plan to store, as their flavor will become muted over time.

There are, however, some preparations that really should be consumed as soon as they've been cooked. For example, a chicken thigh seasoned correctly and cooked with care and attention, until the skin is crisp and the meat is just cooked through, is one of my favorite meat toppings for a bowl of ramen, but many of its virtues start to dissipate precipitously ten minutes after it comes out of the pan. The same could be said about a fresh pork roast, which has a distinctly different texture from that of a cured pork roast, even if the fresh pork roast is still eminently palatable a day after it's been cooked. And the same is true of dashi, the foundational stock of Japanese cuisine; I prefer to make dashi just before using it.

But once you've gotten into the rhythm of making ramen in the way I do, you can easily incorporate those more perishable elements into your bowls. Making dashi takes only about 15 active minutes, and so it's a small thing to prepare a couple of cups of dashi before you start boiling your noodle water; the same is true of cooking a chicken thigh.

There is, finally, another benefit to cooking ramen in this way: it encourages you to view cooking as a continuous process. With many recipes, the cook is encouraged to view the process as having a discrete beginning and end: you start at Point A and gather your ingredients, proceed through Points B to Y as you follow the recipe, and then find yourself at Point Z, with the completed dish in front of you. But preparing ramen the way I'm suggesting isn't intended to produce one singular dish, as if you had planted a single seed and coaxed it into bloom only to achieve a single perfect specimen of fruit. Instead, you are creating the base conditions from which any number of ramen bowls can be prepared, all of a similar quality, much as if you'd tilled a patch of land, chosen for its unique mix of shade and sun, fortified its soil, sown it with various seeds, and then tended this little garden to produce fruit in variety for as long as the growing season allows.

A little effort produces outsized rewards, and once you find how easy it is to prepare broths and stocks and seasonings and toppings at your leisure, you'll realize that this method opens up many avenues for creativity and inspiration, as well as opportunities to reduce waste. And once you understand how many different kitchen odds and ends can be dropped into a soup pot, and how you can use those various soups that result, you'll never look at a picked-over roasted pork shoulder the same way again.

IV

RAMEN: DEFINITIONS AND DETAILS

EVERY bowl of ramen can be broken down into five components.

① **TARE (SEASONING):** The word "tare" translates from Japanese as "sauce," and in the context of ramen, it basically means "noodle sauce." Tare is the primary source of salinity in a bowl of ramen, what determines its flavor. The most common types of tare are shio (salt), shoyu (soy sauce), and miso.

② **FAT/OIL:** Fats and oils add richness and oil-soluble flavors and aromas to the soup and, consequently, to the noodles as they're lifted free of the broth.

③ **SOUP STOCK:** The soup stock provides most of the volume of a bowl of ramen. While the soup stock can be made from all kinds of different meat and fish, it's most often made with pork and/or chicken.

④ **MEN (NOODLES):** These are always, always alkaline wheat noodles, noodles made from a wheat dough that contains alkaline salts. The alkaline salts react with the gluten to give the noodles their distinctive bouncy chew and flavor.

⑤ **TOPPINGS:** A bowl of ramen can be topped with nearly anything, but the most common toppings are slices of roasted or braised pork, marinated boiled eggs, fermented bamboo shoots, blanched spinach, and sliced scallions.

Any soup can be similarly broken down into its constituent elements. Consider the different parts of chicken noodle soup: chicken stock; whatever fat slicks its surface, usually what was used to sauté the vegetables; salt and other sources of salinity (such as a Parmesan cheese rind); and, finally, solid matter, including vegetables and herbs, that flavors the soup (carrots, celery, onions, garlic, parsley, etc.), cooked chicken, and pasta. A pureed soup, like leek and potato soup, can be deconstructed in the same way the liquid medium is the chicken stock or water the vegetables are cooked in, the seasoning is the salt, the fat is what you use to sauté the leeks, and the solid matter is what you end up blitzing, giving the soup body.

Looking at any dish as the sum of its parts is useful for identifying ways to make that dish as a whole taste better, but it requires an understanding of the role each part plays. Then you will see why, for example, a chicken noodle soup can be enlivened at the last moment with the addition of a little fruity olive oil or a squeeze of lemon, or why your leek and potato puree has a better texture when you use a gelatin-rich stock rather than a thin meat broth or water.

One of the advantages ramen has over other dishes is that each component is clearly identifiable and exists distinct from its counterparts, even in the final bowl of soup. The challenge inherent in making a great bowl of ramen is ensuring that those disparate elements, prepared separately, come together in a coherent whole that tastes like a singular bowl of soup rather than a mishmash of ingredients.

Shoyu tare and sliced naga negi

① TARE (SEASONING)

The three ingredients most commonly used to provide the concentrated dose of salinity in ramen tare are salt, soy sauce, and miso. In fact, these ingredients are so pervasive that they constitute the three main flavors of ramen, and ramen shops often have at least one of each on their menu: a shio (salt) ramen, a shoyu (soy sauce) ramen, and a miso ramen.

These distinctions, however, are descriptive, not proscriptive. While a shio tare may get most of its salt content from salt, it may also contain soy sauce; while a shoyu tare is primarily made up of soy sauce, it can contain salt; and a miso tare will often contain both salt and soy sauce. Any one of these tare may also include other flavorful ingredients, like MSG, dashi, meat stock, dried seafood, dried mushrooms, dried spices, or the range of prepared sauces and pastes used in a variety of Asian cuisines, like oyster sauce, dark soy sauce, and doubanjiang.

When thinking about tare, it's helpful to understand what makes soy sauce such a powerful flavoring agent. Japanese soy sauce is quite salty, of course, but because of the roasted wheat included in its fermentation process, it is also quite sweet. Soy sauce is rich in glutamates, which provide savoriness, or umami,* and, since it is a fermented product, it is also noticeably acidic (pH ~4.5; for reference, distilled vinegar has a pH of 2.5). Finally, because of the fermentation process, soy sauce is aromatic, particularly in the moments after heat is applied, as the alcohol-soluble aromatic compounds evaporate with the trace amounts of volatile alcohols. Soy sauce, then, amplifies the salinity, savoriness, sweetness, acidity, and aroma of anything it seasons.

Not every tare must hit the same flavor notes as soy sauce. However, the soup in a bowl of ramen must hit similar notes if it's to taste good, and the tare offers the cook the opportunity to make up for whatever their soup stock or their choice of fat may lack. A plain chicken stock, made with the carcasses of chickens and a few aromatic vegetables like ginger and garlic, can be improved upon with the addition of salt, glutamates, acid, and sugar, something that can be accomplished with a simple shoyu tare of soy sauce and mirin, or a shio tare of salt, dashi, sugar, and vinegar. The flavors of the two bowls of ramen will be drastically different, but the principle is identical. The same is true of a meticulously constructed soup stock, one that incorporates, say, pork, chicken, dried seafood like scallops and kombu, and sweet aromatic vegetables such as leeks, daikon, and Napa cabbage. Because the broth will provide many of the flavors you want in your final bowl of ramen, the tare can simply be a fair amount of salt added to the bowl, or, and quite commonly, a mixture of salt and MSG. However, a tare can also be quite complex, incorporating dried fruit, dried seafood, dried mushrooms, and a blend of soy and other seasoning sauces.

Since most of the ingredients included in a tare are very flavorful on their own, mixing them together almost invariably produces something tasty. But once you consider the range of possibilities available to you from various ingredients and the ways in which you can combine them, you will understand how tinkering with tare formulations and processes can be an expression of a ramen cook's creativity: there's a lot of space for making a tare your own.

* For more on this subject, see "What Is Umami?" (page 113).

Shoyu tare, sliced naga negi, and aromatic lard

② FAT

A good bowl of ramen—a good bowl of noodle soup, really—has an ample quantity of fat. The fat serves two purposes: it gives the noodles and soup texture and adds oil-soluble aromas and flavors. Since the most immediately obvious function of fat is the latter—as soon as a bowl of ramen is put in front of you, much of the aroma that wafts up into your nostrils comes from the oil that slicks its surface—we'll start there.

It is perfectly acceptable to rely on the fat that is rendered out of the animal parts used in the broth-making process. Some ramen shops don't add any other flavors to the fat, since chicken and pork contain naturally aromatic and flavorful fat, which is then further flavored by whatever else is added to the broth. There is an elegant economy to this practice, a total use of whatever ingredients go into the pot, the broth extracting all the ingredients' water-soluble flavor compounds and the fat that rises to the top extracting all their oil-soluble flavor compounds, so the final bowl of ramen has all of these flavors incorporated into it.

The difference between fat-soluble and water-soluble flavors is straightforward: some compounds easily dissolve in fat but not in water, and vice versa. However, some ingredients contain both oil- and water-soluble flavor compounds. Aromatic vegetables like garlic, ginger, and onions have both in large quantities, which accounts for their ubiquity in dishes in a variety of cuisines all over the world: they provide a lot of flavor, whether boiled in water or fried in fat. However, the dramatic differences between the two kinds of flavors is perhaps best illustrated by a dried chile pepper, particularly a potent one, such as a habanero. A habanero chile has a Scoville rating of 100,000–350,000, which means it is painfully spicy. But since capsaicin, the compound that registers as spiciness in the pain receptors in our mouths, is oil-soluble, if you steep or boil a dried habanero in water with no added fat, the water will be flavored with everything in the pepper that's water-soluble, which means the more floral, fruity notes that recall raisins and sun-dried tomatoes. Add that same habanero to sizzling oil, before or after steeping it in water, however, and the oil will become exhilaratingly spicy.

You can use these qualities to your advantage when preparing fats for inclusion in a bowl of ramen. Because alliums like garlic, onions, and shallots have plenty of fat-soluble flavors, they are often used to flavor the fat, and the same goes for ginger. Chilies, whether dried or fresh, are also often used to flavor oils, although chile oils are often used in addition to other flavorful fats, the better to modulate the spiciness in each bowl of ramen. Dried spices and herbs also possess fat-soluble flavors in large quantities: I once had an incredible bowl of vegan ramen that included rosemary oil, and it was the perfect complement to the burnt-onion broth. As with tare, there aren't any hard-and-fast rules about the aromatic oils you can add to a bowl of ramen, and, as such, there's ample room for a cook's creativity.

Flavor aside, fat gives texture to both the soup stock and the noodles. Fat provides a mouth-coating thickness, an aura of greasiness. Further, the fat that lies on the surface of the soup is picked up along with the noodles, coating them and giving them a welcome silkiness. The type of fats you use can produce very different textural results.

Fats can be classified as saturated or unsaturated, and while both can be used in ramen, saturated fats produce a better texture.

They have a thicker consistency, which is particularly evident when they are at room temperature, when they will be solid. Dairy fats, like butter and the fat in cheese; animal fats such as those derived from pork, chicken, or beef; and coconut oil are all saturated fats. Unsaturated fats, which have a thinner texture and are liquid at room temperature, include many common cooking fats, like peanut, canola, olive, and sunflower oil.

Flavored fats, like lard that's been infused with garlic, if prepared and stored correctly in the refrigerator, are usable for a long time. As you make more and more ramen, you'll find yourself accumulating a small storehouse of different flavored fats, which you can mix and match as you like. Using combinations of different fats offers you yet another avenue for experimentation and variation.

There is one way, though, in which fats dull flavor. An excess of fat will make a dish taste less salty than it actually is, which is why high-fat ingredients like pork belly need to be salted amply (think bacon), or they taste greasy. This is important to keep in mind for ramen, and it is why ramen broth is, by and large, incredibly salty on its own: it must function as seasoning for both the noodles and the fat that sheaths them as they're lifted out of the broth.

Finally, fat has an insulating effect. A bowl of ramen with a thick layer of fat on top of it will stay hotter longer. While this has less relevance for the home kitchen than for a ramen restaurant (I typically don't get the fat for ramen very hot; I just heat it until it's liquid), it can be useful to remember if you're trying to prepare ramen for many people: hot fat will keep the ramen hotter in the bowls for a longer time.

③ SOUP STOCK

All soups are mixtures of solids, fat, and water. Clear soups are a combination of a solution, or water in which salt has been dissolved, and a suspension, or water in which small particles of solids have been dispersed but not dissolved, and most of the fat that's present rises to the surface and pools. Thicker, opaque soups, like the milky pork bone broths that are so popular in the United States or pureed leek and potato soup, are colloids, or solutions of salt in which solid particles and fat are evenly dispersed, and their opacity is due to the light reflecting off the fats and solids suspended in the liquid.

In the context of ramen, the soup can be broken up into three main components: tare, fat, and the base soup stock, which can be made from the flesh and bones of meat or fish, dried seafood products, and/or vegetables. Ramen is primarily a synthesis of Chinese and Japanese techniques, based on the soup-making methods in those two culinary traditions. However, since ramen cooks have adopted all sorts of unconventional methods for making soup, and since the audience for this book is primarily a Western one, it's also helpful to understand Western stock-making techniques, which are primarily drawn from classical French cuisine, as these can shed light on gelatin extraction, one of the most important elements of making stock.

Soup stocks are generally called either "stock" or "broth," and the terms are often used interchangeably. While there isn't a strict definition of either term, there is general agreement that the word "broth" is typically used to denote the liquid left after poaching or boiling meat for a relatively short period, whereas "stock" is more often used to refer to the liquid that results from simmering or boiling meaty bones (which may or may not have been roasted) in water for longer periods of time. The differences in the final products stem from the ingredients immersed in the liquid and how long they're subjected to heating, so a broth will typically be a thin liquid with overt "meaty" flavor, while a stock will have thicker texture and more depth of flavor, but a less "meaty" flavor.

"Dashi," the fundamental cooking stock of Japanese cuisine, is made from kombu, or dried kelp, and katsuobushi, shavings of dried fillets of skipjack tuna (bonito). However, the word is also used to simply denote "broth"—a chicken broth, for example, may be referred to as "tori dashi." Classical Japanese cuisine typically emphasizes light flavors and textures, and as such, using dashi as an equivalent to broth is entirely apt, as meat-based stocks in Japanese cuisine are traditionally light in body and flavor.

Chinese stock occupies a kind of middle ground between French and Japanese stocks, as Chinese stocks are made from a combination of fresh and dried ingredients. For example, many Chinese recipes for "superior stock," the base stock of classical Cantonese cuisine, call for chicken bones, dried ham, dried seafood products, and vegetables. Superior stock, unlike dashi, has a fair amount of body—not as much as a classical French veal stock, but it will have more flavor than a veal stock.

Western Stock

While stock can be made from vegetables, meat, and seafood, veal stock is historically the backbone of French cuisine. Nowadays many consumers have turned away from veal because of the way the young calves have customarily been raised, using methods that many people

Shoyu tare, sliced naga negi, aromatic lard, and chicken and pork stock

now view as inhumane. However, the fact that veal was used to produce the most prized stock in the classical French kitchen underlines the qualities French cooks most value in stock—namely versatility, flavor, and gelatin content. Veal bones were prized for stock-making because they are mild in flavor and have a relatively high proportion of collagen to bone matter, because as animals grow older, much of the collagen in their bodies calcifies into bone. Collagen, when heated in water, transforms into gelatin. That gelatin can in turn transform a liquid into a stable gel at or below room temperature. The Jell-O you used to eat in the school cafeteria, the panna cotta you order at your local Italian restaurant, and the elaborate preparations of cooked foods preserved in aspic in classical French cuisine all take advantage of gelatin's gelling abilities. For ramen, gelatin's role is to add texture and mouthfeel to the soup, and to help stabilize the weak emulsions in the milky stocks known as paitans.

There are two kinds of veal stock, white and brown, and the ingredients for both are the same—water, meaty veal bones, and aromatic vegetables and herbs. But for white veal stock, the ingredients are added raw, and for a brown stock they are first roasted or sautéed. White veal stock is said to have a more delicate flavor, and is typically used in preparations where the cook wants another flavor to be dominant, while a brown veal stock has a roasted flavor profile (more on that in a minute) that isn't overpowering, because of the mildness of veal's flavor. For either stock, bones and vegetables are simmered, not boiled, in water to extract their flavors and render out the fat without emulsifying it into the broth, producing a relatively clear, fat-free, salt-free, flavorful liquid. The hot water cooks the meat and draws out flavorful proteins (as well as flavorful compounds from the vegetables/herbs) in the pot, imparting their flavor to the stock. Simultaneously, the connective tissue attached to the bones and in the meat, which is made up of collagen, gradually transforms into gelatin.

Brown veal stock has an additional flavor component produced by twin groups of chemical reactions that take place at temperatures above the boiling point of water (212°F/100°C): caramelization and Maillard browning. When foods are subjected to temperatures higher than 230°F (110°C) and then 285°F (140°C), proteins and sugars begin to undergo caramelization and Maillard browning, respectively, and a series of chemical reactions produces a plethora of new sugars and protein molecules. These reactions are the reason why the crust on a loaf of bread or a well-seared steak tastes so deliciously complex. Since these reactions will not occur in a pot of boiling water at normal atmospheric pressure (as the temperature of the water cannot exceed its boiling point), they must be produced separately first, which is why the veal bones and aromatic vegetables used in a brown veal stock are roasted before adding them to the pot (grilling or sautéing the meat, bones, and vegetables would have a similar effect), and the brown residue that accumulates in the bottom of the cooking vessel, known as "fond" in French, is then scraped up and added as well. Thus, brown stock contains not only the flavorful compounds extracted from the meat and vegetables, along with any gelatin converted from collagen, but also a host of flavorful compounds produced by caramelization and Maillard browning, giving the stock a deeper, roasted flavor profile.

Brown veal stock recipes often call for the addition of a tomato product, typically tomato paste, to provide a concentrated dose of an extremely flavorful group of proteins known as glutamates.* Glutamates, the salt form of glutamic acid, are likely familiar to most cooks from the ubiquitous monosodium glutamate (MSG) and

* For more on glutamates, see "What Is Umami?" (page 113).

discussions about umami and savoriness. Stocks are in many ways merely a vehicle for transferring glutamic acid from meats of all varieties to our mouths. All meats contain glutamic acid in varying quantities; seafood has a higher concentration of glutamic acid than meat from land animals, and tomatoes have similarly higher concentrations.

Brown veal stock is essentially a gelatin-rich flavor bomb that contains a range of flavorful molecules that humans are primed to enjoy.

With a few minor differences, all of the above applies to any stock made from animal meat and bones in the Western kitchen. All are rich in gelatin, the better for use in sauces and lip-smackingly thick soups and stews, and all have ample amounts of glutamic acid.

Dashi

Classical Japanese cuisine relies almost solely on seafood-based stocks that fall under the general category of dashi. Like French stocks, dashi is very flavorful and fat-free; unlike French stocks, dashi contains no gelatin. And dashi takes only minutes to prepare, as opposed to the long simmering times of French stocks.

The primary ingredient of dashi is kombu, a dried kelp rich in glutamic acid. A simple dashi is made by soaking kombu in water and then bringing that water to a simmer, after which the kombu is removed. A kombu dashi can serve as a broth, but it is also a base ingredient for sauces, braises, and soups. You can also use dashi to poach fish or vegetables, imparting a glutamate boost to the flavors of whatever you're cooking.

The most common type of dashi in classical Japanese cuisine is made from kombu and katsuobushi, a processed dried fish product that is unique to Japan. Katsuobushi is made from fillets of skipjack tuna (also known as bonito in English, katsuo in Japanese). Essentially, all the moisture and fat from the fillets is removed, which allows them to be preserved indefinitely. An initial poaching step locks into place katsuo's relatively high concentration of inosinic acid,* which would otherwise dissipate with time, and a smoking process then encourages both caramelization and Maillard browning. The result is a block of intensely flavorful fish, which can be shaved into flakes and then steeped in water to produce an intensely flavorful broth filled with inosinates and all the flavorful compounds of a browned piece of meat in minutes.

The main salient point of dashi is that it is a very flavorful broth that has little to no body; its consistency is nearly identical to that of water. Unlike veal stock, dashi is prized almost entirely for its flavor and, crucially, its aroma. Dashi is often served as a minimally seasoned soup, either by itself or as a kind of backdrop for other ingredients that have been prepared separately.

Chinese Soup Stocks

While much of the information above is reductive, painting Japanese and French culinary traditions in broad strokes, any overview of Chinese soup stock–making practices will by necessity be even more reductive, given China's long and varied culinary history.

However, there are certain generalizations you can make about these practices. For example, in contrast to French/Western stocks, Chinese stocks rarely use roasted bones; instead, it is common practice to soak and blanch the bones prior to making the stock, to promote clarity in the final stock by removing myoglobin and to get rid of meaty aromas, which are considered undesirable. Unlike classical French stocks, Chinese stocks regularly include pork, pork products, and bones. Chinese cooks also tend to use far fewer vegetables in their stocks, confining themselves for the most part to alliums and ginger, which, in addition to flavoring the

* For more on inosinic acid, see "What Is Umami?" (page 113).

stock, have the benefit of removing or lessening unwanted meaty aromas. Chinese stocks also incorporate certain ingredients that the Western cook has always been instructed to omit, notably daikon radish and Napa cabbage, as they can produce sulfurous aromas and flavors that are, for lack of a better term, kind of "farty."

It's also common for Chinese cooks to use different kinds of meat in one stock, and to combine meat and dried seafood. Cantonese superior stock, for example, uses chicken, aged ham, and dried seafood like scallops and shrimp. Similarly, cooks will often add whole muscles to the stockpot, instead of confining themselves to meaty bones, giving their stocks a stronger meaty flavor. The primary difference between Chinese superior stock and dashi is the body the gelatin from the meat and bones imparts to stock.

One of the ways Chinese stock differs from Japanese and French stocks is that there is an entire category of stocks that are cloudy or milky rather than clear. For both dashi and veal stock, clarity is prized, and a lot of effort is devoted to ensuring that a stock is as clear as possible, through the use of both temperature control and careful straining. Boiling can emulsify particulate matter and fats into the stock, so French and Japanese cooks prevent their stocks and dashi from boiling, and finished stocks and dashi are filtered through fine-mesh sieves lined with a finer material, such as cheesecloth, to further improve their clarity. (In classical French cooking, there is also consommé, a fortified stock that's so clear you can see a penny placed at the bottom of the pot, and this is produced by stirring a mixture of egg shells, egg whites, ground meat, and chopped vegetables into a cold stock and bringing it to a boil; the solid matter forms a kind of "raft" as the stock heats and the proteins bond together, which then both filters and flavors the stock as it rises to the top.)

Chinese cooks also value crystal-clear stocks, but they appreciate the virtues of emulsified stocks, which take on a milky appearance because of the way light reflects off the evenly dispersed fat molecules. These stocks, called baitang, are often used as soup bases, either for noodles or for dishes like hot pot, and they partly demonstrate the degree to which ramen is indebted to Chinese culinary traditions. One of the most famous types of ramen is a milky tonkotsu—that is, a pork bone broth—which is a direct descendant of baitang. And one of the ways that Chinese culinary influence is manifested in current ramen culture is that soups can be categorized as either clear or milky, using Japanese words borrowed from the Chinese "chintang" and "baitang"—namely, "chintan" and "paitan."

Secondary Stocks

One practice that each of these traditions shares is making secondary stocks. Called remouillage in French, niban dashi in Japanese, and ertang in Chinese, a secondary stock is made using the spent materials from the original stock, whether they be veal bones for veal stock, kombu and katsuobushi for dashi, or the mix of chicken bones, ham, and dried seafood used in superior stock. The low simmering temperatures that are prescribed for first stocks to preserve clarity are mostly abandoned in favor of harder boils, a practice that underlines the fact that making secondary stocks is a utilitarian enterprise.

Secondary stocks can serve as a base for a stew or be used as a poaching medium for vegetables and meats, to fortify their flavor. For ramen, secondary stocks can be the base for a braising liquid for a meat topping or a poaching medium, and they can also be considered a tasty by-product of your ramen-making. Because the light, clear meat broths favored for some ramen styles almost necessarily fail to wring out every bit of flavor, fat, and gelatin from pork or even chicken bones, those bones can be used to make an emulsified second stock for the base of the milky ramen broths known as paitans.

Shoyu tare, sliced naga negi, aromatic lard, chicken and pork stock, and 40%-hydration noodles

④ NOODLES

Noodles, or men or soba, are the defining element of ramen, its sine qua non ("without which it cannot be"). The noodles give the dish its two names, as "ramen" is the Japanese pronunciation of "la mian," the word for alkaline wheat noodles in Chinese, and "chuka soba," the other name by which ramen is widely known (in addition to "shina soba") means "Chinese noodles." As such, you cannot have ramen without alkaline wheat noodles.

I've taken great pains to emphasize that there aren't many rules when making ramen, but this is an ironclad one: a bowl of noodle soup cannot be called ramen unless it contains alkaline wheat noodles.

This means that there is no such thing as gluten-free ramen. You cannot put rice noodles or other noodles, like shirataki noodles, in a bowl of ramen broth and call what you're eating ramen. The same is true of other kinds of wheat noodles, such as lo mein, in a bowl of ramen broth, as was done for many years at an iconic American noodle bar that, irony of ironies, is widely credited with popularizing ramen in the Western world. This is not a matter of pedantry surrounding semantics; it is a matter of pedantry about the nature of the dish, because the texture and taste of alkaline wheat noodles are unique.

Describing the texture of noodles in English is a little difficult, as we have an impoverished vocabulary with respect to the qualities of noodles. However, ramen noodles are typically characterized as having a "snappy" or "bouncy" texture, attributable to the alkaline salts in the dough. But because there are many other noodles out there that can be described as "snappy" and/or "bouncy," even nonwheat noodles, it's useful to understand why ramen's "snap" or "bounce" is distinct from, say, lo mein or pasta.

Lo mein, like many types of fresh pasta, is made with wheat, water, and eggs. The "snap" and "bounce" of these noodles is the result of the interaction between the protein in the egg whites and the starches in the wheat flour, which produces a strong starch gel that is both soft and rubbery. When you bite down, your teeth pierce the gel fairly easily, but they encounter a little bit of resistance. That soft resistance is generally what we refer to when we say a pasta is "bouncy."

However, the "snap" that we attribute to lo mein and pasta comes from the interaction of water and proteins in wheat flour, which forms the substance we know as gluten. Gluten, when hydrated, forms a strong network of protein chains, which can, if sufficiently strengthened, act as a scaffolding on which a starch gel can support itself. A loaf of bread, particularly one of those loaves with impractically open crumbs so popular on Instagram, is an excellent illustration of this phenomenon. The webbed crumb structure that surrounds and defines all those holes in the bread is made up of a well-developed gluten network, and everything else that isn't those wide-open holes—the parts of the bread that are able to soak up butter—is the starch gel. In a noodle, of course, the gluten network and the starch gel are smushed together into a thin strand, but the architecture is essentially the same: a strong network of gluten that holds a starch gel in place. The "snap" we speak of when talking about biting through noodles is essentially the resistance of that gluten network to being cut by our teeth; the more resistant it is to being chewed and cut up, the more we think, "Hey, those are some snappy noodles!"

The introduction of alkaline salts into a noodle dough fundamentally changes the nature of that snap, because alkaline salts alter the behavior of the gluten network, and different alkaline salts alter that network in different ways. For example, potassium carbonate can make that gluten network more brittle, which translates to a harder "snap," while sodium carbonate makes that network more resilient, making the "snap" seem a little "squeakier." For these reasons, a wheat noodle that contains no alkaline salts has an entirely different texture from one that does.

If it were simply a matter of texture, it might be more acceptable for people to be producing gluten-free ramen, but alkaline salts affect the taste of the noodles as well. First, alkaline wheat noodles are slightly basic, which gives them a (kind of) pretzel-like flavor and aroma (pretzels don't have alkaline salts in the dough, but they are boiled in a basic solution of lye water prior to baking). Second, mixing a wheat flour with an alkaline solution produces a sulfuric taste and aroma, which can vary from very pronounced to barely noticeable, depending on the concentration of alkaline salts, as well as the inclusion of other ingredients, like riboflavin or egg. Ramen soups have evolved to complement these flavors in the noodles and are consequently slightly more acidic and more heavily seasoned than other noodle broths. A good test of this might be using pho rather than ramen in a ramen soup or substituting ramen for the noodles in a pho broth: both will taste odd, although the pho in the ramen experiment will likely work better than the ramen in pho, as the ramen broth is likely to be more heavily seasoned.

Because you really need alkaline noodles for a bowl of ramen, the dearth of high-quality manufactured ramen in most American supermarkets means that one of the biggest obstacles to making ramen at home is finding good noodles. When I first started making ramen, it was very difficult to purchase good fresh noodles, and there wasn't all that much information about how to make them, so I resorted to using the noodles from instant ramen packages. While this works, it is a serious compromise, and you may find yourself wondering, as I did, whether it's worth it to expend a ton of effort on making everything else in a bowl of ramen only to use a brick of fried noodles from a packet.

Nowadays, though, if you have access to a Japanese supermarket or a well-stocked Asian market, you will be able to find a range of ramen, both dried and fresh, and, of course, a fair selection is available online. I recommend avoiding the dried noodle products, which have a drastically different texture from fresh ramen, and instead picking up fresh noodles, typically found in the freezer section. Sun Noodle is one of the more widely available brands, and many ramen restaurants across the country are supplied by Sun. Yamachan and Myojo are two other large ramen producers in the U.S. who have at times made noodles available for sale at the retail level. Any of these brands would work well with the recipes in this book.

However, after years of making my own ramen, I have become something of an ideologue when it comes to fresh ramen. I can't say objectively that the ramen I produce in my kitchen is better than the ramen from these large noodle producers, but I can confidently say I prefer mine over any noodle I can purchase. In part, this is because my noodle formulas produce relatively bland noodles, where the focus is on producing the correct texture, and thus they work much better with my relatively lightly seasoned soups. When I use, say, Sun

Noodle noodles, which taste more sulfurous (not in a bad way) and cereal-like because of the relatively higher proportions of ingredients like alkaline salts and riboflavin, I find I must add more seasoning to the bowl; when the noodles themselves are more flavorful, the soup needs to be more flavorful as well.

There are limitations to making noodles yourself. For example, unless you buy a dedicated noodle-making machine designed to handle a stiff, low-hydration ramen dough, it's difficult to make the kind of noodles that are typically found in a bowl of Hakata tonkotsu ramen: thin, dry, and more hard than snappy, these noodles are extremely well suited to the thick, unctuous broth. If you want to make that kind of ramen, it really is best to use noodles from a large noodle manufacturer.

On the other hand, if you use a pasta machine—mechanized or manual—to make your noodles, you have more options in terms of noodle shape, texture, and flavor than if you rely solely on the catalog of retail products available. You can make thick noodles, thin noodles, wavy noodles, or wide noodles, or noodles with a range of different flours, such as masa and rye and whole wheat. You can make light noodles that swim in your mouth as you drink up your soup, or you can make dense noodles that have a pronounced chew. Small changes in noodle formulae produce appreciably different results, so making your own noodles offers yet another avenue for experimentation and creative inspiration.

Shoyu tare, sliced naga negi, aromatic lard, chicken and pork stock, 40%-hydration noodles, and bias-cut naga negi

⑤ TOPPINGS

If I ask you to picture a bowl of ramen, you'd likely imagine a noodle soup with roasted pork, half a boiled egg, a tangle of seasoned bamboo shoots or greens, a rectangle of nori, a pile of scallions, and a coin of processed white fish cake sporting a pink spiral. These are the classic accompaniments to the noodles and broth.

However, ramen does not really need most of these things; all a bowl of ramen needs to be complete is soup, noodles, and a scattering of sliced scallions. Toppings are entirely optional, and, at times, superfluous. It's nice to have a bit of meat in the bowl, or an egg, but if I don't have either in my refrigerator or freezer, or I don't feel like preparing them, I won't feel like my bowl of ramen is incomplete; it will merely be spare.

Toppings can throw off the careful balance you can achieve between the noodles, broth, and fat, or they can complement and enhance those other elements. Further, toppings can even be the defining element, as in a bowl of mabo men, where mabo tofu is the defining flavor profile of the bowl.

I find it helpful to consider toppings from three vantage points. The first is to view the toppings as a way to "bulk up" a bowl of noodle soup, transforming it into a complete meal. The second is to see the toppings as adding textural complexity, providing everything that soft, snappy noodles and silky soup lack: the crunch of pickled vegetables, the satisfying chew of a piece of meat. The third is to view the toppings as adding more or contrasting flavors, such as the heightened savoriness of fermented bamboo shoots, the subtle marine essence a sheet of toasted nori releases into the soup, or the relatively bland reprieve from the salinity of the soup and other toppings provided by a bit of blanched spinach.

While the first view of toppings is the likely origin of the practice of putting things other than noodles in the bowl, I think it's the worst way to approach adding toppings. That's not to say that a bowl of ramen loaded up with toppings is necessarily bad; there are whole styles of ramen that feature an overabundance of toppings, like jirokei ramen, topped with an inches-high pile of boiled pork slices, bean sprouts, cabbage, and raw garlic. But overloading a bowl of ramen with toppings requires adjusting the seasoning of the soup and adding extra seasoning to the toppings if you want everything to taste like it goes together.

The second approach has many merits, and some of the best bowls of ramen emphasize the textural qualities of toppings over any contributions they might have in terms of flavor. For example, the classic bowl of chuka soba served at Eifuku Taishoken in Tokyo has little more than a pile of pickled bamboo shoots and a few slices of lightly seasoned boiled pork, which take most of their flavor from the surrounding soup. The pork is slightly chewy, not meltingly soft; its flavor offers a kind of bland counterpoint to the intensely seasoned soup and the generous amount of flavorful lard, in which thin rounds of lightly wilted naga negi (Welsh onions) float; the bamboo shoots, while seasoned rather aggressively, as most good pickled bamboo shoots are, are most noticeable for the pronounced crunch they offer as a counterpoint to the soft noodles and pork.

The third approach might seem to be the one that makes the most sense to most people;

after all, how could adding extremely flavorful anything to an already extremely flavorful bowl of noodle soup be wrong? And yet, I have had many bowls of ramen where the toppings outshine everything else so it seems the soup is bland in comparison. This is often the pitfall of more "cheffy" ramen restaurants in the United States, where a lot of time and energy and care is devoted to making insanely delicious meat toppings, often cooked to a gelatinous softness, but very little has been expended on the noodles or soup.

When you think about how to top a bowl of ramen, ideally you'd use a mix of the latter two approaches and disregard the first one almost entirely. The components of a good bowl of ramen should have synergy in terms of both texture and flavor.

1

4

PICTURED OPPOSITE: Tare (1), fat (2), soup stock (3), noodles (4), folded noodles (5), toppings (6)

2

3

5

6

EQUIPMENT

A KITCHEN that's well equipped for making ramen looks basically like a kitchen that's well equipped to produce almost anything, with the addition of a few noodle cooking baskets (which can be used for cooking things other than noodles!).

This list includes both essential equipment and equipment that's simply nice to have, arranged by category, with essentials up front. (The equipment necessary for making homemade noodles can be found on page 49.)

SHARP THINGS

A CHEF'S KNIFE. I most often use a Tojiro gyuto, which is a Japanese blade with a Western blade geometry; it costs about $100. You can also use a Western chef's knife or a Japanese santoku. All that matters is that your knife is sharp and you do your best to maintain that sharp edge. Don't cut on hard surfaces, like bamboo or marble or glass; don't use your knife to chop through bones (unless it's designed for that purpose); don't leave your blade wet after cleaning; don't rest it on hard surfaces; and don't use it for opening packages, for cutting up boxes, or as a flat-head screwdriver when you can't find yours. Learn how to sharpen your knife, or take it in for sharpening at least once a year, several times a year if you cook frequently. A dull knife is a dangerous knife.

A PARING KNIFE. Compact, nimble, and convenient to use, paring knives are very useful to have around, well suited for tasks where a chef's knife's longer blade is unnecessary or unwieldy: peeling shallots, slicing lemons, etc. I recommend buying inexpensive paring knives, because they're just as functional as expensive ones, and you won't feel obliged to pay to sharpen them; when they get dull, you can just buy new ones.

A BONING KNIFE. Western boning knives have thin, flexible blades that make them easy to maneuver when filleting fish or jointing chicken. I prefer to use a honesuki, or Japanese poultry knife, for cutting up meat, and a deba, or Japanese fish butchering knife, for cutting up fish. For most home cooks, though, I recommend sticking with Western boning knives, which are cheaper and require less care. If you want to use a honesuki or a deba, learn how to sharpen it yourself, as these are far and away superior to Western boning knives, but only when very sharp.

A SERRATED BREAD KNIFE. A serrated bread knife is useful for slicing delicate things like chilled chashu. It isn't a necessity for ramen—a chef's knife will do the job—but every kitchen should have a good bread knife.

Y-PEELER. You're going to be peeling vegetables, particularly for clear stocks, and if you're peeling things, you might as well get the best peeler there is, a Y-peeler.

BOX GRATER/ MICROPLANE. Every kitchen should have a tool that can finely grate garlic, ginger, citrus zest, and carrots (for gyoza!).

CUTTING BOARDS. Invest in a good, sturdy wooden cutting board (not bamboo, which is too hard and will dull your blades) for much of your kitchen work: chopping raw or cooked vegetables, slicing cooked meats, dough work, etc. Get the nicest board you can afford, and take care of it. That means washing it by hand *and drying it* after every use and periodically oiling it with mineral oil to keep the wood supple and prevent it from cracking. A well-made wooden cutting board will last a home cook a lifetime if it's properly cared for.

For butchering and handling raw meat and fish, purchase relatively inexpensive cutting boards made of solid plastic; skip the cutting boards that have grooves in them or have plastic feet, as these can warp, and they also bend when pressure is applied to them, which makes cutting difficult. Buy them in two different colors and designate one for fish and seafood and one for meat. When they get banged up or notched with cuts, toss them and buy new ones.

BENCH SCRAPER. A bench scraper is a necessity in any kitchen, even if you only cook occasionally. When you chop vegetables, this tool is the best way to pick them up off the cutting board (don't use your knife to do that!). I like using one to cut up noodle sheets too, and for cleaning up my counter after dusting things with starch or flour.

WHETSTONE AND FIXER. If you own (or want to own) nice knives or specialty knives, I strongly suggest you buy a whetstone and learn how to use it. If you get one, you'll also want to buy a "fixer," which will even out the whetstone's surface.

FISH SCALER AND FISH TWEEZERS. If you'll be cutting up whole fish, you'll need a scaler and a sturdy pair of fish tweezers, to pull out pin bones. I prefer Japanese-style copper fish scalers.

MANDOLINE AND CUT-PROOF GLOVES. Mandoline slicers are very useful tools. I like the bare-bones ones produced by Benriner. Regardless of whether or not the mandoline comes with a guarding mechanism for preventing you from slicing off your fingers, you should purchase a pair of cut-proof gloves—and use them every time you use a mandoline. I guarantee they will save you at least one trip to the emergency room.

POTS AND PANS

TALL HEAVY-BOTTOMED POT, WITH A 6- TO 8-QUART CAPACITY. You can't make ramen without stock, so you need a stockpot. However, many stockpots have thin sides and bottoms, which is particularly bad for making stock with dense, heavy animal bones, like pork bones, as the relative lack of conductive material will lead to scorching wherever the bones are in contact with the bottom of the pot. A Dutch oven is not an acceptable substitute for a tall heavy-bottomed pot: Dutch ovens have relatively low sides and wider bases, which means any stock made in the pot will have a relatively large surface area, which will increase evaporation and thus decrease yield.

So I recommend buying a 6- to 8-quart stovetop pressure cooker; I own one of each size, and these pots are what I use to make most of the stocks in my kitchen, even when I'm making stocks that aren't pressure-cooked. Look for stovetop pressure cookers with relatively tall sides and narrow bases; these have thick sides and bottoms as a matter of course. They are made of nonreactive stainless steel; they are easy to clean; and, unlike a stockpot, they can be used for a range of things other than simmering some water with stuff in it. A 6-quart pressure cooker will be more than sufficient for most of your ramen-making needs, but for cooking large, unwieldy pork bones without resorting to having to crack them with a hammer, an 8-quart pressure cooker can be convenient.

The stockpot, or the pressure cooker pot, is also what I use for boiling water for noodles, particularly when I'm making more than one serving of ramen at a time. They can accommodate a large volume of water; their thick sides mean they retain heat well, and the water can be kept at a rolling boil even after the addition of multiple bundles of noodles; and they can usually accommodate more than one noodle basket at a time.

PRESSURE COOKER. Pressure cookers make amazing stock! And it takes far less time to make a full-bodied stock in a pressure cooker than by simmering it on the stovetop. For that reason alone, you should buy a pressure cooker if you don't already have one. While I own an electric multicooker with a pressure cooker function, I don't use it very often; instead I use my two stovetop pressure cookers far more frequently, both as stockpots and as pressure cookers. But electric multicookers with a pressure-cooker function are useful for any number of reasons that have little to do with the confusing bank of options on their displays: they are insulated, so they heat up your kitchen less than a pressure cooker or stockpot on the stove; their cooking temperatures are regulated, so you don't have to pay as much attention to them; and they won't take up space on the stovetop.

3-QUART SAUCIER. A saucier is a pot with a rounded bottom, which makes it easier to whisk things like sauces that might congeal or scorch in the corners of a straight-sided pot. A 3-quart saucier is a versatile piece of kitchen equipment: it is large enough for boiling pasta (or noodles) and steaming or blanching vegetables, and it's obviously great for the applications for which it's designed, like custards and sauces. I think its capacity and its rounded bottom also make it ideal for most families for boiling soup stock, whether you're using light clear stocks, or thick emulsified stocks, which can scorch when boiled vigorously. This is also the pan I use to make dashi and aromatic oils, and it can be used to make tare.

10- TO 12-INCH CAST-IRON SKILLET. Cast-iron pans are durable and versatile. They're excellent for searing, pan-roasting, and even roasting meats, but they can be used in a pinch for shallow braises. I have two 10-inch cast-iron pans, which I use more frequently than my 12-inch stainless steel skillet for most things related to ramen: searing chashu, pan-roasting chicken thighs or breasts, toasting spices, and charring onions.

14-INCH CARBON-STEEL WOK. A wok is the most versatile cooking vessel in the world. You can use it to boil, steam, sear, sauté, and smoke; you can even flip it over and, provided it's nicely seasoned, cook flatbreads on it. They are indispensable for making stir-fried vegetables, and for ramen that's built with seared tare. A cast-iron pan and a 3-quart saucier could serve as substitutes for a wok for these two purposes, but the wok's general versatility makes it a necessity in any kitchen. If you have a wok, you should also have a wok spatula.

RIMMED ALUMINUM SHEET PAN WITH FITTED WIRE RACKS. These are indispensable for roasting meats and vegetables, for cooling cooked foods, for defrosting frozen foods, for drying various things, and for resting cooked foods. They also are the best vessel for all kinds of prep work, whether that's making gyoza or stashing chopped vegetables. For home cooks, I recommend at least two half sheet pans, four quarter sheet pans, and four eighth sheet pans, and at least two wire cooling racks that fit into the half sheet and quarter sheet pans, respectively. Once you have a couple, you'll probably want more. I think I could have ten of each and still use more.

STRAIGHT-SIDED 2-QUART POT. This is an entirely optional piece of equipment, but I find it useful for making tare, particularly in the relatively small quantities that are best suited for home cooks. The straight sides mean that a small volume of liquid will be deeper than in a pan with sloping sides, which helps with soaking and steeping the relatively high proportion of solid materials (kombu, shiitake, katsuobushi). It is also a great size for making single portions of instant noodles, as well as for boiling a single portion of fresh ramen. (When I make ramen for lunch for myself, I use a 3-quart saucier for the stock and a 2-quart pot to boil the noodles.)

BOWLS, CONTAINERS, AND ACCESSORIES

STAINLESS STEEL MIXING BOWLS IN A VARIETY OF SIZES. These are indispensable, useful for storing prepared vegetables, like the large volume of chopped vegetables used in stocks, as well as, well, mixing things like gyoza or wonton filling. The larger bowls are great for straining hot stock into, and when they are set on an aluminum sheet pan, they greatly reduce the time it takes to cool a stock to room temperature.

MASON JARS, DELI CONTAINERS, AND CAMBROS. You will need storage containers for your stock, tare, and oils. Tare and oils will easily fit into Mason jars, which have the benefit of being made from glass rather than plastic. Deli containers are cheap and, provided you don't add hot liquids to them, can be reused many times. Cambros, large heavy-duty plastic storage containers with volumetric measurements etched into their sides, are useful for large or small amounts of stock, and, since they're rectangular or square, they're easily stackable, and they also fit quite well in most refrigerators. Larger Cambros, like 6- to 8-quart containers, can be used as the water bath for most immersion circulators. Most of mine are 4-quart Cambros, which I use both for stocks and for storing flour: one can comfortably hold a 5-pound bag of flour.

KITCHEN TORCH. I went for years without a kitchen torch, and while they're very convenient and easy to use, they're an entirely optional piece of kitchen equipment for most home cooks. A broiler will perform the same function. I use my torch almost exclusively for chashu.

COOKING WEIGHTS. A weight designed to be placed on top of meat to maximize its surface contact with a hot pan is very useful for searing. I use them for steaks and chops regularly, as well as roasts, but in the context of ramen, I most often use one for pan-roasting chicken breasts or thighs before slicing them up to use as toppings. The breasts or thighs become more compact, and the skin gets much crispier. These weights come in various shapes and sizes, but I prefer the ones made by Chef's Press, which are flat rectangles of metal with vents that allow steam to escape.

TOOLS

SCALE. Every kitchen should have a scale accurate to 1 gram. I use a scale for measuring out the ingredients for tare (most liquids can be assumed to have the same density of water, as they're primarily water, and thus 1 gram of liquid equals 1 ml of liquid); to weigh meat to determine how much salt to use for curing it; and, crucially, for measuring out the ingredients for noodle doughs. If you don't make noodles, you can get away with not having a scale; however, I strongly recommend you buy one!

FINE-MESH SIEVE. If you're making ramen, you'll be pouring a lot of things through sieves: stock, tare, fat, noodles, vegetables, wontons, etc. To me, this is a nonnegotiable piece of equipment. It is best to have a fine-mesh sieve; those with larger perforations aren't as versatile.

SALAD SPINNER. While you aren't going to be making much salad for ramen, you will likely deal with a fair number of leafy vegetables, particularly spinach. I swear I've spent about half of my time cooking ramen washing spinach, since spinach, particularly the good, mature, leafy kind, is a very, very dirty vegetable.

SPRING-LOADED TONGS, COOKING CHOPSTICKS, AND/OR OVERSIZED TWEEZERS. All of these tools are used to manipulate foods, whether a tangle of noodles or a piece of meat. If you are very adept at using chopsticks, you don't *need* anything more than a pair of cooking chopsticks, which are just very long chopsticks. But even if you are a chopsticks master, it's likely you'll still find a pair of spring-loaded tongs or oversized tweezers very useful.

LADLE, PREFERABLY A 350-ML ONE. Ladles are the best tool for transferring liquids between containers. They are also very useful for measuring out liquids, particularly when constructing bowls of ramen. Most of the ramen recipes in this book call for 350 ml of stock per bowl, but, of course, a 175-ml ladle will also work.

MEASURING SPOONS AND CUPS. A good set of measuring spoons and several measuring cups of varying volumes help to ensure you are using the precise amounts of ingredients called for. Since most of the ramen recipes in this book call for 30 ml of tare and fat to be added to each bowl, it's helpful to have two tablespoon measures (a tablespoon is 15 ml) for measuring out those ingredients without cross-contamination.

NOODLE BASKETS. One of the few tools that is entirely noodle specific, a noodle-boiling basket isn't a fixture of most kitchens. Designed to boil single portions of noodles, these baskets aren't really essential, as a strainer can perform the same job. Their virtue lies in the fact that they can easily be submerged in and then pulled out of a large pot of water, and multiple baskets can be used at the same time, provided the pot of water is large enough. And noodle baskets are very convenient for blanching small quantities of ingredients.

WOODEN SPOON. An essential tool for any kitchen: any time you need to stir or scrape something around in a hot pot, you're going to want to reach for a wooden spoon.

HEAT-RESISTANT SPATULA. Useful for stirring and folding, a heat-resistant spatula is most valuable for its ability to efficiently scrape mixtures from one container into another. They are very useful for dealing with aromatic oils, whether simply transferring them from a pot to a container or getting every last bit of oil out of a blender canister.

SLOTTED FISH SPATULA/ TURNER. The thin blade of a slotted fish spatula is also useful for turning pieces of meat or anything else that might threaten to stick to a hot pan or grill grate. Every cook should have one, even if you rarely, if ever, cook fish.

FINE-MESH SKIMMER SPOONS. These tools are intended for skimming the surfaces of stocks or other liquids and can also be used as diminutive strainers for small quantities of liquids (like aromatic fats).

PICTURED LEFT TO RIGHT: ladles, noodle basket, tablespoon measure, hashi, renge, and serving bowls

OTHER DEVICES AND GADGETRY

MEAT GRINDER. Whether manual or electric, a meat grinder is a powerful tool that transforms whole muscles into ground meat. It is the most efficient and best way to grind meat for a variety of applications, like sausages, meatballs, and dumpling fillings. It can grind meat to a range of textures, from coarse to fine, depending on the grinding plate used. If you buy whole chickens or larger cuts of meat like pork shoulder and cut them up with any kind of frequency, having a meat grinder is useful, and the hand-crank ones are inexpensive. However, since you can chop meat using other gadgets or methods, and since ground meat is widely available at grocery stores, I can't say a meat grinder is a necessity for most cooks. But if you own one and use it properly, you'll find that the ground meat you produce is superior in texture and quality than anything you can buy or produce with another method.

FOOD PROCESSOR. Food processors can chop, slice, or julienne vegetables; puree soups and sauces; form and knead doughs; and grind meats. They are convenient to use, but an entirely optional piece of equipment.

BLENDER. Having used several different high-end countertop blenders, I can confidently state that they produce better results than hand-held immersion blenders, whether you're blending aromatic oils or blending a portion of an emulsified stock to improve the stock's emulsion. But the high-end blenders are *too* powerful for some applications, like blending up bones for emulsified stocks, as they blitz them to such a fine consistency that you'll have difficulty straining the emulsified stock through a fine-mesh sieve. If you're going to pick one, pick a hand-held blender.

IMMERSION CIRCULATOR. Sous vide is a powerful method for cooking all kinds of ingredients at precisely controlled temperatures. But an immersion circulator is an entirely optional piece of equipment; every element of ramen that can be made sous vide can be cooked using conventional cooking methods.

MICROWAVE. Microwaves are one of the most powerful cooking tools in the modern kitchen, but by and large they're used only for heating up leftovers. I mostly use mine to warm up serving bowls, but they do render fat efficiently.

KITCHEN TIMERS. While the timer on your phone works just as well, it's useful to have a dedicated kitchen timer, particularly when cooking noodles.

NOODLE MACHINES

If you are planning on making your own ramen, you'll need some kind of machine to help you form sheets of dough and knead those sheets. Commercially available pasta-making machines are your best option here, but since pasta-making machines are designed specifically for egg-based pasta doughs, which contain a higher quantity of water, are more supple, and are consequently easier to work with than ramen dough, it's imperative that you understand that the relatively stiff and dry dough used for ramen can wreak havoc on these machines. Carefully read the instructions for making fresh ramen noodles (see page 162) when using one, and proceed with caution.

STAND MIXER WITH PASTA-MAKING ATTACHMENTS. KitchenAid stand mixers have attachments that can form dough into sheets and assist in cutting those sheets into noodles. The main drawback here is that you must use a KitchenAid stand mixer (preferably one of their "Professional" series, which have all-metal parts), and these machines are expensive.

MANUAL PASTA MACHINE. Manual pasta machines, such as those produced by Marcato Atlas, are perfectly suitable for making ramen. The process is more difficult than with an electric machine, as the sheets must be manually run through the rollers and cutters using a hand crank. It's helpful to have an extra pair of hands assisting you if you are using one of these machines. Some manual pasta machines come with motorized attachments, for an additional cost. (This will still be less expensive than buying a KitchenAid with its pasta-making attachments.) If you have absolutely no use for a stand mixer, I recommend getting a Marcato Atlas with a motor attachment. But if all you can afford is a manual pasta machine, rest assured that you'll still be able to produce fresh ramen; the process will just be more time-consuming.

SERVING

RAMEN BOWLS. There are several different styles of bowls commonly used to serve ramen. None of them are required, but they share design elements meant to make ramen look more attractive. When combined, the soup, noodles and toppings will typically come up to about the 70- to 80-percent mark of the bowls, meaning these bowls usually accommodate about a liter of liquid. They often, but not always, have flared sides, to make it easier to sip from the bowl, and they'll often have a little foot at the bottom, which insulates the bowl slightly and keeps the ramen hot. You can find bowls specifically made for ramen online and at specialty Japanese kitchen equipment stores. Of course, you can use other bowls, but they should be able to accommodate a similar amount of liquid.

RENGE. These are flat-bottomed soupspoons (pictured on pages 4 and 47) that are typically served with noodle soups in Japan and other Asian countries. They are very well designed for their purpose, and I strongly suggest picking up a set.

HASHI. Ramen is meant to be eaten with chopsticks. Japanese chopsticks are different from Korean and Chinese chopsticks in that they are typically shaped like an elongated conical prism, whereas the shape of Chinese chopsticks is more like a rectangular prism and Korean chopsticks are usually flat and made of metal. But any chopsticks will do.

ASSORTED SMALL PLATES. Small serving plates are useful for serving accompaniments like lime wedges or pickles on the side. Slightly larger ones are useful for serving tsukemen toppings if you don't want to cover up the noodles.

INGREDIENTS

KOMBU. Kombu is kelp, specifically large specimens of brown algae. Dried kombu is one of the foundational ingredients of Japanese cuisine, as it is the primary ingredient in dashi, and it is often referred to as "dashi kombu." Much of the kombu in Japan is harvested on the island of Hokkaido, and there are several varieties that are especially prized for making dashi: hidaka kombu, rishiri kombu, makombu, and rausu kombu. Each of them produces a dashi with different characteristics, different concentrations of sweetness and glutamates, and slight differences in appearance. While there are other sources of kombu, I generally recommend Japanese kombu. Feel free to experiment with different varieties—for home cooking, the preparation for all of them is identical.

KATSUOBUSHI. Katsuobushi is another foundational Japanese ingredient, and it is also one of the main ingredients in dashi. Made from katsuo (skipjack tuna, or bonito), katsuobushi is the most famous example of a category of dried-smoked fish called "fushi"—for example, smoke-dried mackerel is called "sababushi."

Katsuobushi is prepared in a multistep process that takes about 100 days to complete. Fresh skipjack tuna are deheaded and gutted, then filleted. The fillets are poached at temperatures between 170° and 200°F (76° and 93°C) to firm up the meat and cook it through; cooking the fillets also locks in the inosinic acid concentration in the flesh. Once cooked, the fillets are deboned and then smoked numerous times to dry the flesh. After smoking, the fillets are cleaned up, with all the tar and fat that has accumulated on their surface wiped off. Some of the smoked fillets are then inoculated with a beneficial mold. The mold further dries out the fillets and removes fat even as it encourages fermentation, which gives the fillets their fruity aroma. Then the fillets are sun-dried and the mold is brushed off. The process produces rock-hard fillets—they clink when knocked against one another—that are sold whole or are shaved to varying degrees of thickness.

The number of times the fillets go through smoking and mold-inoculation determines their quality, with those that have undergone repeated smoking and mold-inoculation commanding the highest prices. Mold-inoculated katsuobushi is called "karebushi" and is relatively difficult to find in the United States. Non-mold-inoculated katsuobushi is called "arabushi," and it is what you're more likely to find in specialty markets and Asian grocery stores here.

Katsuobushi is further distinguished by whether or not the fillets still contain some of the dark meat near the bloodline (chiai) and by the way it's sold. Shaved katsuobushi flakes are called "kezuribushi," and the size of those flakes is categorized by the following: usukezuri are very thin, large shavings; atsukezuri are thick (about 0.2 mm), large shavings; and itokezuri are very thin, narrow shavings, which are used for topping dishes rather than for making dashi.

The type of katsuobushi you use will determine many of the characteristics of the resulting dashi. While each one will produce an aromatic and flavorful dashi, katsuobushi that contains some of the chiai will make a darker dashi. A dashi made from karebushi that does not contain chiai will be very refined, with a smoky, almost fruity aroma and a very pale color.

In terms of preparation, large, thin shavings of katsuobushi should only be steeped in hot water for a few minutes. Thicker shavings can be steeped for a longer period of time without muddying the dashi or making it too fishy.

Katsuobushi declines in quality as soon as it's shaved. Packages of fushi are injected with inert gas to extend their shelf life, but as soon as you open the pack, the quality will begin declining. It's best to use katsuobushi as quickly as you can to get the most out of its flavor and aroma, although it will still be perfectly safe to use for months.

FUSHI. The range of other fushi products available in the United States is small. There are some widely available mixed fushi products, which contain the shavings of a variety of smoked fish, like mackerel and scup, and, if you see a packet of shavings that includes fish other than katsuobushi, I heartily recommend picking it up. These tend to be stronger in flavor and aroma, fishier, more in your face. They are important in gyokai preparations—that is, soups that include a large amount of dried fish (these are typically emulsified).

NIBOSHI. The term "niboshi" translates literally as "cooked and dried," and it refers to a range of small fish that are boiled and dried whole. The most common type of niboshi is katakuchi iwashi, made from immature sardines (although these are often referred to as anchovies). Niboshi come in a variety of sizes; the smaller ones are often used for making snacks, and the larger ones are generally used for dashi.

YAKIBOSHI. Prized by ramen cooks in Japan, but sadly difficult to find in the U.S., yakiboshi are fish that have been grilled and then dried.

SHIITAKE. Dried shiitake mushrooms are a common ingredient in dashi because they contain large amounts of guanylic acid, which acts synergistically with the glutamic acid in kombu and the inosinic acid in dried fish. You can find dried shiitake at several different price points, and while the more expensive varieties do offer more flavor and aroma, some of them can cost hundreds of dollars per pound.

SALT. All salts should, in theory, consist only of crystallized NaCl, and so they should all taste the same. However, since there are various harvesting methods for salt, the geometry of those crystals can vary wildly, which translates to significant variances in behavior. Flake salt, for example, like fleur de sel and sel gris, may have relatively large or relatively damp crystals, which affects the way these fall and sit on foods, whereas finer salts, like table salt, fine sea salt, and some kinds of kosher salt, have relatively small, dry crystals. When dissolved in a solution, however, all salts are functionally identical.

That's not to say that different salts can't have different flavors. Kala namak, or black salt, is an Indian salt that's roasted, and the trace amounts of other compounds in the salt result in a sulfurous

PICTURED OPPOSITE:
Commonly used ingredients: niboshi (1), katsuobushi (2), kombu (3), dried scallops (4), dried clams (5), dried shiitake (6), soy sauce (7), mirin (8), and sake (9)

3
2
8
2
2
5
3
6
1
4
7
2
9
3

Soy Sauce

While most traditional soy sauces are made with fermented mold-inoculated soybeans, Japanese soy sauces contain a fair proportion of wheat and, as a result, taste sweeter than Chinese soy sauce and Korean joseon ganjang, which are made with soybeans only.

There are two main kinds of Japanese soy sauce: koikuchi, or dark soy sauce, and usukuchi, or light soy sauce. Koikuchi is the style you find on most grocery shelves, and it shouldn't be confused with Chinese dark soy sauce, which is a darker, thicker, syrupier, and less salty product. Usukuchi is typically saltier, and it has a thinner texture. A lot of the usukuchi sold in the retail market is a blended product of soy sauce mixed with mirin and sake and sugar—I tend to avoid it, but you can find excellent brewed usukuchi at specialty Japanese stores. As a general matter, these soy sauces are interchangeable. For those who use both types, usukuchi is often used to keep the color of the final dish light, which is obviously important aesthetically for ramen.

Mass-market brands like Kikkoman and Yamasa offer "marudaizu" shoyu, which means "whole bean" shoyu, for a slightly higher price than their standard koikuchi soy sauce. The term "whole bean" refers to the fact that the soy sauce was made using whole soybeans, rather than soybean mash, which produces an inferior product that is consequently less expensive. I strongly recommend trying marudaizu shoyu—it is noticeably better than their standard offerings.

Other less common forms of Japanese soy sauce include shiro shoyu, or white soy sauce, and saishikomi shoyu, or double-fermented soy sauce. Shiro shoyu is made with a higher proportion of wheat than other soy sauces, and it is pale and clear. It has less flavor than koikuchi, but the lighter color is aesthetically appealing. Shiro shoyu is often used in shio ramen to add umami depth without any caramel coloring. Saishikomi shoyu is made in the same way as koikuchi, but rather than brining the mold-inoculated soybeans and wheat in a salt solution, brewed soy sauce is used.

flavor and aroma after roasting. Other salts are similarly impure, and thus they carry with them additional flavors; while faint, these are nevertheless present.

I always use Diamond Crystal kosher salt to develop recipes. If you use teaspoons and tablespoons to measure salt, rather than weight, this is important to know. Different salts have different densities, based on the shape of the salt crystals; a teaspoon of Diamond Crystal contains almost half as much salt as a teaspoon of table salt.

MISO. Miso is a paste made from fermented soybeans and grains that include rice and barley. The soybeans and grains are cooked and inoculated with *Aspergillus* mold, then left to ferment for months. Different proportions of soybeans to grains yield different kinds of miso. (Miso can be made from other legumes and grains using a similar process.)

The main types of miso you'll find in the grocery store are shiromiso (white), akamiso (red), and awasemiso (a blend of red and white miso). White miso gets its color and mild flavor from the relatively low proportion of soybeans used in the mix; akamiso uses a higher proportion of soybeans, and it is often aged. There is also a darker miso, hacho miso, which is made entirely with soybeans and is aged extensively.

Although tamari is often referred to as shoyu, or soy sauce, it is a distinct product. Tamari is in fact the "proto" soy sauce, and it was used for seasoning in Japan long before the production method for soy sauce was introduced from China. Tamari is a by-product of the miso-making process: soybeans are inoculated with mold, packed into containers, and left to ferment. As they do so, they produce liquid runoff, which is tamari.

Shiro shoyu, saishikomi shoyu, and tamari are generally used as dips or finishing sauces. These are fair game for inclusion in tares.

There are two main kinds of Chinese soy sauce: light and dark. Unlike Japanese soy sauces, the light version is the more all-purpose soy sauce (it is actually very similar to Japanese dark soy sauce), and dark Chinese soy sauce has more limited applications. There are several mass-market Chinese soy sauces available across the U.S., and they can all be used to great effect in ramen tare or for seasoning toppings and such. The one thing to keep in mind about light Chinese soy sauce is that it is less sweet than Japanese soy sauce, because it doesn't contain any wheat.

I strongly recommend seeking out artisanal Chinese soy sauces and experimenting with them in your own cooking.

The same can be said about the different types of Korean ganjang. Varieties that use only soybeans are called "joseon ganjang," and those that incorporate some wheat are called "yangjo ganjang." Both can be used interchangeably with koikuchi soy sauce.

Avoid soy sauces made from hydrolyzed soy proteins, using a chemical process that mimics what happens when soybeans are inoculated with mold and fermented. As a rule, chemically produced soy sauces have a harsher, saltier flavor, and little in the way of sweetness and complexity to ameliorate those harsh flavors. When in doubt, consult the ingredient list; a good soy sauce should contain nothing more than salt, soybeans, wheat, and water (and sometimes alcohol, as a preservative).

MIRIN. Mirin is a sweet rice wine. It adds a rounded sweetness to foods, as well as umami, as it's made with *Aspergillus*-inoculated rice. Its sugar content helps to produce an attractive glaze on cooked foods. Much of the mirin available in Japanese grocery stores and specialty shops in the U.S. is not true mirin, but a mirin-like product, often sold as "aji mirin," which basically means "tastes like mirin." There are also nonalcoholic mirin-like options available, including honteri mirin. For most home cooks, these products can be used interchangeably, but "hon mirin," or true mirin, has a greater complexity of flavor.

SAKE. Sake is a rice wine made with polished rice that's been inoculated with *Aspergillus* mold and fermented. Sake is used in various ways in cooking, providing acidity and sweetness, as well as some umami. It's commonly used to ameliorate or mask meaty and fishy smells in dishes.

OYSTER SAUCE. One of the crowning culinary achievements of the nineteenth century, oyster sauce was created by Lee Kum Sheung, a chef in southern China, when he accidentally boiled down an oyster soup stock into a thick sauce. Oyster sauce has a sweet and savory flavor profile that is basically inimitable and makes everything taste delicious. It adds a savory depth to tare and bowls of ramen. It is an essential ingredient for any home cook.

FISH SAUCE. When people speak of fish sauce, they are usually referring to Vietnamese or Thai fish sauce, a fermented sauce made from anchovies and salt and little else, although many brands add sugar and MSG. There are a variety of Japanese fish sauces, made from anchovies, squid, and other fish, but they are relatively hard to find. I like Red Boat fish sauce because it contains no additives, but most any Thai or Vietnamese fish sauce can be used in its place (with the understanding that some may be sweeter or more . . . MSG-ier). Fish sauce is essentially liquid packed with glutamates and inosinates, so it's perhaps best viewed as one of the most delicious flavor enhancers in the world, and should be used accordingly—that is, with almost everything.

DOUBANJIANG. Doubanjiang is a fermented paste made from broad beans (fava beans), soybeans, and chili peppers. A signature ingredient of Sichuan cuisine, it's one of the defining flavoring elements of famous dishes like ma po tofu. As is true of many Chinese ingredients, there is a Japanese version, which goes by the name "tobanjan," but I prefer to use doubanjiang. Pixian doubanjiang is generally considered to be superior, as it has a deeper flavor profile because of its longer fermentation process. There is also another somewhat similar product called "hongyou doubanjiang," which is a less fermented, more oily cousin to doubanjiang and is excellent in soups. I recommend picking up both kinds. Mala Market is a very good source for these pastes, as well as a range of other high-quality Sichuan ingredients. Some doubanjiang, like the one sold by Lee Kum Kee, contain MSG. While the Lee Kum Kee product is inferior to pixian doubanjiang, it is still eminently tasty.

MSG/HAIMI. For information on these chemical flavor enhancers, see page 115.

SPICES. Whenever possible, I suggest buying spices in their whole form and grinding them yourself as necessary. Whole spices keep far better than ground spices, and the freshly ground spices have more flavor and aroma.

PEPPER. There are many kinds of pepper, and even more kinds of "peppercorns" (see below). The most common form of pepper used in ramen is white pepper. All the recipe amounts given for white pepper in this book are suggestions, since the vast majority of white pepper on the market is the preground stuff, which varies widely in terms of aroma and flavor. Since whole white peppercorns also vary in intensity of flavor and aroma depending on their source of origin and age, it's very difficult to provide precise measurements. As with any spices, buy whole white peppercorns if you can and grind them yourself; the results are almost always funkier and more interesting than preground white pepper.

The other kinds of "peppercorns" called for in this book are Sichuan pepper and sansho pepper, neither of which are actually peppercorns; they are the dried flowers of trees related to citrus. Both create a kind of numbing sensation on the tongue; both also contain a not-negligible amount of sodium, and so they make things taste saltier. Mala Market is the best source of Sichuan peppercorns; sansho peppercorns can be purchased from various spice vendors.

LARD. Lard is an essential ingredient in ramen, so finding a good source for it is imperative. You could, of course, render lard yourself from solid pork fat, but it is a smelly process, and good-quality lard can be found at most good butchers and some supermarkets. Avoid hydrogenated lard, which is sold in bricks in the refrigerated section; it does not taste as good as plain rendered lard.

NOODLES, STORE-BOUGHT. See Noodles, pages 33–35.

SPINACH. Spinach is a wonderful, delicious vegetable; baby spinach is not. Try to find mature leaf spinach, with long hardy stems and big, curly leaves. Good alternatives are other heartier, flavorful greens, such as chard, kale, or mustard greens.

WAKAME. Wakame, a thin, edible kelp often sold dried or cured, is excellent in soups.

WONTON SKINS AND DUMPLING SKINS. Wonton skins are distinct from dumpling (gyoza) skins in that their dough is, like ramen dough, alkaline. That means they can be cooked very thoroughly and then submerged in hot soup but still retain a bit of snap and chew. You can find both in the refrigerated and freezer sections of Japanese and Asian supermarkets.

DRIED CHILIES. Dried chilies are basically interchangeable for the recipes in this book—with obvious differences in heat levels and flavors—so try all the ones available to you. Dried chilies should have supple, leathery skins and smell distinctly like the dried fruit they are; avoid dried chilies that have papery skins and are falling apart.

SESAME PASTE. Chinese roasted sesame paste is distinct from tahini, a related product that is more widely available. Tahini is made from unroasted sesame seeds, while the seeds used to make Chinese sesame paste are roasted, and the paste has a deeper flavor. The two can be used interchangeably, but the results will be markedly different (not *bad*, but different).

VII

HOW TO MAKE RAMEN

1. SOUP STOCK
2. FAT
3. TARE
4. TOPPINGS
5. NOODLES

① SOUP STOCK

Many of the qualities that define a bowl of ramen come from the stock or broth, which makes up most of the volume of liquid in the bowl. These qualities include flavor, aroma, texture, and appearance. Ramen stocks are typically categorized in three ways: by primary ingredients, by clarity, and by texture.

PRIMARY INGREDIENTS: These can be almost anything that produces a flavorful and aromatic broth: dried seafood, like kombu, katsuobushi, or niboshi; meats, like chicken, pork, or beef; fresh fish and shellfish, such as snapper, sea bass, fluke, crab, or clams; and vegetables and dried legumes, such as onions, cabbage, chickpeas, and beans.

CLARITY: No matter what ingredient you use for stock, the stock can be made in such a way as to produce a clear or a cloudy stock. Clear stocks are typically referred to as "chintan" stocks; cloudy stocks are referred to as "paitan" stocks.

TEXTURE: Stocks are typically characterized as being either thin ("assari") or thick ("kotteri"). The texture of a stock can be affected by four different qualities: the amount of particulate matter it contains, the amount of dissolved starch in the stock, the amount of fat emulsified into the stock, and the amount of gelatin it contains.

These definitions are important to understand as a ramen cook because they give you clearly articulated goals. Depending on the qualities you'd like your final bowl of ramen to have, you have to use not only specific ingredients but also specific methods for each of those ingredients. For example, while the chemical and physical processes for making a chicken paitan and a pork paitan are essentially the same, the methods used to produce the two stocks are quite different.

The following pages (62–110) detail how to prepare stocks made from dried seafood, meat, fish, vegetables, and legumes separately, but because the same principles govern the clarity and texture of stocks regardless of the ingredients used, I'll address these two qualities first.

THE MECHANICS AND IMPORTANCE OF CLARITY

There are several factors that affect the clarity of a stock, although in the end the determining factor comes down to how much *stuff* exists in suspension in the liquid. That stuff can be the proteins released by meats and vegetables, or broken-down starches, or minuscule globules of fat, or it can be all of these things. The clarity of a stock is determined by the degree to which light is refracted or reflected as it passes through the liquid; even the color of a stock can be seen as a function of clarity, as whatever color your eyes perceive the stock to be is produced by wavelengths of light that aren't absorbed by whatever is floating in the stock.

While clarity, or the lack thereof, in a ramen stock is not determinative evidence of its quality, it does offer physical evidence of what the stock does and doesn't contain. Most importantly for the cook making ramen, the clarity is a good indicator for how aggressively the stock should be seasoned. For this reason alone, any home cook should possess a basic understanding of how to prepare a clear stock—even if the only thing you really care about is how your bowls of ramen taste.

You can make a clear stock in two ways. The first is to take as much care as possible to prevent fat and particulate matter from emulsifying and becoming suspended, respectively, in the stock; the second is to remove as much of the fat and particulate matter as possible after the stock has been prepared.

Since the clarity of a stock depends on the amount of material that is suspended or emulsified in the liquid—that is, the amount of material that is mixed with, but not dissolved in, the liquid—the best way to produce a clear stock is to minimize the amount of agitation the liquid is subjected to during its preparation. While this agitation can take many forms—including stirring, blending, sloshing, and pouring—the most important ones when cooking a stock are simmering and boiling. More precisely, the best way to limit the amount of agitation when preparing a stock is to control its cooking temperature.

At normal atmospheric pressure (i.e., air pressure at sea level), the boiling point of water is 212°F (100°C). As water is brought to that temperature, the water molecules will have enough energy to overcome the pressure exerted on the liquid by the surrounding atmosphere, transforming them into water vapor, which manifests as bubbles in the liquid. These rising bubbles agitate the liquid, literally pushing around the water molecules that remain in their liquid state as they rise to the surface, along with anything suspended within it. The size of these bubbles of vapor, and the speed with which they rise, are determined by the temperature of the liquid.

The terms we use to describe a pot of hot liquid at or near the boiling point of water are "simmering" and "boiling," and while the way in which these words are used is descriptive, and thus qualitative, they can be translated to specific temperatures. At normal atmospheric pressure, liquid starts to produce errant small bubbles of vapor at about 185°F (85°C). The quantity of those bubbles and the frequency with which they rise to the surface steadily increase until the liquid reaches about 205°F (96°C).

LEFT TO RIGHT: katsuobushi dashi, chicken chintan, chicken paitan, and roasted pork chintan

Above that temperature, the bubbles grow larger, culminating with very large bubbles churning constantly toward the surface of the liquid when it reaches the boiling point, commonly referred to as a "roiling" or "rolling" boil.

If your goal is to produce as little agitation as possible from boiling as you cook your stock, the solution is to bring the temperature of the water to just under 185°F (85°C) and then maintain that temperature for the duration of the cooking time. This is simple enough to do, but it requires a certain degree of fussy attention, as well as a reliable thermometer, and for most stocks, but particularly stocks made from meat, it requires extending the cooking time significantly to produce a stock with a comparable flavor and texture to one prepared at a higher cooking temperature.

Going to the opposite extreme, you can use a pressure cooker. The way a pressure cooker works is that once the pot is sealed and the liquid inside is heated, the pressure that builds up between the surface of the liquid and the top of the pot exceeds normal atmospheric pressure. Pressure cookers designed for home use are fitted with weighted valves that maintain a pressure of about 12 to 15 more pounds per square inch than at normal atmospheric pressure—if the pressure exceeds that amount, it will be sufficient to lift the weight sitting on top of the valve, which then allows excess vapor to vent. Adding pressure to the surface of the liquid means that the water molecules must be heated by a directly proportional amount of energy to transform them into water vapor and escape the liquid. That means that the temperature of liquid in a sealed pressure cooker can exceed the boiling point of water at normal atmospheric pressure, rising up to about 250°F (121°C); it also means that the liquid will not boil and, consequently, won't be agitated until and unless the temperature inside the pot exceeds that upper limit and the pot is allowed to vent.

These two methods—adjusting the temperature of the liquid so it remains just at or below simmering or adjusting the pressure of the liquid so that it cannot boil even at temperatures far over the normal boiling point of water—are the best ways to produce a clear, flavorful stock. The first method will, for most meat stocks, take anywhere from 6 to 12 hours (or longer); the second takes only 1 to 2 hours.

Straining and clarification

Even if you produce a very clear stock right from the get-go, you will still need to get it out of the pot while leaving all the solid material in the pot, which brings us to mechanical means of clarification.

The most common form this takes is straining—passing a stock through a fine mesh so that any solid matter is separated from the liquid. While it may seem like a simple matter to pour stock from its cooking vessel through a strainer into another container, there are a few details to consider if you are trying to produce the clearest stock possible.

The first is mesh size. If you pour the stock through a colander, large pieces of solid matter like bones and bits of flesh will be strained out, but smaller bits will easily pass through the colander's large holes. Pass the stock through a fine-mesh strainer, and, of course, fewer smaller bits will pass through. You can take this principle to an extreme: you could, for example, buy medical-grade sieves with extremely small holes that measure in microns; if you use one of these to strain your stock, it will certainly be clearer than one that's been sieved through your standard-issue fine-mesh strainer. However, a more practical solution is to fold up some dampened cheesecloth and line your strainer with it. Passing the liquid not just once, but twice or several times, through a cheesecloth-lined strainer will produce even clearer results.

LEFT TO RIGHT: Coagulated proteins rising to the surface of a stock just after it's come to a boil; the same stock after simmering for several hours

Another way in which you can use a strainer to facilitate achieving a clear stock is by skimming the water with a fine-mesh skimmer as it initially comes to a boil, removing what is typically referred to as "scum." This is common practice for all kinds of stock, and the intent is to remove any obvious bits of particulate matter that might make your stock cloudy. Meat stock will produce a fair amount of foamy stuff in the first hour after it comes up to about a simmer, as myoglobin proteins denature, solidify, and rise to the surface.

The same principle of removing matter at the beginning of the process to ensure a certain degree of clarity (and color) is at work when a cook soaks or blanches the meat and bones before preparing the stock. Soaking meaty bones in cold water will remove a significant amount of myoglobin, which is evidenced by the pinkish-red tinge the water will take on after about 5 hours. If clarity and color are of the utmost importance, the cook can then blanch these soaked meaty bones—that is, place them in a pot of fresh water, bring it to a boil, and allow the water to boil for a short period of time, anywhere from 15 to 30 minutes—and then drain the bones and rinse them of any dark, scummy matter before starting the stock-making process in a clean pot. The primary benefit of these two techniques is that removing a lot of the material that can make your soup cloudy up front allows you to be a little less diligent about controlling the temperature (and thus the agitation) of the stock when you're preparing it, since there's less dark stuff that can end up suspended in the soup.

Just as you can remove such material before you start making the stock, you can remove it after the fact by using a clarifying raft. After you've prepared your stock, chilled it, and defatted it, place it in a pot along with a mixture of egg whites and finely chopped vegetables, and/or ground or finely chopped meat, and bring it to a boil as you stir it constantly. Then, once the egg whites begin to set, you stop stirring, and the egg whites, along with the other solid material, congeal to form a "raft," which rises up through the stock, picking up and holding onto anything suspended in it. You keep the liquid at a strong simmer until the raft solidifies completely, then carefully ladle the stock out of the pot and pass it through a strainer, at which point you'll have what the French call "consommé"—a crystal-clear stock.

A clarifying raft works in two ways: The first and most obvious is that as the egg whites solidify and rise, the raft acts as a sieve; as it rises through the liquid, larger bits of particulate matter are caught in the raft, and when the egg whites fully cook and solidify, those bits of particulate matter are trapped. The second, less obvious way has to do with the fact that egg whites are also almost entirely protein, and cooked proteins have a kind of natural affinity and almost magnetic attraction for other cooked proteins. When heat is applied to a protein molecule, it denatures, which means its physical structure changes.* It can help to visualize a protein as a single string, bunched together; when it's heated, that bunched-up string unfurls. The string itself is unchanged, but the alignment of its parts changes, exposing more of the proteins to the surrounding environment. When many denatured proteins are in proximity and being jostled, as in a hot stockpot, they collide and become tangled up. So, with an egg white raft, as the proteins in the egg white and ground meat cook and denature, the denatured proteins in the stock get stuck in the raft and become attached to it. In Chinese cuisine, stocks are often clarified using lean pieces of meat rather than a raft, but the principle at work is identical; as the meat cooks, other bits of protein in the stock will attach to it, leaving the stock clearer after the cooked meat is removed.

There is one last method for promoting clarity in stocks of all kinds, which relies on the fact that suspended solids in a stock will, with gravity, settle over time. You can use this to your advantage by allowing a stock to sit for a while and then carefully ladling or pouring off only the clear upper portion. The stock remaining in the pot, while somewhat cloudier, will still be quite clear, and it can be used when the clearest stock possible isn't necessary.

* For a fuller description of protein denaturing, see Harold McGee, *On Food and Cooking: The Science and Lore of the Kitchen* (Collier Books, 1988), pp. 594–96.

THE MECHANICS OF TEXTURE

We often describe soups as having "body" or "texture." Even though those terms typically refer to the holistic experience of eating the soup, they are the result of multiple factors.

As mentioned earlier, the body and texture of a stock are directly related to the amount of suspended solids, the amount of emulsified fat, and the amount of dissolved gelatin and other thickeners in the stock, and the quantities of each in the final stock are determined by the cooking temperature, the cooking time, and the points during the process when you strain out material.

Let's use a simple chicken stock to illustrate the mechanics, one made with chicken bones and meat, a few aromatic vegetables, and water that has been brought to near boiling. At the beginning of the process, as the water starts to come to a boil and scum rises to the surface, there isn't much else floating around in the water. The meat is still holding onto its fat, flavor (which is essentially protein), and, importantly, gelatin. The vegetables are similarly still largely intact. You could still manipulate the liquid in the pot to produce a clear stock by reducing the temperature or through careful straining, simply because there isn't much material in there.

If you let the stock boil for a while, however, that changes. Not only is more stuff being released into the stock as the ingredients cook; the quantity of dissolved starches and gelatin increases as well. Starch and gelatin are both thickeners, which means they effectively bind with water and make the liquid more viscous, and they are, consequently, also both emulsifiers, so they make it easier to disperse fat evenly through liquid. The higher the concentrations of starch and gelatin in the stock, the easier it is to bind up both fat and other particulate matter in the stock; conversely, higher concentrations make it more challenging to produce a clear stock.

The starches aren't as much of a concern as gelatin, as they constitute a tiny portion of the total solid matter in the stock. In other stocks, the amount of vegetable matter that's added to the pot, and the point(s) at which those vegetables are added, will have greater or smaller effects on the body of the stock, but for this one, you can disregard the vegetable matter and focus solely on the chicken bones and meat.

The rate at which fat, gelatin, and proteins are extracted from the chicken and bones depends on the size of the chicken parts, the temperature at which the stock is being cooked, and the duration of the cooking time. Much of the flavor will be extracted within a couple of hours, no matter the cooking temperature, since chickens and chicken parts are relatively small. The fat, which for clear stocks will be removed later in any case, begins rendering out at a temperature below simmering (about 140°F/60°C), but it takes time to render it out completely; chicken meat that has been cooked for 6 hours in a stock will still have a fair amount of fat, which is evident in the fat that's produced if you use those spent chicken bones to produce a secondary stock (see page 98). In the context of the stock's texture, however, the most important element is gelatin extraction; actually, not gelatin *extraction*, but gelatin *conversion*.

Gelatin is not a substance that simply resides in the bones and meat, waiting for a quick dunk in water to slough it off and dissolve into the liquid. Instead, it is produced when collagen is heated in water. Collagen is one of three proteins that make up the connective tissue in animals' bodies—"protein structures that surround the live cells that made them," as Harold McGee describes its makeup in *On Food and Cooking*. Connective tissue, as the name suggests, links muscle fibers to one another and to the skeleton of an animal's body. The reason all stock recipes call for bones is not that bones themselves possess flavor of any kind; in fact, they have very little inherent flavor, and in clear stocks, the minerals they contain (mostly calcium) don't even end up in the liquid. Bones are called for because they will normally have a lot of connective tissue attached to them, along with bits of meat attached to that connective tissue, and, as such, are a rich source of collagen.

The rate at which gelatin dissolves into water is dependent on the temperature of the water. Collagen begins to break down and turn into water-soluble gelatin at around 130°F (54°C); as the temperature increases, the speed at which the collagen converts into gelatin increases. If we decide to keep the liquid in our simple chicken stock at 160°F (71°C), it will take many, many hours—something like 8 to 12—to convert enough collagen into gelatin to give the stock ample body. However, if we boil the stock at a hard boil (212°F/100°C), we can produce a full-bodied stock in far less time, more like 4 hours. And if we use a pressure cooker and raise the cooking temperature above the boiling point of water, to 250°F (121°C), we can produce a full-bodied stock in only 1 or 2 hours.

Trying to produce a clear stock that has a significant amount of body means you are working toward two goals that exist in tension with each other. Low cooking temperatures benefit the goal of clarity, but they make gelatin conversion a lengthier process; high cooking temperatures make it more difficult to produce a clearer stock, but they facilitate gelatin conversion. A pressure cooker can solve both problems at the same time, as it can cook a stock at an extremely high temperature with very little agitation, producing a clear stock with a lot of gelatin in a fraction of the time it would take using a conventional pot.

EMULSIFIED STOCK

Making an emulsified stock can require less attention than making a clear one. You can take the same combination of chicken parts and vegetables, cover them with water, bring the liquid to a rolling boil, and just let it boil for several hours, covered or uncovered, topping it off as needed with more water so the pot doesn't boil dry, and you'll produce a milky stock rich with gelatin, fat, and flavor.

However, as with a clear stock, you can pick and choose what you include in your emulsified stock, depending on your goals. For example, if you'd like your emulsified stock to be very pale, taking its color almost entirely from the fat emulsified into the liquid, you may want to soak the raw bones and meat in water overnight to leach out some myoglobin, which will transform into dark scum once the stock starts cooking. You could also blanch the bones and meat, rinse off any dark material, and then start making the stock with fresh water. Alternatively, you could simply skim off the initial scum produced by boiling. Or, as is often the case, you can employ all three techniques in combination.

All of these techniques will have an effect on the stock's appearance, of course, but they will also affect its flavor, which can be thought of as the sum total of all the elements that are swimming around in the liquid. An emulsified stock made with blanched chicken bones that has been skimmed in the first hour of boiling will be whiter than an unskimmed stock made starting with raw bones, but it will also taste "cleaner," as it will contain less of the brownish particulate matter exuded by the meat.

The way you add other ingredients to an emulsified stock has a similar importance for appearance, texture, and flavor. You can, for example, add onions and garlic and ginger early in the process and, regardless of whether or not you strain them out at the end, they will contribute a fair amount of starch and sugars to the liquid. You can add them only toward the end of the cooking process and then strain them out, which means they will contribute a minimum of starch. Or, you can do a little bit of both. You can also add vegetables that have very little effect on flavor but have profound effects on texture, such as potatoes. After prolonged cooking, potatoes will have contributed a fairly large amount of bland starch to the liquid, making it easier to produce and maintain a strong emulsion but also diluting some of the stock's meaty flavor.

For these reasons, I don't recommend dumping all your ingredients into a pot of water and letting it boil for hours if you want to make an emulsified stock. Instead, I cook it in stages, adding and removing ingredients as necessary to produce the results you want. I follow a similar approach to the one I use for clear stocks for emulsified stocks, as it's more hands-off—you don't need to watch the water level in the pot for hours—and gives you more control over the final product. You'll produce a relatively clear stock, cooked at a higher temperature to facilitate the rendering of fat and the conversion of gelatin, and then at the end, you'll use agitation in one form or another to emulsify the broth, incorporating only those elements you want.

HOW TO MAKE DASHI (AND INCORPORATE DRIED SEAFOOD INTO STOCK)

Dashi is used in soups, as a cooking base, and as a seasoning. Many of the same techniques used to make dashi have been adapted and applied to making ramen broths and tare.

While a dashi can be made with only kombu, in which case it's typically called "kombu dashi," the word "dashi" most often refers to a soup stock made with kombu and katsuobushi, shavings of processed dried skipjack tuna loin. Dashi may also include other dried seafood products, such as dried scallops and clams, as well as ingredients like niboshi, or boiled and dried immature sardines, and dried vegetables, particularly dried mushrooms, such as shiitake. The importance of dashi in Japanese cuisine has led to a fair amount of research into these ingredients, the chemistry behind why they are so flavorful, and how best to extract their flavors.* This research has, in turn, resulted in several best practices concerning their use, each rigidly followed by professional Japanese cooks. These methods are designed to maximize the flavor and aroma of dashi and limit or eliminate any "off" flavors these ingredients can produce. While there's no way to describe them other than "fussy," understanding why they are observed is useful for making ramen.

Many of these practices differ sharply from the way in which Korean and Chinese cooks use the same ingredients; for example, while boiling dashi ingredients is generally looked down upon by Japanese cooks, Korean cooks boil dashima (kombu) and dried anchovies as a matter of course. Further, since ramen-making techniques draw heavily on Chinese culinary conventions, and because ramen is in many ways less "refined" than classical Japanese cuisine, the proscription against boiling dashi ingredients is often ignored, particularly when preparing thicker emulsified ramen broths.

But as with any set of rules, it helps to know why they exist before you break them.

Kombu Dashi

The simplest dashi of all is kombu dashi, with only two ingredients: kombu and water.

The consensus ideal cooking temperature for kombu extraction is 140°F (60°C); studies have shown the density of glutamic acid in kombu dashis made with identical quantities of identical ingredients are much higher when the dashi is held at that temperature rather than 170°F (76°C).† It isn't so difficult to maintain a temperature of 140°F (60°C) in a pot of water for an hour, but it does require careful monitoring, and you can't step away from the kitchen while the dashi is cooking. For this reason, some cooks now use immersion circulators to make kombu dashi, as these machines provide near-absolute temperature control.

However, this is one instance where you

* See "What Is Umami?" (page 113).

† The Japanese Culinary Academy, *Flavor and Seasonings: Dashi, Umami, and Fermented Foods* (Shuhari Initiative, 2017), p. 46.

need not let perfect be the enemy of the good. A kombu dashi cooked at 170°F (76°C) for an hour may not be as flavorful as one cooked at that lower temperature, but that doesn't mean it isn't powerfully flavorful; it is also unlikely that you (or I!) would notice any deficiency in it, barring a side-by-side taste test.

Cold-soaking kombu in water for an extended period is another, and completely hands-off, method for maximizing the extraction of glutamic acid. If you soak kombu in cold water overnight, you will produce a strong dashi; if you then heat that water along with the kombu, you'll produce an even stronger dashi. The efficacy of soaking is dependent on the type of kombu you use. Some types contain higher quantities of alginic acid than others,* and, when they are hydrated, the alginic acid forms a viscous gum that coats the surface of the kombu leaves, limiting their exposure to the water that surrounds them and, consequently, the amount of flavorful compounds you can extract from them. For this reason, it's helpful to periodically agitate the kombu in its soaking water.

What you do with the kombu and its soaking water is up to you. You can simply remove the kombu and use the soaking water as is, or you can bring the kombu and water up to 140°F (60°C), hold it at that temperature for an hour, and then remove the kombu. Or you can do what many home cooks do and put the kombu and water in a pot, bring the liquid to the barest of simmers (tiny bubbles will begin to form on the surface of the water), which translates to a temperature around 170°F (76°C), then turn off the heat. All of these methods will produce a fully flavored kombu dashi, of varying strengths. For the sake of convenience, I recommend this last method. The kombu dashi requires very little attention, you don't need to break out a thermometer, and the results are good.

Regardless of the method you choose, the kombu used in these preparations isn't entirely spent, and it can be used for other preparations, whether that's a second, weaker but still flavorful dashi, which can be used as a flavor base for a braise or marinade, or for cooked preparations like tsukudani (simmered seasoned kombu) or furikake (a seasoning for rice).

Kombu dashi can be fortified with other ingredients to amplify its flavor. The most common are katsuobushi and dried shiitake mushrooms.

Kombu Shiitake Dashi

Dried shiitake mushrooms are often paired with kombu to make dashi because shiitake, when heated in water, produce relatively large amounts of guanylic acid, a flavorful compound that has been found to work synergistically with glutamic acid. That means that a stock that has a combination of glutamates and guanylates is much more flavorful than a stock that has only one of those compounds.

The method for making dashi with shiitake mushrooms is like the method for making dashi with kombu. To make a dashi with shiitake, you rehydrate (soak) the mushrooms in cold water, then remove them from the liquid, heat the liquid to, ideally, 140°F (60°C), add the shiitake back to the liquid, and let the mushrooms steep at that temperature for a short period of time.

Be sparing in your use of shiitake. Dried mushrooms are flavorful and aromatic, so much so that they can be overpowering; soaking a large amount of mushrooms in water overnight and then using the soaking water and those mushrooms can yield a dark and very mushroom-y dashi, which may or may not be what you want.

---

* The Japanese Culinary Academy, *Flavor and Seasonings*, pp. 46–47.

Dashi made with katsuobushi, shiitake, and kombu

Dashi with Kombu and Katsuobushi

In classical Japanese cuisine, the way katsuobushi is used in dashi is intended to maximize extraction of flavorful compounds and appealing aromas while minimizing any "off" flavors or aromas. These off flavors aren't necessarily those you'd associate with the idea of a block of dried fish, as they aren't "fishy," per se (they are in fact more sour than anything else), but the main problem is that they seem muddy. However, if you make dashi using kombu and katsuobushi in the manner prescribed by classical Japanese technique, it will be clear, full of flavor, and possessed of an intoxicating but light smoky aroma, and it will above all else be "clean."

That process, like all the others involved in dashi-making, has to do with temperature control. First you make a kombu dashi. After you remove the kombu, you bring the dashi to about 185°F (85°C), add quite a lot of katsuobushi, shut off the heat, and let the mixture steep for anywhere from 30 seconds to 30 minutes, depending on the thickness of the katsuobushi flakes. Pass the liquid through a fine-mesh strainer, and you have a clean-tasting, aromatic dashi.

The short steeping time may seem surprising, but it is entirely sufficient to extract much of the flavor from the katsuobushi flakes, as they are generally shaved very thin, which maximizes the surface area. There isn't any need to cook the katsuobushi for long, as is necessary with fresh meat and fish, because its flavors have already been developed by its protracted production process. It possesses smoke flavor from smoking, compounds created by Maillard reactions in the smoking process, and a high concentration of inosinic acid because of the initial poaching treatment the katsuo fillets are put through.

But why not boil the katsuobushi, or at least let it steep for longer? The best illustration of why you shouldn't do this, and of the muddy aroma and flavor of a badly made dashi, is niban dashi, a secondary stock made by boiling kombu and katsuobushi that has already been used once in fresh water for at least 10 minutes to make another dashi. Niban dashi is a way to get the most out of expensive dried seafood, and that seafood is boiled, rather than simmered, to quickly extract as much flavor as possible. However, the aroma of a niban dashi is noticeably inferior to that of an ichiban dashi, and its flavor is muddier and noticeably more sour and fishy. In a soup in which dashi figures prominently, that sour fishiness would be distracting; in other preparations, though, such as when a niban dashi is used as the basis of a braise or as poaching liquid for strong-flavored vegetables, like bitter or sweet greens, that flavor is less noticeable.

Niboshi Dashi

Niboshi are a class of boiled and dried fish products made from a wide variety of small fish. Unlike katsuobushi, which is made from skipjack tuna loin, niboshi use whole ungutted fish. They produce a stock that is far more "fishy" than a dashi made with katsuobushi, but it has none of the smoky aroma or flavorful compounds created by Maillard browning reactions. However, niboshi have a lot of inosinic acid because of the boiling step that precedes drying, and they contain a fair amount of glutamic acid. Each kind of niboshi has its own subtle but enticing aroma.

The most common forms of niboshi you'll find in the U.S. are made from iriko or iwashi, which are both kinds of immature sardines, although they're often labeled as anchovies. When making dashi, niboshi are treated slightly differently from katsuobushi, mostly because they are whole fish, no matter how diminutive, and thus don't have the large amount of surface area of shavings of katsuobushi. Unlike katsuobushi, niboshi are often soaked in cold water along with kombu before being simmered to make dashi. However, as with katsuobushi, it isn't generally recommended that you boil niboshi when making dashi, to avoid the extraction of bitter and "off" fishy flavors. Niboshi are also often beheaded and gutted before being used in dashi, as the head and guts would contribute stronger, fishier flavors.

Applying Dried Seafood Stock-Making Practices to Making Ramen

So how do these best practices apply to making ramen? Are you obliged to get out your instant-read thermometer and always check the temperature of your stocks and tare? Must you throw out your dashi if its cooking temperature rises a hair above 140°F (60°C)? Is it a waste of ingredients to not soak your kombu?

Although you could follow all these practices to the letter, home cooks can actually pick and choose among them, particularly the ones that are entirely hands-off, like soaking, and use visual cues, like the formation of bubbles in heating liquids at various temperatures, to estimate cooking temperatures. This gives you a nice compromise between maximizing flavor extraction and minimizing the fussiness of preparation.

Here are a few simple rules to follow when making dashi and dashi-related products where clarity and clean flavors are the goal:

SOAK YOUR KOMBU IN COLD WATER BEFORE MAKING DASHI. Soaking the kombu for an hour before making dashi will yield a noticeably more flavorful dashi. And a longer soak time, up to about 24 hours, is almost always better than a shorter one. If you are using dried seafood other than katsuobushi, it is also a good idea to soak it in cold water.

AGITATE THE SOAKING KOMBU. At least once or twice during its soaking time, slosh the kombu and its water around. This helps move aside any mucilaginous stuff that can get in the way of extracting more flavor out of the kombu.

AVOID BOILING OR SIMMERING KOMBU. Boiled kombu contributes a slightly odd aroma and a sometimes distracting flavor to dashi. Use a thermometer or temperature cues offered by the bubbles formed in heating water to prevent the water from coming to a simmer.

REMOVE THE KOMBU BEFORE ADDING OTHER INGREDIENTS. If you're making a shiitake dashi, or a dashi with niboshi or katsuobushi, remove the kombu before raising the temperature of the liquid in anticipation of adding the shiitake or katsuobushi.

DON'T BOIL SHIITAKE OR DRIED SEAFOOD PRODUCTS. Boiling produces "off" or otherwise too-strong flavors in these ingredients, and it also agitates the liquid, which can make it cloudy.

LEFT TO RIGHT: kombu-shiitake dashi after soaking and niboshi-kombu dashi after soaking

WHEN TO BREAK THE RULES

All these rules and suggestions are important for producing the kind of dashi used in classical Japanese cooking, but ramen isn't classical Japanese cooking.

The proscription against boiling dried seafood products is less an inviolate rule than an expression of taste preferences, reflected by the fact that these ingredients are often used in other cuisines without that proscription. For example, in Korean cuisine, it's very common to boil dashima (dried kelp that's essentially identical to kombu) and dried anchovies together to make a basic stock. If you've ever eaten Korean food, you know that any so-called "off" flavors aren't particularly noticeable. This contradiction is also evident in niban dashi, where the ingredients are boiled rather hard to extract their flavors as quickly as possible. Niban dashi is used to cook vegetables and as the basis of braises, so the off flavors don't seem to bother Japanese cooks.

If you intend to use a dashi as a light, clear soup in which to serve a piece of poached fish, the goal is to accentuate the flavor of the fish and provide a savory backdrop. If the dashi is too fishy, the subtle flavor of the poached fish will be muddied or lost. If, however, you're using dried seafood products in something like a paitan, where animal protein and fat are blended into the stock to yield a rich, milky broth, the presence of any "off" flavors is far less noticeable and, in the right circumstances, these can actually complement the other flavors in the broth. For example, a tonkotsu or chicken paitan with a fair amount of niboshi boiled and then blended into the broth is delicious, as the bitterness of the niboshi acts as a counterpoint to the relative sweetness of the meat and vegetables in the stock. Add some katsuobushi, and the sourness produced by boiling the shaved fish flakes in a rich stock can provide a similarly welcome counterpoint. However, in a chintan stock, the bitterness of niboshi or the sour-smokiness of katsuobushi can be distracting, if not actually unpleasant.

CHICKEN STOCK; OR, WHY YOU SHOULD BUY WHOLE CHICKENS

The two main meat stocks used in ramen are chicken and pork. While there are some kinds of ramen made from lamb, beef, duck, and other stocks, they are relatively rare, but the principles that apply to chicken and pork stocks are transitive and can be applied with little to no modification to other meats. For example, you can make a duck stock as you would make a chicken stock, and you can make a beef stock in the same way you'd make a pork stock.

Chicken stock is a fundamental ingredient in kitchens across the world because it's incredibly flavorful, yet not overpowering. The quantity of chicken stock convenience products at your grocery store is evidence of its versatility and importance. Chicken stock is also inexpensive and relatively easy to produce.

I think part of the hesitation on the part of home cooks about making chicken stock at home is they do not understand how easy it can be to prepare. Brown chicken stock isn't particularly difficult to produce, but it is a multistep process: you first brown the chicken bones in a hot oven or in a hot pan, then transfer them to a pot, along with the brown sticky bits they have left in the pan, cover them with water, add roasted vegetables and herbs, and simmer this mixture together for several hours. Strain the stock, and you have a gelatin-rich, lip-smacking liquid with all the flavors and aromas of a roasted chicken dinner.

Although brown chicken stock is a culinary marvel, white (or blond) chicken stock is equally marvelous. It is made without any browning of the ingredients. When it is hot, it is a tawny shade of near-gold, but when chilled, it takes on a whitish cast, pale as a cartoon ghost. And all you have to do to make it is cover chicken bones with water, add a few peeled aromatic vegetables like onions and garlic, simmer the water for a couple of hours, and then strain it.

Brown chicken stock may have the edge on white chicken stock because of the toasty flavors produced by Maillard reactions, but white chicken stock has the benefit of maximum versatility. White chicken stock can be used wherever brown chicken stock can be, with just a small sacrifice of flavor, but it can also be used wherever brown chicken stock's more assertive flavor profile could be distracting, as in braised vegetable dishes, or as a base for stocks fortified with more expensive ingredients, like game birds, or in something like a bowl of ramen, where you simply want a gelatin-rich liquid medium to act as a vehicle for the other flavors.

For these reasons, I recommend that all home cooks make white chicken stock regularly. Its base ingredients—meaty chicken carcasses—are sold for a couple bucks a pound at most grocery stores. But it can be made even more cheaply, and can serve as a kind of easily obtainable education on the fundamental elements of whole animal butchery, stock cookery, and kitchen waste reduction, if you choose to buy whole chickens and cut them up yourself.

breast halves
tenders
wings
deboned drumstick and thigh

KINDS OF CHICKEN

If you only shop at a small grocery store like the one that's a couple blocks from my apartment, your options for chicken are likely limited to several brands, one of which is probably Perdue, and the Perdue stuff will probably be the cheapest in the refrigerated case.

Apart from the branding, the packaging contains useful information, like how the chicken has been processed and whether it's been brined. My recommendation is to buy "air-chilled" chicken, not "wet-chilled" chicken, and to avoid chicken that has been brined. Chickens that have been brined and/or been "wet-chilled" will contain more water, the first by design and the second incidentally, and that excess water dilutes the flavor of the bird.

If you can afford to buy a better bird—"air-chilled" birds, chickens raised on small, independent farms, fresh-killed chicken—then please do so.

HOW TO CUT UP A CHICKEN

There are many ways to cut up a chicken. The technique you use is typically determined by how you're going to use the bird's disparate parts. For the recipes in this book, if you are buying a whole chicken, all you need to know is how to remove the breast halves, legs, and wings and how to debone the legs.

To start, you'll need a sharp knife, a stable cutting board (preferably one dedicated to preparing raw meat), and a couple of receptacles to hold the cut-up parts as you remove them.

For the cutting board, the material matters less here than that it is completely stable. You do not want your cutting board sliding around underneath the bird while you're going at it with a sharp knife. To prevent that, lay a damp cloth towel out on your work surface and place the board on top. Try to push the board around once you've laid it down; if it moves at all, you'll likely need another layer of damp cloth to anchor it.

The receptacles for the chicken parts are also important, if only because you want the cutting board free of clutter so you have room to maneuver the bird. Small sheet pans are excellent for this purpose. I like to have a couple of quarter sheet pans at hand, one for meatier, serving portions of chicken (the breasts, the legs) and another for pieces destined for stock (neck, head, carcass, scraps).

Start by removing the head and neck, if they are still intact: Place the bird on its back on the board and extend the neck. Make a small slice with the tip of your knife at the neck to expose the vertebrae, then set the knife aside and, using your hands, bend the neck over itself so that it snaps at the exposed vertebrae. Then you should be able to simply twist and pull the neck and head away from the bird. Place them in the receptacle for stock pieces.

If the chicken came with its feet attached, remove them next. Using the tip of the knife, make a small incision at each ankle of the bird to expose the tendons and the bone. Bend the feet back over the ankle to pop the bone out of its socket, then slice the tendons and flesh that connect the feet to the leg. Place the feet in the receptacle for stock pieces.

Remove the wishbone: Turn the bird so its legs are pointing away from you and you have a good view of the opening into the breast cavity. Using your fingers, find the telltale wishbone shape (it is located exactly where your collarbone would be if you were a bird). Using the tip of your knife, make small incisions along either side of the bone to expose it on both sides. Set your knife aside and, using your fingers, push the flesh back to expose the bone more fully, which will allow you to get a better grip on it. Slide your fingers around both tines of the wishbone, close to the point where they meet at the top, pull back (this will require a fair bit of force), and remove the bone. (If it snaps apart, you can dig around in there with your fingers to pull the bone bits out; careful, they're sharp.)

Remove the wings: Extend one of the wings and give it a little waggle; you should be able to see the joint moving under the flesh and skin at the point where the wing attaches to the body. ① **Using the tip of your knife, make a couple small incisions through the skin and flesh to expose the joint.** Turn the bird onto its side, with the wing you're working on facing up. Gather the wing's drumette, flat, and tip together in one hand (as if you were squeezing one of those spring-loaded grip exercisers), and position the wing so it's flush with the body. ② **Holding the chicken steady on the board with your other hand, bend the wing back over the joint; this should pop the drumette out of the socket in the shoulder.** ③ ④ **Using your knife, cut away any flesh and skin that keeps the wing connected to the body and remove the wing;** set it aside in the serving-portion receptacle. Repeat with the other wing.

Turn the bird so that its legs are pointing toward you. (5) **Using your knife, slice through the skin between the leg and the breast on one side.** Using both hands, turn the chicken on its side, with the side where you cut through the skin facing up. (6) **With one hand, compress the leg so the drumstick is flush with the thigh and the entire leg is flush with the body and then, holding the rest of the chicken down with your other hand, pull the leg up and back toward you, which should pop the thigh bone out of its socket.** (7) **Using the tip of your knife, make a few small cuts through the flesh that connects the leg to the body, and** (8) **remove the leg.** Set it aside in the serving-portion receptacle and repeat the process with the other leg.

Turn the bird breast side up again. Using the tip of your knife, make a shallow incision down one side of the line of bone and cartilage that separates the two breast halves. Once you've made the initial incision, go into it again with the tip of your knife to slice down to the breastbone. Still using the tip of your knife, slice through the skin and flesh where the breast is attached to the shoulder joint. Set down your knife and, with one hand gripping the chicken near the shoulder joint and the other gripping the breast half, pull the breast half away from the body. The breast should come off cleanly, still attached only by a strip of skin near the lower part of the breast; slice through this to free the breast. Repeat with the other breast half.

Use your fingers to pull the tenders away from the body; they should come off easily. If you plan on using the tenders for a purpose other than stock, you'll want to remove the tendon that runs through the center of each and protrudes like a little tab out of the thicker part of the tender. To do this, anchor the tab of the tendon to the cutting board using your index finger and a paper towel or kitchen towel, then scrape away from your finger with the knife, taking care not to cut the tendon. The tender can then be placed in the serving-portion receptacle; the tendons can be placed in the receptacle for stock scraps.

At this point, you have two skin-on breasts, two skin-on legs, two tenders, and two whole wings in one receptacle; in the other, you have the chicken carcass, its neck and head, its feet, and the tendons if you've removed them from the tenders. You may also have the bird's heart, liver, and gizzard. If you want to use everything to make chicken stock, you can throw everything but the liver into a pot; if you plan on using the breasts and legs and wings, either for toppings for ramen or another dish, you may or may not want to cut them up or otherwise trim them for serving. This decision is dictated in part by how thrifty you want to be, but also by how using each of these parts can affect the flavor of a stock.

For the whole wings, at the very least I like to remove the wing tips and use them for stock. Wing tips are primarily made up of skin and connective tissue, and while they're fun to eat, they are very good for stock; removing them from wings you're going to prepare some other way is a small sacrifice you can make for a better broth. Using the tip of your knife, make a small incision at the joint to expose the tendons and bone, bend the wing backward over itself, and then slice away any remaining tendons, flesh, and skin to remove the tip. If you like, you can then cut the wing into two pieces—drumette and flat—using the same method. Save the wing pieces for another use: you can toss them into a freezer bag and hold onto them until you have enough to make it worthwhile to deep-fry some wings, or do as I do and just salt them heavily and broil them as a cook's reward for cutting up the chicken.

For the breasts, I cut off any gnarly-looking bits, and I sometimes square off the breasts for even cooking, since that'll yield a better presentation, and any scraps will be put to good use in the stock. Whether or not you remove the skin is up to you: if I'm going to make a pan-roasted chicken breast for dinner (or as a topping for ramen), I'll leave the skin on; if I'm going to make cutlets or poach the breast, I'll remove the skin and toss it into the stockpot (or reserve it for rendering the fat).

For the legs, decide whether you're going to keep the bone in or not. For stewed, braised, or roasted legs, I'll leave the bone in; for anything else—stir-fries, using the meat for meatballs, or some grilled preparations—I'll take it out. The easiest way to remove the bone is to first split the leg into the thigh and drumstick. The process is identical to taking off a wing tip or separating the leg from the body of the bird: make an incision around the joint between the two parts and then bend the joint in the opposite direction from the way it naturally wants to bend, which will pop

the bone of the drumstick out of the kneecap. Use the tip of your knife to cut away any tendons and flesh connecting the two parts and pull them apart.

Once you've separated the two parts, start by deboning the thighs. The bone runs right through the middle of the thigh. (9) **Turn each thigh skin side down and, using the tip of your knife, make a shallow incision down the length of the bone to expose it.** Use your knife to cut the flesh away from the bone with small cuts until the entire bone is exposed, then slide the tip of the knife under the bone to cut the flesh away there too. You should be left with an exposed bone still attached at either end to the thigh. (10) **Use the tip of your knife to cut away the flesh connected to the bone, then** (11) **pull the bone free.** Place the bones in the stock receptacle and the deboned thighs in the serving-piece receptacle.

For the drumsticks, starting at the point at which each one was attached to the thigh, use the tip of your knife to make an incision down its length, using the central bone as a guide. Using small slices, cut the flesh away from the bone to release it, at which point it will be connected only at the joints that connected to the thigh and the ankle. Lodge your knife between the bone and the flesh and cut through the skin, severing it completely just above the ankle. Stand the leg up on the cutting board, with the joint that was attached to the thigh resting on the board, and scrape down along the bone to release the flesh. Place the bones in the stock receptacle and the deboned drumsticks in the serving-piece receptacle.

CHOOSING CHICKEN PARTS FOR STOCK

It's customary to think of bones as being the base ingredient of many meat stocks, but the bones of animals contribute little to the flavor and texture of broth. Bones are made up of calcium and collagen; calcium isn't soluble in water, and it's difficult to convert the collagen they contain into gelatin without prolonged cooking. The real reason bones are added to stock is that even the most diligently butchered animal will still have a lot of meat and connective tissue attached to the bones. When deciding which parts of an animal to use for making stock, it's most useful to consider how much skin, connective tissue, cartilage, flesh, and fat they contain, and their relative proportions.

Chicken breasts are leaner muscles that get relatively little use. They are tender and best suited to quick-cooking preparations. In fact, extended cooking of the breasts can make them dry and chalky. For stock, this means that chicken breasts primarily contribute meaty flavor.

Chicken legs, which are fattier and, because they see a lot of use, have a relatively high proportion of connective tissue, are best suited to longer-cooking preparations, the better to tenderize their tougher meat and to convert the collagen in the connective tissue into gelatin. For stock, this means that chicken legs contribute flavor and gelatin.

The skin that covers the legs and breasts is primarily made up of collagen and fat, which means it contributes mostly gelatin to clear stocks, as the fat that renders out and rises to the surface is generally skimmed off.

Chicken wings, which are a mix of darker, more-worked meat (in the flat of the wing), and whiter, less-worked meat (in the drumette), and a lot of skin and connective tissue, contribute both flavor and gelatin to stock.

Chicken feet and heads, which are made up mostly of skin and connective tissue, primarily contribute gelatin.

The varying proportions of these chicken parts used in a stock will determine the stock's character. If, for example, you make a stock entirely with skinless chicken breasts, it will have a lot of sweet, fleshy chicken flavor but very little body; the result will be a light, very chicken-y broth. If you make one entirely with chicken legs, it will have slightly less chicken flavor, but it will have far more body, as the amount of dissolved gelatin from the connective tissue will be much greater. When chilled, a breast-only stock will still be liquid, while a stock made from chicken legs will likely form a strong gel. A stock made entirely of chicken wings (though expensive), would have even more body than a stock made entirely from chicken legs, and more flavor too, given the relatively large proportion of white meat in the drumettes. In terms of pure chicken flavor, it would be slightly inferior to a stock made from just breasts, but it would more than make up for that with the fact that it has more dissolved gelatin.

A chicken carcass, with some flesh still clinging to the bones and all the cartilaginous bits in the joints and in the back, as well as a small amount of skin, offers a nice middle ground for flavor and gelatin conversion, which is one reason chicken backs are often called for in stock recipes. The main reason, however, is that there aren't many uses for the carcasses other than turning them into stock.

If your goal is to simply produce "the best" chicken stock, one that is full of both flavor and gelatin, one that tastes like the essence of chicken while also having that lip-smacking quality that is the sign of a well-made nourishing soup, then it makes sense to use all parts of the bird.

Yet if cost is part of your concern, and you, like me, like to get the most out of the ingredients you pay for, it seems like a missed opportunity to chuck the breasts and legs (and wings! My god, the wings!) into stock. For a bowl of ramen, those various parts can be cooked to serve as toppings. The breasts can be poached and sliced or shredded, pan-roasted and sliced, or slivered and used for a stir-fry. The leg meat can be similarly slivered and stir-fried, whole bone-in legs can be braised and the meat shredded, and the thighs (bone-in or boneless) can be pan-roasted and the meat sliced; or the meat of boneless legs and thighs can be ground up and used for meatballs or wonton filling. The choice is up to you. In the recipes in this book, I offer examples for most of these preparations for use in a bowl of ramen. Generally speaking, for sliceable toppings, I'll use the breast and the thighs; for ground-meat preparations, I will use just the leg meat, because of its relatively high proportion of fat and connective tissue, which yields less dense, juicier cooked meatballs and dumplings. Drumstick meat is also best used for ground meat preparations.

If, however, you choose to use any or all these parts to make your stock, cut them up to increase their surface area, which will result in more flavor and gelatin extraction. This can mean something as simple as cutting the breasts into several pieces each, separating the thighs from the drumsticks, and cutting the wings into tips, drumettes, and flats. But for maximum surface area, and for improving the clarity of the stock, I recommend removing the meat from the bones and chopping it into a relatively fine mince, grinding it in a meat grinder, or pulsing it in a food processor.

HOW TO MAKE CHICKEN STOCK FOR RAMEN

The process of making chicken stock for ramen is straightforward, and it is essentially the same regardless of whether you're making a clear stock or an emulsified one, or a brown stock or a white stock, either in a pressure cooker or in a stockpot on your stovetop: you simmer the chicken meat and bones, either roasted or raw, in ample water to cover, along with a few peeled aromatic vegetables, until their flavor and gelatin has been extracted, after which you steep additional vegetables and any soaked dried seafood like kombu in the liquid. The goal is to produce a very light-colored but full-bodied, flavorful stock.

Here are general guidelines for making stock for ramen:

EVERYTHING IN THE POT SHOULD BE COMPLETELY SUBMERGED. If your ingredients aren't submerged in the water, they won't contribute as much to the stock.

DON'T BOIL THE STOCK. To keep the stock clear, you should avoid boiling it for the reasons I've already discussed. However, even for emulsified stocks, it's best to avoid boiling the stock for most of the cooking time because boiling will lead to evaporation, which means you'll have to pay more attention to the stock and top it up with more water as needed to keep the ingredients submerged.

ADD A FEW PEELED AROMATIC VEGETABLES AT THE BEGINNING OF THE COOKING PROCESS. Adding aromatic vegetables like garlic, ginger, and onion at the beginning of cooking will produce the long-cooked flavor known as "kokumi" (see page 110), which translates to a kind of "roundness" of flavor and lessens the "meaty" aroma of simmering bones and meat without clouding or darkening the stock. Keeping the vegetables whole rather than slicing or dicing them prevents them from breaking down too much during cooking, and the skins/peels will impart color to the stock.

ADD A LARGER QUANTITY AND VARIETY OF CHOPPED AROMATIC VEGETABLES TOWARD THE END OF THE COOKING PROCESS. If you want to add more vegetables to the stock, add them toward the end of cooking so they don't overcook, which would make the stock sweeter and darker. Overcooked vegetables also act like a sponge, soaking up some of the flavorful stock and reducing the yield, unless you press them thoroughly when straining—which could make the stock cloudy. Vegetables like onions, scallions, naga negi (Welsh onions), garlic, ginger, leeks, celery, and carrots should be diced before adding them to the pot at this stage, as the greater surface area will facilitate extraction of flavor. (Napa cabbage is an exception, as it already has a lot of surface area.) These vegetables should be simmered for only about 45 minutes.

ADD SOAKED DRIED SEAFOOD, ALONG WITH ITS SOAKING WATER, AT THE END OF THE COOKING PROCESS. If you are adding dried seafood to the stock, you should soak it beforehand in water, preferably overnight, to maximize flavor extraction. Adding the seafood and its soaking water at the end of cooking is an easy way to control the temperature of the stock; the soaking water will help drop the temperature of the stock below the temperatures that would lead to, for example, the kombu producing "off" flavors.

STRAIN THE STOCK THROUGH A FINE-MESH STRAINER LINED WITH DAMP CHEESECLOTH. You can simply strain a stock through a fine-mesh strainer, but adding a layer of damp cheesecloth to the strainer is a cheap and convenient way to improve the efficiency of the straining process.

USE THE STRAINING PROCESS TO RAPIDLY COOL DOWN THE STOCK. Transferring the stock from the stockpot to a large metal mixing bowl will immediately start to cool it down; the stock will lose heat to the air and to the bowl. Then transferring the stock to storage containers will cool it down further. You can also chill the bowl and other containers; you don't need to freeze them, simply fill them with cold water from the tap, then drain them before you strain in or add the stock. You can also take advantage of the conductive properties of aluminum sheet pans and metal bowls by setting the bowl containing the strained stock on

LEFT TO RIGHT: roasted chicken chintan, chicken paitan, and regular chicken chintan

a sheet pan set on a cooling rack, which will help to rapidly cool the stock.

CHILL THE STOCK THOROUGHLY BEFORE REMOVING THE FAT. While you can skim the fat off the top of a pot of stock relatively easily, it is much, much easier to chill the stock before removing the fat. The fat will rise to the surface and solidify, and you can then use a spoon to scrape it off. If you are in a rush and need to remove the fat immediately, you can fill a large ladle with ice water and dip it into the hot stock; the fat will congeal and cling to the surface.

USING A PRESSURE COOKER TO MAKE STOCK

Be careful when using a pressure cooker, not because they are dangerous (modern pressure cookers are very safe), but because they can make a mess if you use them improperly. You should always abide by the instructions in your pressure cooker manual, and pay particular attention to two of them: Never exceed the maximum fill line, and always check that the pressure valve is unobstructed before using the cooker. In both cases, you run the risk of blocking the pressure valve, which can lead to excess pressure blowing the safety gasket and creating an eruption of boiling-hot stock so powerful that you'll need to clean the ceiling. (It is not fun!)

HOW TO MAKE AN EMULSIFIED STOCK

As explained on page 69, an emulsified stock is produced by agitating stock to disperse the particulate matter and fat evenly throughout it. In ramen shops, and in some ramen recipes, this is achieved by boiling the stock hard, which both agitates the contents of the pot and speeds up flavor extraction and gelatin conversion. I find it quicker and more convenient to agitate the stock using a blender, either an immersion blender or a high-powered countertop blender.

Mike Satinover, a ramen chef who runs Akahoshi Ramen in Chicago, has noted in his recipes that using a high-powered countertop blender to blend just a portion of the stock will yield a very strong emulsion once that blended portion is reincorporated into the stock, and I have adopted this technique as well.

To make an emulsified stock, simply make the stock as you would a clear stock but omit the steeping step at the end. Then, when the stock is done, emulsify it by either immersing a stick blender in the stock or breaking up the material in the pot with a potato masher or a wooden spoon (if you go the latter route, it helps to then boil the stock for about 30 minutes or so, to mimic the agitation a blender accomplishes in minutes). Once the stock has been strained, you can steep soaked dried seafood and/or chopped vegetables in it, and then strain it again. For a stronger emulsion, you can transfer a portion of the stock to a high-powered blender, blend it, and stir it back into the rest of the stock.

It can also be helpful to add starch in the form of a small amount of peeled, cubed russet potatoes to the stock as it cooks. When the stock is done, the potato's starch will be completely gelatinized, which means it will be fully dissolved in the liquid, and it will help strengthen the emulsion without distracting from the other flavors in the stock (as russets are relatively flavorless).

PORK STOCK

A pork stock is made using essentially the same technique as a chicken stock, but there are a few key differences. For one thing, pigs are larger animals, and thus their bones are larger; they are mammals, so their bones are denser and some of them contain marrow (avian bones are hollow); and, finally, pigs, of course, are not generally purchased whole, and you will have to use the variety of cuts available at your local supermarket or butcher, or special-order them from an online purveyor.

Kinds of Pork

Most supermarket pork, generally referred to as "commodity pork," is of middling quality. The pigs are effectively clones of one another, and they have been bred primarily with an eye toward consistency and mildness of flavor, the better to live up to what might possibly be the most misleading marketing slogan of all time: "The other white meat." Of course, pork is not a white meat—it is red meat, but if the only pork you've ever seen is the kind usually available in American supermarkets, you might be forgiven for being ignorant of that fact. Good pork should have a deep red hue; it should not be pale pink shading into ivory. Pork of this kind is typically from heritage breeds that have been abandoned by the larger pork-producing industry in favor of the leaner breeds used for commodity pork.

Considering the pig's importance to ramen—its meat and bones are used for stock; its belly, shoulder, and loin are used as toppings; and its rendered fat is used as both topping and as an aromatic oil—it's preferable to use high-quality pork. Fortunately, it's relatively easy to find good pork online or at retail whole-animal butchers.

While I recommend buying pork from heritage breeds, using good pork means you must embrace inconsistency. For example, while commodity pork bellies are all generally of the same size, with a relatively even distribution of fat to meat from one end of the belly to the other, a pork belly cut from a heritage breed pig might be enormous at one end and thinner at the other, with a very uneven distribution of fat to meat.

If you're following a chashu recipe that calls for rolling up a slab of pork belly that weighs four pounds and you buy a piece of commodity pork belly for it, you'll be able to produce a neat round of chashu without difficulty. However, if you go to a good butcher and ask for four pounds of pork belly, you might get a piece that is an even slab, or you might get a narrow but relatively tall hunk of pork belly that is predominantly fat. That inconsistency is the reason commodity pork producers have settled on the breeds they have; a belly from a farm in Iowa and one from Upstate New York will be almost identical in size and shape, ready to run through an industrial abattoir without any need to adjust the machinery, and the end consumer, whether a home cook or a giant bacon producer, will always be supplied with a consistent product.

Because most of the pork that's available in the U.S. is commodity pork, the recipes in this book were tested primarily with that type. But I urge you to seek out good-quality pork, keeping in mind that you may need to make adjustments, particularly the time it takes to cook a braise or roast. On the other hand, when turning pork bones and meat into soup, it doesn't matter what kind of pork you use from a technique standpoint; the only difference will be in how good the soup tastes.

How to Choose Pork for Stock

Pigs, like chickens, are broken down into different parts for consumption. But a home cook is unlikely to break down a whole pig. Instead, we work with what's available at our local grocery store or butcher, and the selection of pork cuts available will largely be determined by the prevailing tastes of the population those businesses serve.

However, as with chicken, it's less important to use specific parts of the pig than it is to consider what those different parts contribute to the stock, and the same principles that apply to chicken parts apply to pork parts: the skin and connective tissue provide collagen, which will convert to gelatin; the skin and the fat that lies within the muscle tissues and surrounds it will provide fat; and the flesh itself will provide sweet, porky flavor. Thus, a pork stock made entirely with a lean cut of pork like the loin will be thin in body but will have a lot of meaty flavor. A stock made entirely with pig's feet, or trotters, will contain so much gelatin it will set up when chilled into a solid block of pork Jell-O with a rather large fat cap on top, and it will have relatively little meat flavor.

There are certain key differences between pork (and other mammals) and poultry: one is bone marrow. As mentioned earlier, birds have light, hollow bones, while pigs, cows, and sheep (and us!) have dense, solid bones, some of which contain marrow, a spongy substance located in bone cavities. There are two kinds of bone marrow—red and yellow—and different bones have different concentrations of each. There is a lot of discussion among ramen cooks about how different pork bones affect the flavor of a stock. My suspicion is that whatever the differences in flavor produced by using these various parts, the effects are likely due to the relative proportions of meat to connective tissue to bone marrow, as well as the relative proportion of the different kinds of bone marrow.

For most home cooks, the importance of bone marrow is somewhat beside the point. For a ramen restaurant that makes stock in 50-liter batches, it can be important to use a high proportion of marrow-rich bones. For a home cook working with a 6-quart stockpot to make about 4 liters (4 quarts) of stock, it's more important to use a mix of pig parts that yields a flavorful and gelatin-rich stock.

However, a stock made with marrow bones will be more flavorful than one made without, a truth that is evident in the stock- and stew-making practices of cuisines around the world. A good way to experiment with marrow bones is to have your butcher cut some femur bones crosswise on their bandsaw, which exposes the marrow and will reduce the cooking time.

Another key difference is size and weight. As a pig is far larger than a chicken, its bone structure is correspondingly larger and denser. This means the bones are also much heavier, which presents a few challenges.

The first is that, as I've mentioned before, bones themselves don't have any inherent flavor; they are basically calcium scaffolding to which all the flavorful stuff in an animal is attached. A pound of meaty chicken bones will have a much higher ratio of meat and connective tissue than a pound of meaty pork bones, and if you use each of those to make a liter of stock, the chicken stock will have far more flavor.

The second is that because of their density, pork bones will sink in water. And wherever the bones are in contact with the bottom of the stockpot, there is a high likelihood that they will scorch, even though they are submerged in liquid. As a result, you must move pork bones around while cooking and/or use moderate heat to prevent your stock from taking on a burnt, acrid taste.

The third challenge is that, because of their size, it can be difficult to fit pork bones in the pots typically used in a home kitchen.

Finally, the relatively large size of everything related to pork—the muscle groups, the bones, the areas of connective tissue as well as their thickness—means that pork stock must be cooked for longer than chicken stock, regardless of the cooking temperature. This is simply a matter of surface area relative to mass: it will take longer to extract the flavor and convert the collagen in a 5-inch cube of pork than it will to extract the flavor from a 1-inch-thick chicken breast, much as it will take far longer to convert the collagen in a wee chicken foot than it will take to turn a pig's foot the size of your forearm into a wobbly, gelatinous mass. If you are intent on incorporating marrow into the stock, to access the marrow within bones like the femur and tibia, it's customary to cook the bones until they become brittle enough to break easily, and making a good pork stock with marrow ends up being a protracted process, one that, because of the risk of scorching, requires a fair amount of attention.

Taking all of that into consideration, most home cooks are better off buying a bone-in, skin-on pork picnic shoulder for stock. Widely available and relatively inexpensive, a picnic shoulder has a nice mix of meat, fat, connective tissue, and skin that produces a flavorful, gelatin-rich stock, and it can be used for both clear and emulsified stocks. With some light butchery, which you can do yourself or have the butcher accomplish for you, a pork shoulder can also provide you with a pork roast to use for braised or roasted chashu and a fair amount of ground meat for use in gyoza, wontons, or meatballs—although that ground pork can instead be thrown into the stockpot, which will help improve the stock's clarity and, because of the vastly increased surface area produced by grinding the meat, shorten the cooking process.

There are, of course, other widely available cuts that can be used for stock, and chief among them are pork neck bones, which have a similar ratio of meat to fat to connective tissue, although they have a relatively higher proportion of skin (if the skin is left on). Meaty shanks are similarly good for stock—I roast them and use them to make Roasted Pork and Dried Clam Stock (page 230). Ribs provide a nice mix of connective tissue to meat, although they are a little bone-heavy. And bellies are a little heavy on fat, but they have ample connective tissue and meat. Lean cuts, like the loin and tenderloin, aren't particularly great for making stock by themselves, but they can be used to add more pork flavor to a stock, and since they don't have much fat, they can also be used to improve the clarity of a stock.

Pig's feet, or trotters, make an excellent addition to stock, but don't use them on their own. Because they are primarily made up of tendon, connective tissue, bone, and skin, they have very little meat, and so they won't add much flavor to the pot. What they lack in flavor, however, they more than make up for in the amount of collagen they provide, which will result in an extremely gelatin-rich stock. Pigs' feet are also great because once you've used them for enriching a stock, you can turn them into a delicious terrine (see page 292).

HOW TO CUT UP A PORK PICNIC SHOULDER

Cutting up a pork shoulder is a relatively simple task, made all the simpler because there's very little need to come up with perfectly fabricated pieces. The goal is primarily to separate the meat from the bone and the skin from the meat, and it doesn't matter all that much if you do it neatly, since you'll be dropping pretty much everything into a pot to make stock. While you could, if your pot is large enough, throw in the whole shoulder, because of its size, you'd have to cook the stock for longer to produce a good one. Cutting up the pork shoulder, even if you're uninterested in producing a roast for use as chashu or ground meat to use in various ways, helps to increase the surface area of the parts, facilitating both flavor extraction and gelatin conversion.

Pork shoulders are sold in several different ways. You can buy whole bone-in, skin-on pork shoulders, or you can buy boneless ones. You can also buy smaller cut-up sections of the shoulder, which are typically labeled "butt" or "Boston butt" and "picnic shoulder," either bone-in, skin-on or boneless and skin-off. The former refers to the top half of the shoulder, which consists of the shoulder blade and the large amount of meat that surrounds it, creeping up to the neck area; the latter refers to the section consisting of the upper arm bone and its surrounding meat. For the purposes of a single pot of pork stock, either one or the other of these pork shoulder halves will suffice. The butt has more meat, and the meat, because the muscle groups are worked relatively less hard during the pig's life than those in the area of the upper arm, is well-marbled, with not too much connective tissue, the reason it's prized for pulled pork and roasted pork preparations. The best pork shoulder chashu is made with roasts cut from the butt portion, specifically the group of muscles known as the "coppa" or "money muscle," which you can easily purchase.

The picnic has much less meat and a far higher proportion of connective tissue, as well as a higher ratio of skin (if it has it) to fat. The picnic is the smaller of the two cuts. For the home cook making about 4 liters (4 quarts) of pork stock, the size and the ratios of skin to meat to bones to connective tissue in a picnic shoulder make it ideal, so that's what I focus on here. A picnic also has the benefit of having a relatively straightforward bone structure; it's mostly a single bone running through the meat, like a cartoon ham.

The method I describe will produce a boneless roast, a bunch of trim, and the central bone with a lot of meat and connective tissue attached, which can be used for stock or seasoned with salt and roasted slowly in the oven (see page 281). And that slow and roasted shoulder, once picked of meat, can then, in turn, be used to make a ramen stock (see page 182).

The first step is to remove a cylindrical roast from the picnic shoulder, for chashu or another use. This first step brings a lot of the mysterious interior of the shoulder to light and makes it less likely that you'll just aimlessly hack away at the thing. ① **If you look at the larger side of a picnic roast, you should be able to identify where the bone has been cleaved in two, and the ring of meat that surrounds it;** one side will look much meatier than the other, and you'll want to focus on that side.

Next, make an incision that will mark off the length of the final roast. A small nick is all that's necessary.

(2) **Make a shallow incision down the length of the roast, aligned with the central bone, to mark off the lateral side of the final roast.** At this point, because the overall shape of the final roast has been outlined, you should be able to visualize it easily.

Run the knife along the shallow incision, cutting deeper into the roast to expose the bone that runs down the center.

With the tip of your knife flush against the bone, make small cuts to release the meat entirely from the bone.

Once the meat is freed from the bone, cut deeper into the initial incision you made to mark the end of the roast. At this point, the chashu roast should be connected to the picnic roast only along its bottom side .

Roll the picnic shoulder over and, using the tip of your knife, make a shallow incision down the length of your almost fully cut away chashu roast. (3) **Repeat this process until you can pull the entire chashu roast away from the picnic roast.**

Now you can roast the picnic shoulder, cut off chunks for use in stews or as ground meat, or simply toss the whole thing into a pot and make a stock.

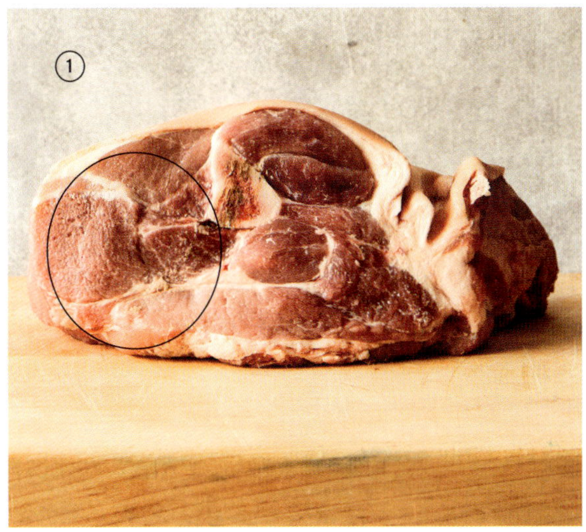

HOW TO MAKE PORK STOCK FOR RAMEN

There are key differences between making pork stock versus a chicken stock for ramen.

A PORK STOCK TAKES LONGER. This is mostly a function of the size of pork cuts and the rate at which the collagen in the parts is converted to gelatin, but it also has to do with extracting flavor. You can reduce the amount of time it takes to make the stock by having the butcher cut up the bones into smaller pieces and grinding up the meat you will use for the stock. Using the relatively low cooking temperatures required for a clear stock, it can take anywhere from 6 to 12 hours to yield a gelatin- and flavor-rich stock from pig parts, and even at the longer end of that spectrum, those parts will still likely have a lot more to give (and could be used for a secondary stocks).

PORK BONES ARE HEAVY. You must be careful about controlling the cooking temperature, as any points of contact between the heavy pork bones and the pot can result in scorching; this is particularly true of pots made with thinner and more conductive materials, like aluminum or stainless-clad aluminum. For a stovetop chintan, where you are already modulating the temperature to keep the liquid at a bare simmer, this is less of a concern, as the heat generated at those points of contact will be dispersed throughout the liquid. But if you are, say, boiling the stock to emulsify it, particularly for extended periods of time, you run the risk of scorching. The same is true if you use a pressure cooker. Stirring the bones as they cook will help you reduce the chances of scorching, but as that's impossible in a sealed pressure cooker, you should avoid using high heat to bring it up to and keep it at pressure.

MAKING PORK STOCK IS SMELLY. Boiling or simmering pork bones is a stinkier affair than cooking chicken bones. Add in the fact that pork stock is cooked for longer than a chicken stock, and your house will smell powerfully like boiled meat. There really isn't any way around this, but there are ways to ameliorate it. The first is to add ginger to the pot, a common technique for masking the smells of boiled meats of all kinds. Ginger is aromatic, and it has the added benefit of imparting long-cooked flavors to the stock. Alternatively, use a pressure cooker, as it reduces the cooking time significantly and, because the pot is sealed, limits the amount of smelly stuff released into the air.

PIG PARTS ARE BLOODY. Well, not exactly bloody, but myoglobin-y. Pork has a greater amount of myoglobin than chicken. Myoglobin is a protein found in muscle that's responsible for storing oxygen, but it also stores iron, which accounts for the red color. When cooked, myoglobin loses its ability to hold onto iron, and that is why a steak, when cooked from raw to rare to medium-rare to medium to well-done, gradually changes in color from red to pink to pale gray to brown. The relatively high concentration of myoglobin in pork means that if you make a stock with it, that myoglobin will gradually turn brown, and it will impart that color to the stock. As a result, many ramen cooks try to remove that myoglobin so that the finished stock has a pale, light color, whether it's a chintan or a paitan.

There are two ways to remove myoglobin from meat: soaking the raw meat in fresh water or blanching it, and these can be used singly or in combination.

To soak your pig parts , submerge them in cold water to cover in your fridge for anywhere from 8 hours to as long as 24 hours. Changing the water several times will remove more myoglobin.

To blanch the parts, cover them with fresh water in a large pot, bring the water to a boil, and let it boil for 15 to 20 minutes. Drain the parts, then rinse them thoroughly under cold running water to remove any denatured myoglobin that's stuck to them, as that brownish/grayish stuff will color your stock. Then the parts can be thrown back into the (cleaned) pot to make stock with fresh water.

Removing myoglobin is primarily an aesthetic concern, so if the appearance of your stock isn't important to you, you can ignore this step entirely. If you want to make a tonkotsu broth that looks like milk, you will want to soak and/or blanch your pork parts before making stock.

HOW TO EMULSIFY PORK STOCK

The same principles that apply to emulsified chicken stocks apply to emulsified pork stocks, along with the same caveats. Since boiling the stock both speeds up the processes of flavor extraction and gelatin conversion *and* helps immensely with emulsifying the stock, it is common practice to simply boil an emulsified pork stock from the beginning. However, I do not recommend doing this at home for many reasons already outlined: the risk of scorching, which requires that you pay more attention to the stock than you would if you merely simmered it; the increased evaporation, which means you have to top off the pot periodically to ensure the various parts remain fully submerged; and the smell it generates.

I strongly advise using a pressure cooker to make an emulsified pork stock, as it takes far less time to render out the fat, extract the flavor, and convert the collagen to gelatin at the higher temperatures a pressure cooker can achieve; those higher temperatures also do a great job of making pork bones brittle, if you're intent on cracking them open to access their marrow. However, most home pressure cookers have a severe space limitation. While an 8-quart pressure cooker can relatively easily hold a whole pork shoulder bone and enough water to cover if you are going to simply simmer it in water, it won't if you are going to put on the lid and bring it to pressure. The bone may fit, but you'll have to use far less water in order to avoid going above the maximum fill line, which means you'll have a lower yield.

Considering how long it takes to fully render the fat, convert the gelatin, and extract the flavor from pig parts, it's easier to make a second flavorful and full-bodied emulsified pork stock from parts that have already been used to make a clear stock. (While you can do the same thing with chicken parts, it's less effective, as chicken parts give up what they have relatively quickly.)

HOW TO MAKE SECONDARY STOCKS

Making secondary stocks from animal parts that have already been used to make a stock is common practice at ramen restaurants because it's economical. These parts still have stuff to give up, whether that's fat, flavor, and/or gelatin, and throwing that away would further tighten the already tight cost margins under which restaurants operate. Typically, these second stocks are emulsified stocks, as the animal parts have already been hammered by the original stock-making process, and so they are primarily providing gelatin and fat, with relatively less flavor.

Thrifty home cooks can also take advantage of this practice, but home cooks operate under a set of limitations that restaurant cooks don't have, which include but aren't limited to the number of large stockpots at their disposal, storage space, and time. For example, if you decide to make a pork chintan and cook it for 8 hours, you may not want to spend another 2 to 3 hours making a secondary stock, and you would consider the 2 quarts of secondary stock you lose out on as an acceptable trade-off of convenience over cost efficiency.

However, following a few simple guidelines, you can wait until later to make a second stock, and that second stock need not be a pale ghost of the first one in terms of flavor.

PREVENT OXIDATION. Cooked meat, particularly plain cooked meat, will oxidize rapidly after cooking, producing unpleasant aromas and flavors. These "off" flavors will be familiar to everyone, as they are present in any leftover cooked meat, a phenomenon known as "warmed-over flavor." But if that meat is prevented from oxidizing, it won't take on those unpleasant aromas and flavors as quickly. (This is an important consideration for meat toppings used in ramen; see page 126).

Although the best way to limit oxidation in the meaty bits left over from making stock is to make a second stock immediately after the first, so the cooked meat has no chance to oxidize, you can immediately cover the drained bones and meat with cold water and store them in the refrigerator until you're ready to make the secondary stock, preferably on the following day. When you're ready to make the stock, simply transfer the water and the bones and meat to a clean pot, add a little more water, and start cooking.

USE LESS WATER FOR THE SECONDARY STOCK. The meat and bones may still have more stuff to give up, but they don't have a lot of it, so if you used the same quantity of water as you used for the first stock, the second stock would be so diluted in flavor and gelatin content that it would be fairly insipid. A good rule of thumb to keep in mind is that those spent bones will probably yield about half as much second stock of decent quality as first stock.

ADD A SMALL AMOUNT OF FRESH MEAT AND BONES TO THE SECONDARY STOCK TO IMPROVE ITS FLAVOR. This is the way niban dashi is made; the spent kombu and katsuobushi from ichiban dashi is supplemented with a handful or two of fresh katsuobushi to improve its aroma and flavor. Since the spent parts from a first stock mostly contribute fat and gelatin to a secondary stock, and relatively less flavor, I like to add ground meat to second stocks for a flavor boost.

USE STRONG FLAVORS TO SEASON THE SECONDARY STOCK. Composed mostly of fat and gelatin, second stocks are a prime vehicle for strong flavors, which means they're great for gyokai stocks, stocks with a fair amount of dried seafood products, such as niboshi and katsuobushi steeped or simmered into them.

MAKING FISH STOCK WITH FRESH FISH

It isn't that common for ramen shops to offer ramen made with fresh fish stock, but it isn't unheard of. For home cooks, ramen offers a delicious and relatively easy way to use up parts of fish you'd otherwise be inclined to throw away. The head and carcass of a finfish contain a lot of flavor and gelatin and can quickly make a flavorful and richly textured stock.

While the process for making a fish stock is similar to making chicken and pork stocks, there are a few key differences. The bone structure of a fish and the connective tissue contained within it are optimized for movement in water. Water offers more resistance to movement than air, so fish have a much higher proportion of muscle to bones and connective tissue than chickens and pigs, as they need it to propel themselves quickly through water—to escape predators, to capture prey. However, since a fish lives in water, it does not require the bone structure and connective tissue of a land animal in order to counteract the full downward force of gravity, so the bones are less dense and the proportion of connective tissue is far lower; the connective tissue is also far less dense.

These characteristics explain the relative tenderness of fish flesh compared with that of land animals, as well as why fish parts need to be cooked only for a relatively short time to extract the flavor and convert the collagen to gelatin. The delicate nature of fish flesh also means it is far more important to avoid boiling it when making a stock, as extended heating combined with agitation will have the effect of pulverizing the flesh, which in turn makes it more difficult to produce a clear stock.

Fish fat also oxidizes quickly and will produce unpleasant aromas and flavors when it does. That oxidation of the fat represents one of the biggest obstacles for makers of prepared fish products. This is why the process used to make katsuobushi includes the diligent removal of any traces of fat in the fillets through boiling and mold inoculation; the katsuobushi fillets then become far more shelf stable and can be used to produce a fragrant, delicious stock with no off flavors.

Kinds of Fish

The best kinds of fish to use to make a full-flavored, gelatin-rich stock with few off flavors and aromas are "white-fleshed" fish, or non-oily fish. These include snapper, bass, cod, bream, sole, and fluke; they do not include salmon, mackerel, sardines, anchovies, and tuna. (Careful readers will note that many dried fish products used to make dashi belong to this latter category, which underlines the degree to which the processes for making dried Japanese seafood sidestep many of the issues presented by using these fish for fresh fish stock.)

If you live along any U.S. coast, you should have no problem finding fish that are appropriate for making a fresh fish stock. A good fishmonger will have whole fish for sale, which they should be happy to break down for you; a great fishmonger might even sell fresh fish bones for stock. If you do not live along a coast, your best bet is to find a reputable online source for good-quality fresh fish. But online purveyors will not fillet the fish for you and give you the bones, so you'll have to know how to do that yourself.

Another drawback to buying fish online is that you have no opportunity to inspect what you're buying, and so you're left at the mercy of the purveyor's discretion and will be paying a premium for the fish and its shipping costs, despite purchasing it sight unseen. Thus it is far preferable to buy fish from a good fishmonger. But even there, the quality may vary considerably from fish to fish, so it's important to know what to look for so you can assess fish for their freshness.

The fish should not smell fishy in the slightest; its gills should be bright red, not dun- or rust-colored; its eyes should be quite clear, not cloudy, and they should be bulbous and seemingly wet; the flesh, when pressed, should be quite firm, not at all mushy; and the skin should be shiny, even iridescent. The freshest fish will also be coated in a mucilaginous substance that is produced to prevent the scales and skin from drying out.

Occasionally you may see fish that is still in a state of rigor mortis, its head and tail raised together, bending the body like a strung bow. If you are lucky enough to get incredibly fresh fish that is still in rigor mortis, it's best to let the rigor mortis pass, so the flesh loosens and the body flattens out, and it will be easier to cut up. Store it in your refrigerator until it relaxes.

Storing Fish

For most home cooks, the best way to store a whole fresh fish is to not store it at all. A fresh fish that's not in a state of rigor mortis should be dealt with immediately; its viscera and gills should be removed from the body, its fillets prepared for cooking or for storage/aging, and its carcass used for stock.

If you *must* store your just-purchased fresh fish for any amount of time, make sure it is kept as cold as possible; it should be as close to the freezing point, without going lower, as you can get it. Home refrigerators are typically set to just under 40°F (4°C), a suboptimal temperature for storing fresh fish, and its quality will deteriorate quickly. This is the reason why many fish markets store their fish on sheet pans or trays set on crushed ice; the sheets, made of aluminum, are conductive, which means they are efficient at transferring heat away from the fish flesh to the ice, keeping the fish as cold as possible. You can mimic this same setup at home by covering a sheet pan with crushed ice and placing the whole fish (less preferable) or the prepared fillets on a smaller sheet pan and setting that on the ice.

Another way of keeping your fresh fish in good condition is to cure it slightly. This is only effective with fillets, and it will give the fish flesh a slightly firmer, cured texture, but it will extend the amount of time you can leave it in the fridge before you absolutely must cook it. Curing also heightens the flavor of the fish, because it makes it salty and removes some of the moisture within the flesh, concentrating its flavor. And curing also makes fish proteins less likely to stick in a hot pan. To cure fish fillets, simply sprinkle them on both sides with salt. How much is up to you, but know that a relatively heavy cure, one that will make your fish fillets as salty as gravlax or shiozake, would use 1.5% to 2% of the weight of the fish in salt.

The carcass and head of a filleted fresh fish, rinsed of any viscera, can be stored briefly in the refrigerator, but it's best to stash these in the freezer in a freezer bag, with as much excess air removed from it as possible, until you're ready to make stock with them. Freezing will not affect their flavor, unless they become freezer-burned, which can happen if they are stored improperly or for too long.

skin-on fillets
skinless tail portions
scraps

fins, skin, and other trimmings
head and central skeleton

HOW TO CUT UP WHOLE FISH

Just as learning how to cut up a chicken will familiarize you with the anatomical structure of other poultry as well, and learning how to cut up a pork shoulder gives you some insight into the anatomical structure of other land animals, the approach to cutting up one fish can be applied to others. However, fish fall into two general categories—flatfish and roundfish—which are treated differently. But for our purposes, I focus on medium-sized roundfish like red snapper and black sea bass, as those are the ones called for in this book.

There are various techniques for cutting up fish, depending on the style of cooking and the conventions of the specific cuisine, but the methods I describe here are basic: the goal is simply to remove the viscera and gills and remove the flesh so that you're left with the carcass and head and the fillets. Although the ability to produce meticulously well-cut fillets comes only with practice, for making ramen stock, leaving strips of flesh here and there can actually be a boon to your bowl of ramen. In any case, once you remove the fillets, there's a range of possibilities: chop them up for meatballs or dumpling fillings or trim them into presentable portions to sauté or sear for topping ramen or for serving as part of another meal. Any trim can, of course, be thrown into the stockpot.

Here are general tips for butchering fish:

USE A SHARP KNIFE, PREFERABLY ONE DESIGNED FOR THE TASK. You can use a filleting knife, a deba, or a santoku.

KEEP YOUR FISH COLD. If you are filleting more than one fish, work with one of them at a time and keep the other fish in the refrigerator until you're ready to use them. Keeping fish cold helps preserve their flavor, prevents deterioration in quality, and makes them easier to butcher.

SCALE THE FISH IN A LARGE PLASTIC BAG IN YOUR SINK. The bag helps catch any scales that fly around.

WORK AS QUICKLY AS YOU SAFELY CAN. This has to do with keeping the fish cold. That being said, *do not rush this process*. You are working with a slippery, wet, oddly shaped object and a very sharp knife. If at any point you are feeling overwhelmed, put down your knife, step back, take a few breaths, and reset.

AFTER SCALING, DRY THE EXTERIOR OF THE FISH THOROUGHLY WITH A KITCHEN TOWEL OR PAPER TOWELS. A dry fish is a less slippery fish.

The Process

Using kitchen shears, cut off the fins at the point where they attach to the fish.

Scale the fish using a fish scaler, then run your fingers over it to make sure you've removed all the scales. Rinse the fish under cold running water, then dry it thoroughly using a kitchen towel or paper towels.

Using the tip of a sharp filleting knife, deba, or santoku, make a shallow incision from the fish's anus up to its gills. Using the knife or kitchen shears, sever the two halves of the collar. Using your hands, spread open the incision to reveal the internal organs.

Run the tip of your knife between the gills and the gill plate to release the gills. With the tip of the knife, sever the topmost part of the gills, where they attach to the head, on either side. Using your fingers, pull the gills out of the body; the viscera should come out along with them. Using a kitchen towel or paper towels, dry the interior cavity thoroughly, and mop up any blood.

Lay the fish on its side on your cutting board, with the top of the fish toward you. Using the tip of your knife, with your blade parallel to the work surface, make a small incision right behind the head, inserting your knife flush with the central line of bones that divides the fish in half. Again using the tip of your knife, make a long, shallow incision by following the line of the central line of bones all the way down the fish until you reach the end of the fillet at the tail.

Again using the tip of your knife, cut a little deeper into the incision you've already made, using the central line of bones as a guide; if this is done correctly, the knife tip should make a clicking sound as it passes over each bone. (1) **If you find it helpful, you can use the fingers of your other hand to lift the fillet away from the carcass to give you a better angle to expose the flesh as you cut.** Repeat these shallow incisions until the tip of the knife rides along the fish's spine all the way down the fish and the fillet has been fully released from that side of the spine.

Turn the fish around, so its belly is facing you. Starting at the tail, using the tip of the knife, with your blade parallel to the work surface, make a shallow incision extending from the tail to the belly of the fish, using the central line of bones as a guide. Just as you did on the other side, deepen the incision until the tip of the knife rides along the fish's spine. The fillet should be completely freed from the skeleton of the fish except at the head and at the tail and where the pinbones in the fillets connect to the spine.

Slide your knife blade between the spine and the fillet and, with the knife flush with the spine, cut back toward the tail, using the spine as a guide, to sever the pin bones from the spine and cut through the skin where the fillet is still attached to the tail.

Turn the fish around once again, so that its back is facing you. Make a deep incision behind the spot where the pectoral fin is located, cutting at an angle across the fish and into the flesh down to the spine so that the cut meets up with the initial cut behind the head. Holding the blade parallel to the work surface, slide it between the fillet and the backbone and cut toward the head of the fish, using the spine as a guide, and free the fillet entirely.

REPEAT THIS ENTIRE PROCESS ON THE OTHER SIDE OF THE FISH. If you find it difficult to lay the fish flat on the cutting board, place it so that its head and collar jut off the end of the cutting board, which will make the rest of it lie flatter.

You now have 2 fillets and the frame of the fish. Rinse the frame of blood and any dark material.

To trim the fillets into serving portions, start by removing the membrane and rib bones located on top of the belly meat. In small-to-medium fish like black sea bass, the belly meat is quite thin, so you can simply cut off that area and toss it into a stock, although that will change the look of the fillet—not a huge issue. But you can also (2) **cut along the top of the fillet to free the rib bones** and then use them as a guide to help you slice the rib bones and the membrane that covers them off the fillet while leaving some belly meat intact.

For use as ramen toppings, I like to remove the back half of each fillet, which is made up of tougher muscle tissue (as that half of the fish is what is used to propel it through water) and use it for meatballs. However, rather than simply cutting it off, I skin that portion first, as it's easier to remove the skin from a whole fillet than from a cut portion of one.

To skin the fillets, lay each one flat on the cutting board, skin side down. Make an incision at the base of the tail into the meat, angled back toward the end of the fillet but not through the skin: this will give you a little tab of skin that you can use as a handle. Holding that tab with your nondominant hand, position your knife angled slightly downward with its cutting edge at the point where the skin and flesh meet.

Using a gentle sawing motion, make small cuts until you can slide the blade between the flesh and skin and position the blade flat against the board. (3) **Pull the tab of skin with your nondominant hand while continuously using a gentle sawing motion with the knife—** the force required to cut away the flesh should come primarily from your hand pulling the fillet toward the sawing knife edge. As you do so, try to keep the blade flat. Continue pulling until the skin is completely separated from the fillet.

Alternatively, if you are using just the tail end of the fillet for meatballs, remove only the skin that covers the part of the fillet you will cut off. Then remove the skinned portion of the fillet, along with the skin, by cutting the fillet crosswise in half.

This will leave you with 2 skin-on portions of fillet and 2 skinless tail portions, plus the skin you removed from the tail portions, which can be used for stock.

HOW TO MAKE FRESH FISH STOCK FOR RAMEN

The main challenges a fresh fish stock presents are shelf life, clarity, and aroma. Fish stocks tend to start taking on off flavors even under refrigeration after a couple of days; they are at their best when freshly made, and they quickly decline in quality. Since fish flesh is so delicate, cooking it past the point of well-done makes it disintegrate into tiny particles, which easily get bound up in the stock, as the fish's connective tissues convert to a relatively large amount of gelatin very rapidly. And cooking fish stock is a smelly business; your house will smell like fish.

All of these challenges can be addressed by controlling the cooking temperature. However, compared to making a chicken or pork stock, you'll likely start off with far less raw material and will consequently use a smaller quantity of water, and controlling the cooking temperature of a smaller volume of water is more difficult. I like to use a double boiler for making fresh fish stock, which puts an upper limit on the cooking temperature of the stock.

To do this, put the ingredients for the stock in a metal mixing bowl and cover them with cold water, then set the mixing bowl over a pot filled with water. Bring the water to a boil over high heat, reduce the heat to maintain a steady simmer, and cover the bowl tightly. The steam rising from the simmering water will heat the bowl, which in turn will heat the water it

LEFT TO RIGHT: The fish carcass and trimmings with aromatics before cooking. The finished fish stock before straining.

contains, and it will eventually start to approach the boiling point. But as the water vapor within the bowl rises and condenses on the lid, it will drip back down into the stock, modulating the temperature and preventing it from rising above 206°F (97°C), making this an entirely hands-off way of maintaining a low simmering temperature. The lid not only helps with temperature control but also limits the amount of fishy aromas dispersed into the air.

Because fish has a delicate flavor, I don't use a lot of aromatic vegetables in the stock—just scallions, ginger, and garlic. And, unlike with pork or chicken stock, instead of adding the kombu and its soaking water to the stock at the end and allowing the kombu to steep in the stock, I soak the kombu in water overnight and use the soaking water as part of the base liquid for the stock. This is because of the comparatively lower total volume of stock, and because I do not add vegetables at the end, which would help drop the temperature. Instead, once the stock is done, I add the strained kombu to the hot stock after it has been strained so it can steep while the stock cools (the straining process will drop the temperature of the stock closer to "ideal" extraction temperatures).

Making a second stock with fresh fish bones isn't all that effective since the bones will be almost entirely spent by the first stock-making process. Emulsified fresh fish stocks, while they do exist, are tough to make as they require a large amount of fish bones and heads, far more than would be convenient for most home cooks to procure.

VEGETABLE RAMEN STOCK

As ramen cooks have expanded their offerings to accommodate those who don't eat meat or fish, bean broths have emerged as a good alternative. They are rich in protein and flavorful, and, with judicious use of blending, can mimic both clear and emulsified stocks. Bean broth is also easy to make, as anyone who has cooked a pot of beans can attest.

How to Make Bean Broth for Ramen

I strongly suggest using a pressure cooker to make bean broths. A pressure cooker cuts the cooking time down to a matter of minutes. All you need to do is add the beans; ample cold water to cover; a few aromatic vegetables, like onions, carrots, garlic, ginger, scallions, and celery (bean broths are the only instance in which I use celery for ramen stock); and a bay leaf to the pressure cooker pot; bring it to pressure; and cook for about 10 minutes. Most varieties of dried beans, if soaked beforehand, will be completely cooked at this point, and the broth the process produces will be delicious.

The question of whether to soak your beans or not has bedeviled food writers for generations. Do you have to do it? No. The benefits of soaking lie almost entirely in the fact that the beans will cook more evenly; you'll have far fewer "blown out" beans, or beans that have been cooked to mush, and far more will remain whole even when they've been cooked to a creamy consistency. The structural integrity of the cooked beans has more to do with the salt that's added to the soaking water than anything else, as the salt strengthens the pectin in the beans; the evenness in cooking has more to do with the fact that the beans absorb water during the soak, which means they aren't really being *hydrated* as they cook, they are simply cooking.

Neither of these considerations is particularly important if your only goal is to make a broth for ramen. But if you want to use the beans you use to make your broth for some other purpose, it's best to soak them in salted water for at least 8 hours, or overnight.

To make a kind of emulsified bean broth, you can blend some of the cooked beans into the broth, but don't go overboard. While adding more cooked beans to the broth will produce a richer texture, the broth will also become "heavier," in that it will become more filling. There is no gelatin in a bean broth, so any thickness in texture will come solely from the proteins and starches in the beans.

How to Use Vegetables in Stock

Vegetable stocks are made in the same manner as other stocks, but the cooking times are far shorter. There's little need for long cooking, as there's no collagen to convert into gelatin. And plant cells are more fragile than meat and connective tissue, so exposing them to heat quickly breaks them down, which means you can extract their flavor relatively quickly.

Vegetables release a lot of sugars into the stock liquid, and cooking vegetables in the stock for longer than about 45 minutes intensifies that sweetness to an unpalatable degree. Also, once the cells in the vegetables rupture, they become sponges, soaking up the liquid they're submerged in, meaning cooking a lot of vegetables in stock for too long will reduce the final yield of the stock (unless you express all the soaked-up stock in the vegetables, which would make the stock cloudy).

LEFT TO RIGHT: Emulsified chickpea stock and clear chickpea stock

There has been some research on the way in which long-cooked vegetables produce a kind of roundness of flavor, which in Japanese is called "kokumi." A lot of this research,* or at least the most high-profile examples of it, has been done and promoted by Ajinomoto, the Japanese company founded by Kikunae Ikeda, the chemist who isolated and identified glutamic acid and the originator of MSG. Unlike umami, which is now considered to be a "fifth taste," the term "kokumi" refers to the way the addition of onions and garlic to a dish enhances its flavor, particularly when the onions and garlic are allowed to cook for a long time. Ajinomoto calls this a kind of "mouthfulness," and it claims that its research shows that this phenomenon is both observable and attributable to the presence of a chain of amino acids known as glutathione.

Since Ajinomoto is a manufacturer of products derived from amino acids that are intended for use in cooking, it's wise to take their claims with a grain of salt; on the other hand, Ajinomoto is responsible for one of the most miraculous food additive discoveries in history—MSG—and their research on the flavor chemistry behind umami is so widely accepted that it might as well be the law. The presence of disodium guanylate and inosinate in the ingredient list of your bag of Doritos is a testament to that fact.

You can use Ajinomoto's research into the phenomenon to your benefit when cooking. In the context of making stock (or aromatic fats, or tare, for that matter), that means considering the beneficial flavors produced by quickly cooking vegetables or by slowly cooking them. For this reason, I'll often add an onion, garlic, and ginger to my stock both at the beginning of the cooking process and at the end, to capture the two kinds of flavors, for a more layered flavor profile in the final dish. The longer-cooked vegetables might reduce the yield slightly, but so long as you don't add a ton, the risk of the vegetables adding too much sweetness to the stock is minimal.

Regardless of when you add vegetables to a stock, consider their surface area. A peeled whole onion thrown into a pot of water won't add as much flavor in a given period of time as an onion that has been diced, and the same is true for any vegetable; chopping them up speeds up the rate at which they cook and release their flavors. When making a stock with only vegetables, one you plan on cooking for 45 minutes at a strong simmer, you can throw in vegetables in a relatively whole state and the stock will turn out fine. However, when adding vegetables to a stock to steep at relatively low temperatures, as I often call for, you want to chop them up so that they give up what they have as quickly as possible.

* Ajinomoto, "Kokumi Substances," https://www.ajinomoto.com/innovation/action/kokumi-substances.

Fat is an essential component of a ramen bowl, and the type of fat you use and the flavors you add to it will have a profound effect on the overall flavor profile of a bowl of ramen. You can use both animal- and vegetable-derived fats in ramen, and you can flavor them with anything that is oil-soluble. Typically the fat is flavored with aromatic vegetables like onions, garlic, ginger, and scallions, but it can also be flavored with a range of spices and herbs, as well as dried seafood products.

It is common practice to use the fat that rises to the surface of a stock in bowls of ramen. While that is economical, I tend to avoid using that fat for ramen. It has a kind of flat taste, and its texture is a little watery, both due to the long cooking time and the fact that the fat that rises to the surface of a stock has a slightly higher water content than fat rendered with other methods. You can ameliorate these issues by heating the fat on the stovetop to cook off any water, then adding chopped aromatic vegetables, spices, herbs, and/or dried seafood to it, but I prefer to use this fat, unflavored, for stir-fries.

How to Render Animal Fat

The most basic method for rendering fat is covering hunks of fat and skin (which contains a lot of fat) with water and boiling the water away. As the fat renders, it covers the remaining solid fat and skin completely, and the mixture is heated until as much of the fat as possible is rendered. You can use this method to render the fat from chicken skin, duck skin, pork fatback, or chunks of fat from any animal you can think of. Just as with flavor extraction and gelatin conversion, temperature, time, and the surface area of the bits you're rendering are all important considerations. Cook the fatty bits at too high a temperature, and they'll begin to brown and produce toasty, roasted flavor notes, or even a burnt flavor; cook them at too low a temperature, and not only will the process take forever, but the fat also won't render completely. Rendering large slabs of fat and skin will take much longer and be less efficient than rendering fat and skin that have been finely chopped, pulsed in a food processor, or run through a grinder.

For rendering chicken and other poultry fat, I recommend using the stovetop or the microwave. Both are relatively hands-off methods, although both are also more efficient if you take a little time beforehand to cut the fat and pieces of skin into smaller bits. You can simply cut the fat and skin into ½- to 1-inch pieces, but blitzing them in a food processor or running them through a meat grinder will make the rendering process quicker and more efficient.

Considering the quantities home cooks are typically tasked with, I don't find it too onerous to cut up the fat and skin using a knife. However, if, say, I've stored the skin and fat from several chickens I've cut up in the freezer, with the idea of rendering all of the fat in one go, I'll use a meat grinder. If you're working with an enormous quantity of fat and skin, though, it may be worth compromising and chucking the lot into a pot without cutting any of it up.

To render fat on the stovetop, place the skin and fat in a heavy-bottomed pot and cover them with water. Heat the water to boiling and boil until the water evaporates; the boiling water will render out enough fat to cover the pieces of skin and fat. Once the water has boiled away, the temperature of the liquefied fat will begin to climb above the boiling point of water, which will then in turn render the remaining fat more efficiently. Once the pieces of skin begin to fry—the fat in the pan will begin sizzling—turn the heat off, let the mixture cool, and strain out the remaining skin.

When rendering fat, you want to avoid frying the skin bits until they become brown and crisp. That browning means the temperature of the fat has risen sufficiently to slightly degrade its quality; some of its aroma will be lost, and it will take on a little of that "brown" flavor. In other contexts, that may be desirable, but for ramen, I prefer fats that are neutral in flavor. If you want to eat crispy skin bits, you can strain the leathery bits out of the rendered fat and fry them in fresh oil or bake them until crisp in the oven. (Salt the skins as soon as they come out of the oil or the oven, and eat them with pickles or kimchi.)

Rendering pork fat, or other non-poultry animal fats, is similar, but the process is smellier. Given that good butchers and many supermarkets sell freshly rendered lard, and you end up producing a lot of lard when making stock and chashu, you don't have to render lard yourself if you don't want to.

Another animal fat product that is often used in ramen is seabura, or pork backfat cooked until it's almost falling apart, then chopped or strained. When added to hot broth, instead of melting into a liquid fat, the chopped or strained bits of seabura float in the broth, adding texture and flavor to each spoonful. To make it, you boil chunks of backfat until they're meltingly tender, about 2 hours, then drain them and chop them up or push them through a fine-mesh sieve. Chopping the fat will yield a more interesting texture, while pushing it through a sieve will yield minute particles of backfat. Both processes will yield a fair amount of liquid fat, which can be used wherever you'd use rendered lard. The seabura can be flavored by adding chopped raw garlic, roasted garlic, or even seasonings such as a couple spoonfuls of tare.

Adding Flavor and Aroma to Fats and Oils

The fat you render can be flavored further by slowly cooking and/or frying aromatic vegetables (like garlic, ginger, and onions) or spices and herbs in it. Quickly frying these ingredients will yield a flavorful and aromatic oil, while slowly cooking garlic, onions, and ginger in fat will produce a subtler yet more rounded flavor profile, which is referred to in Japanese as "kokumi" (see page 110), a kind of mouth-coating quality evident in fats that have been used, for example, for confit, where meat is slowly poached covered in oil along with herbs and aromatic vegetables. Combining a slow poach with a quick fry yields a fat with both the rounded, fuller flavor of the first technique and the more aromatic and sharper flavors of the second. When slow-cooking vegetables, it's best to leave them whole or at least in larger chunks, as that will prevent them from dehydrating too quickly and starting to fry and brown. For quickly infusing oils and fats with flavor, though, it's best to finely chop your ingredients.

Depending on the ingredients you use, and how you cut them up before cooking, the process of frying aromatic vegetables in fats and oils can yield by-products that can be put to further use. For example, frying garlic or scallions or garlic chives in oil or animal fat will both imbue the fat with their flavor and yield crispy, dehydrated bits of vegetables, which can be used as a topping for ramen, or blitzed up along with other ingredients to form tasty pastes that, when added to a bowl of ramen, can alter its character considerably.

③ TARE

Because ramen cooks make a big deal out of tare, home cooks may believe that making tare must be complicated, or that it relies on special techniques or knowledge. If tare is sometimes called "the soul of the bowl," then the cook who makes the tare must be a kind of mini ramen god.

The facts of the matter are far more mundane.

Tare is used primarily to season a bowl of ramen with salt. The soup stock and the fat in the soup add a host of water- and fat-soluble flavor to the final bowl, but if you simply combine them and take a sip, that spoonful of liquid will be incredibly bland. Salt isn't fat-soluble, for one thing, and as I've already described in detail, cooks typically limit the amount of salt they add to soup stocks to maximize their versatility. Foods that taste appealingly salty typically have a salt quantity that is about 1% of their total weight—and provided the soup stock and fat are well made and flavorful, you'll end up with a decent bowl of soup.

However, there are many ways to add salt to a soup, and if you use something more than just plain old salt, you'll also be adding a host of other flavors. Soy sauce is a prime example: it adds salt, sugar (particularly if you use Japanese soy sauces), a little acidity, and other flavorful compounds, which include glutamic acid, one of the most powerful flavor enhancers there is. For more on soy sauce, see pages 56–57.

While ramen's emphasis on tare is unique in noodle soup traditions, the idea of a seasoning sauce for noodle soups isn't. Chinese noodle soups rely on a similar system of seasoning as ramen, partly because ramen is, after all, originally a Chinese noodle soup; these soups will often be seasoned with a mixture of soy sauce, vinegar, aromatic vegetables, and spices that's prepared ahead of time. Vietnamese pho typically relies solely on fish sauce for salinity and savor and a bit of lime juice for acidity; the rest of the flavor in the soup comes from the stock and its flavorful fat, fortified with charred onion, ginger, and spices. Thai noodle soups typically take a more deconstructed approach, and a range of seasoning sauces, including fish sauce, are used to provide salinity and flavor, along with sugar, citrus juice, and other acids, many of which are offered to individual diners to tweak their own soup to their tastes.

If there is mystery inherent in the way tare does its job in a bowl of ramen, it has to do with flavors that are set apart from the essential tastes of acidity, sweetness, and salinity. In other words, the mystery of tare has to do with what we call "umami."

What Is Umami?

"Umami" is a word coined in 1908 by Japanese chemist Kikunae Ikeda when he was trying to determine why dashi tastes so good. The word roughly translates as "deliciousness," but it's more commonly translated as "savoriness." Ikeda identified glutamic acid, an amino acid found in vegetable and animal proteins, as the primary source of this savoriness, and his research has since been confirmed, leading to umami being inducted into the pantheon of the five tastes, joining saltiness, bitterness, sweetness, and sourness.

Ikeda found that glutamic acid existed in high concentrations in kombu. Further research has revealed that there are other sources of umami in addition to glutamic acid, namely inosinic acid and guanylic acid, and that these three amino acids work together in multiplicative rather than additive ways. For example, a food that contains both glutamic acid and inosinic acid will taste many times more savory than a food that contains only glutamic acid, and one that contains glutamic acid, inosinic acid, and guanylic acid will taste many times more savory than one that contains just glutamic acid and inosinic acid.

While the synergistic relationship between these three amino acids might seem to be only of academic interest, its application is evident in many of the processed foods stocked on grocery store shelves. Scan the list of ingredients on most bags of chips or any decent instant noodle product, and you'll find monosodium glutamate, disodium inosinate, and disodium guanylate. Their synergistic relationship is also evident in something as mundane as a mushroom cheeseburger or a plate of chicken marsala: meats, like ground beef and chicken, have glutamates and inosinates in quantity, as do cheese and chicken stock, and mushrooms are the main source of guanylate (the amount of guanylic acid is higher in dried shiitake mushrooms than in other kinds). These foods have a rounded savory flavor that a cheeseburger or a pan-roasted chicken breast with a simple pan sauce does not.

So while tare is primarily a source of salinity for a bowl of ramen, it is also a source of elements that provide and exponentially increase the umami of that bowl. This dual role explains why shio ramen, or ramen that has been flavored with a tare in which the primary

Shoyu tare

source of salinity is salt, rather than more flavorful, glutamate-rich ingredients like soy sauce or miso, is one of the most challenging types of ramen to make. A shio tare, almost by definition, operates with a handicap. In short, the challenge of making a good ramen tare consists of packing it with a lot of salt and a lot of umami-producing ingredients.

MSG and Haimi

There is, of course, a very simple way to boost the umami of your bowl of ramen, and that's by adding monosodium glutamate to your tare or directly to the bowl.

MSG provides a concentrated boost of glutamates—and that's it; it doesn't add other flavors or aromas. MSG must be used in conjunction with other flavorful ingredients, plus some source of salt, in order to work effectively. The nature of those other flavorful things will also affect MSG's efficacy as a flavor enhancer; if you use MSG to season a green vegetable like kale, stir-fried with garlic and a little salt, the dish will taste just a little better than those greens simply stir-fried with garlic and a little salt; however, if a little chicken stock is added to those stir-fried greens, they will taste much better, as the MSG will work in conjunction with the inosinates in the chicken stock to produce more flavor. Add some dried mushrooms, with their guanylic acid, and the dish will be even more flavorful.

MSG can be used along with the sodium salts of inosinic acid and guanylic acid to provide a similar, more immediately effective boost in flavor, without any of the additional flavors and aromas that foods rich in inosinic acid and guanylic acid provide. In Japan, you can buy haimi, a combination of these salts—monosodium glutamate, disodium inosinate, and disodium guanylate. Because of its more "rounded" flavor-enhancing profile, haimi is commonly used by ramen shops. (A product available in the U.S. called SuperSalt is essentially the same thing.)

If you're comfortable using MSG and other flavor enhancers to season your food, it may seem as if "more is more" should be the governing philosophy. However, there is a point past which these flavor enhancers' effects have rapidly diminishing returns. Research published in the journal *Food & Nutrition Research** has shown that the boost MSG brings to flavors declines significantly once it exceeds 0.8% concentration, which tracks with the way Ajinomoto, the largest MSG manufacturer, suggests people use the product—at about 1% concentration. Thus, if you season 100 milliliters of already seasoned stock with 0.5 gram of MSG, it will taste significantly more savory and flavorful than the seasoned stock alone; if you season the same amount of stock with 0.8 gram of MSG, it will taste even better. But if you season it with 1 or 1.5 grams of MSG, or 2 or 3 grams, you won't notice as large a boost with each increase.

If you do choose to use MSG or similar products in your ramen, I suggest adding no more than about 0.5% of the total weight, which, for the sake of convenience, you can approximate by simply using volume, treating the soup, tare, and fat in the bowl as if it were water (water's mass is equal to its volume: 1 g water = 1 ml water). For a bowl of ramen soup with about 410 ml of liquid (350 ml soup stock + 30 ml tare + 30 ml fat), that means using no more than 2 g MSG or haimi to season it.

* S. Jinap, P. Hajeb, R. Karim, S. Norliana, S. Yibadatihan, and R. Abdul-Kadir, "Reduction of Sodium Content in Spicy Soups Using Monosodium Glutamate," *Food & Nutrition Research* 60 (2016).

HOW TO MAKE TARE

The goal of making a tare is to produce a liquid that has a high concentration of salt; a high concentration of flavor enhancers like glutamic acid, inosinic acid, and guanylic acid; and a high concentration of the myriad chemical compounds that make things flavorful.

The easiest way to make a tare is to use powerfully flavorful ingredients that possess these qualities, like soy sauce. Mirin and sake, two other common ingredients in Japanese pantries, are often used in tare. Sake is a rice wine that is both savory-sweet and umami-rich, and there are many kinds of sake, each of which has its own unique flavor profile. Mirin is a sweetened rice wine that is primarily used as a sweetening agent, but it also provides a range of flavors, including umami-rich ones. Miso, a paste made from fermented soybeans and grains, is umami-rich, slightly acidic, and quite salty, and it offers a host of pleasing aromas and flavors. Tamari, which is often referred to as a type of soy sauce but is in fact the liquid runoff from miso production, is quite salty, a little sweet, a little acidic, and very flavorful and aromatic.

While all these products can be viewed as substances with varying ratios of the same elements—salt, sugars, umami flavor enhancers, acid, and water—they all share one thing in common: koji. "Koji" refers both to strains of mold (*Aspergillus oryzae* and *Aspergillus sojae*) and to grains that have been inoculated with those molds, and it has been used for thousands of years in East Asia to produce soy sauce, miso, alcohols, and other culinary products.

You certainly don't have to limit yourself to just ingredients commonly found in Japanese pantries. Chinese soy sauces, less sweet than Japanese versions because they aren't made with wheat, are salty, glutamate-rich, and flavorful. Dark Chinese soy sauces, which are more syrupy, sweeter, darker, and less salty than light Chinese soy sauce or Japanese dark soy sauces, can be used in tare, as can other prepared sauces, like oyster sauce, a combination of cooked oyster juices and other seasonings, and often MSG. China has a range of fermented products used for seasoning, like douchi, or fermented soybeans, and doubanjiang, a fermented chili paste made from broad beans (fava beans) and hot chilies.

Feel free to further expand your search for flavorful tare ingredients to include those from Korea (ganjang, doenjang, and gochujang), Thailand (Golden Mountain sauce), or Vietnam (fish sauce), as well as other prepared products from all over the globe, like Maggi seasoning, tomato paste, mustard, ketchup, and Worcestershire sauce. What unites all of these is that they are fundamentally condiments, and as such, they're extraordinarily flavorful.

So, is it simply a matter of mixing some of these ingredients together in a container and adding that mixture to a hot soup? Yes! That's it! The mystery of tare, revealed.

Of course, proportions matter. If you use a lot of ketchup and a little bit of soy sauce, your ramen will taste strange; if you use a lot of soy sauce and a small amount of ketchup, it might taste pretty normal.

Designing a Tare

In the context of a ramen shop, where a single stock may be used for more than one kind of ramen, a tare offers a precalibrated dose of seasoning and flavor to various soups. It obviates the need for the ramen cook to adjust on the fly; each bowl of ramen receives a set quantity of soup, which is seasoned precisely with a set amount of tare, and every bowl will taste the same.

This approach is useful for home cooks too. Because a tare generally consists of very salty, often fermented ingredients and little to no fat, you can make a tare and stash it in your fridge, where it will keep for a very long time. As long as you always use a similar volume of soup stock in your bowls of ramen, that one tare can be used as seasoning for soup stocks in variety. One week, you may have pork stock on hand, and you can make ramen with that stock and your tare; the next week, you may have a chicken stock, or a chicken and dashi double stock, and you can use the same tare with little to no adjustment in seasoning—a pinch of salt, maybe, or a splash of sweetened vinegar. You can also use the fact that tare keep for a long time to expand the number of bowls of ramen you are able to produce at a moment's notice. If you make a shoyu tare one month, a miso tare the next, and a shio the month after that, you'll have three separate tare with drastically different flavor profiles that can be used whenever you like.

You can, of course, design a tare to complement a specific soup. Ramen shops do this, after all, which is how they produce unique bowls of ramen. The benefit to home cooks is that doing this can produce singular, outstanding results if you get it right (if you get it slightly wrong, the results will still be tasty). For the recipes in this book, I designed tare that "match" the soup stocks they're served with. I also tested whether a tare made for specific soups can be used in other soups, and the results are clear: they all taste pretty good. That is because all tare are well-rounded, providing elements that any traditionally made soup stock can benefit from: salinity, sweetness, acidity, and umami.

SALT. The amount of salt in a tare is obviously important. Determining how much salt to put in a tare is fundamentally a matter of personal taste. Here again, however, ramen shop conventions can offer you a guide.

Typically, a tare makes up about 10% of the total volume of the soup. If a ramen shop uses around 300 ml of soup stock per bowl of ramen, the amount of tare added to the bowl will be around 30 ml. This ratio gives you limits within which you can tweak your tare to suit your tastes. If you consider the fact that most "well-seasoned" food is seasoned with about 1% of its weight in salt, with a little basic math, you can see that a tare should be about 10% salt by weight.*

As an example, consider a soup stock that's seasoned only with soy sauce as its tare. Commercially produced soy sauce has about 5 grams of salt per 100 grams—about 5% salt. If you season 300 ml of soup with 30 ml soy sauce, the total volume of soup (330 ml) will then contain about 1.5 grams of salt, which would mean the soup would have a salt concentration of 0.5%, and it will taste a little bland.

To improve its flavor, you can either increase the amount of soy sauce until the salinity of the whole hits 1% salt, which would mean you'd have to use around 75 ml of soy sauce for 300 ml of soup, or you can simply add salt to boost the salinity, which would mean using 1.5 g salt along with 30 ml soy sauce to season 300 ml of soup stock.

While either of those bowls of soup will be sufficiently seasoned, they will have drastically different flavor profiles. The one with 75 ml soy sauce will taste predominantly of soy sauce; many of the nuances of the soup stock will be lost, buried beneath the soy sauce flavor. Conversely, the bowl of soup with added salt will taste more like the soup stock. The two bowls of

* Weight and volumes, in the context of thin liquids like tare or clear soup stocks, can basically be assumed to be equivalent, or near enough that any discrepancies will be negligible.

Commonly used tare ingredients.

soup will also look different: the one seasoned with just soy sauce will be very dark, almost black, and the bowl seasoned with salt and soy sauce will be pale amber.

But neither of the tare in that example will be particularly good; they will simply get the seasoning job done. For fuller flavor, you'll want to add other ingredients to the tare, and whatever other ingredients you add to a tare will necessitate adjusting the amount of salt in it so that it can season whatever soup you're using. Some ingredients, like fish sauce, have a higher concentration of salt than soy sauce, and these can be used both to boost the salinity and to offer other flavors. Other ingredients, like mirin and sake, contain a relatively small amount of salt, and thus you'll want to add salt in some other form to compensate for the dilution of the tare's salinity when adding those ingredients.

Finally, it's important to remember that the 1% target of salinity for foods isn't an ironclad rule. A bowl of ramen contains a fair amount of fat, which will affect your perception of saltiness; the bowl has a mass of noodles in it, which are relatively bland, and they will take a majority of their seasoning from the soup. A bowl of ramen may have a range of toppings and garnishes, and some of them, too, take their seasoning from the soup. That is why good ramen invariably contains soup that is incredibly salty, the better to season everything else in the bowl. While a combination of soup stock and a tare that has about a 1% concentration of salt will be quite tasty when sipped on its own, it will be unutterably bland if sipped with added fat, noodles, and any toppings. The primary obstacle home cooks (myself very much included!) face in making good noodle soups is understanding how salty the soup has to be before it even begins to approach the saltiness of the ramen and pho and other soups served at restaurants. When making tare, the amount of salt you need to add to it to make it work can seem deranged; tasting a good tare is an unpleasant experience, because it will be tongue-curlingly salty.

One of the greatest challenges of making ramen and making tare is hitting a combination of flavor and salinity that results in a final bowl of ramen that is seasoned "just right"—that is, it's incredibly salty, but not so salty that you feel like you might die after eating it.

SUGAR. Tare is also the primary vehicle for adding sweetness to a bowl of ramen. A soup stock may contain a bit of sugar, provided by any vegetables that have been cooked or steeped in it, but a tare will provide most of the sweetness for the bowl, often through the addition of soy sauce, sake, or mirin, which is the sweetest of these three ingredients.

Depending on your taste, you can add other sweeteners to a tare. There are a variety of sugars available to use, from granulated white sugar and brown sugar to unrefined sugars like jaggery and palm sugar. For sweetness with no other flavors, you might turn to white sugar, but if you want to add a bit of complexity of flavor, you might choose an unrefined sugar or brown sugar, for their darker, molasses-y notes, or honey, which can add a range of flavors and aromas.

Cooked vegetables can also be used to add sweetness to a tare. Ivan Orkin, the chef of Ivan Ramen, famously uses a sofrito of vegetables cooked to a jammy consistency, which adds vegetal complexity along with a concentrated dose of sweetness.

I generally don't add extra sugar to tare, as I find that the sweetness provided by soy sauce, mirin, and sake to be sufficient in most cases. If a specific soup stock or bowl of ramen seems like it could be sweeter—this is particularly true of emulsified stocks—I'll add sugar by using amazu, or sweetened vinegar (see page 298).

I also like using sake as a sweetener, which requires cooking the sake down until it is almost dry. This accomplishes several things at once: it boils off the alcohol in sake almost completely, which means the only alcohol present in the final bowl is that provided by the mirin, which will be a tiny amount; it concentrates the acidity of the sake; it prevents the addition of sake to the tare from diluting the salinity; and it slightly caramelizes the sugars in the sake, which gives it an extra dimension of flavor. What's left after cooking the sake down is a syrupy liquid that has a lot of flavor with very little water; this is identical to the process used in French cuisine for adding wine to pan sauces, when the wine is cooked "au sec"—that is, "dry"—before building the rest of the sauce.

You want to avoid adding so much sugar to a tare that the resulting bowl of ramen is noticeably sweet, a pitfall that I've found to be more common outside of Japan, although it exists there too. Sweetness is meant to make ramen's crazy saltiness less noticeably crazy. It isn't meant to make the ramen sweet.

ACIDITY. Home cooks often overlook the importance of acidity in cooking, in part because sour foods are ubiquitous. A sandwich made with salami, cheese, and yeast-raised bread may not seem at first glance to be a great example of a sour food item, yet each of its ingredients possesses a slight acidity, as they are all fermented foods, and fermented foods, by and large, are slightly acidic,* thanks to the lactobacilli and other bacterial colonies that are responsible for giving those foods their flavor and extending their shelf life. Slightly acidic foods simply taste better to us, as is evident in the popularity of prepared condiments like mustard, ketchup, and mayonnaise, as well as in the fact that seafood of all kinds is often served with a wedge of lemon.

For ramen, acidity is doubly important, because a bowl of ramen contains alkaline noodles and a relatively large amount of fat. Acidity counteracts and complements the pretzel-like flavor of ramen and offers a counterpoint to the palate-deadening effects of the large slick of fat that sits on top of it. This latter effect is often described as the acidity "cutting through" the fat, as if the acid were a breaching whale, but I like to think of it as simply offering a point, or, really, many millions of points, of contrast to the salty-fattiness and doughy alkalinity of the other components of the bowl.

Since many tare rely on fermented ingredients for flavor and salinity, acidity may be overlooked by many home cooks because its inclusion is built into the process. Any shoyu tare will be slightly acidic, since soy sauce is inherently acidic and a shoyu tare is primarily made up of soy sauce, and the same is true of a miso tare. Shio tare present a challenge in that they start off at a disadvantage, as salt has no other flavors or flavor enhancers and it isn't acidic in the slightest. Other ingredients typically used in tare, like mirin and sake, as well as some types of katsuobushi, are also acidic, as they, too, are fermented products.

For most tare, the amount of acidity these various ingredients provide is sufficient for seasoning most soups, particularly plainer, lighter ones. Thicker, heavier soups, particularly emulsified soups, can benefit immensely from being spiked with more acid, the better to address the higher concentration of emulsified fat and/or particulate matter. More concentrated soups, like those for tsukemen, also benefit from a higher concentration of acidic ingredients.

There are a lot of these to choose from. Various vinegars and citrus juices are widely available and intuitive to use, but there's no reason to limit yourself. Ingredients like tamarind, green mango powder (amchur), and dried fruit are all good sources of acidity that will also add

* Some fermented foods are actually alkaline, like iru or natto—fermented locust beans and soybeans, respectively.

delicious flavors to the bowl of ramen; even your choice of sake can boost the acidity of the tare.

Since I find that different soups have wildly different requirements when it comes to acidity, I prefer to season soups directly with acid as needed, which is why in many of the recipes in this book, I call for small amounts of vinegar or amazu (see page 298) or souring agents like katsuobushi powder to be added to the bowl along with the tare. Seasoning ramen in this way makes your tare more all-purpose.

UMAMI. Aside from salt, a tare offers an opportunity to provide a concentrated dose of the amino acids responsible for umami: glutamic acid, inosinic acid, and guanylic acid. Many of the ingredients commonly used in tare contain relatively high proportions of these amino acids. Soy sauce, miso, and rice wines like mirin and sake all contain glutamates, as they all are produced using a fermentation process that involves koji. Inosinic acid and guanylic acid are typically added to tare in the form of dried seafood and dried mushrooms, respectively.

Umami is the one element of tare that is very dependent on the type of soup stock you use. Soup stocks made from meat and fish contain large amounts of inosinic acid, and depending on whether or not you steep kombu or dried mushrooms in the stock, they can also provide a significant amount of glutamic and guanylic acid. For example, a double-soup consisting of a 1:1 ratio of chicken stock and dashi made with kombu, katsuobushi, and shiitake will contain enough umami-producing compounds that it's relatively unimportant for the tare that seasons it to add anything more than salt, sugar, and acidity in order to taste delicious, whereas a soup that consists of a simple chicken stock will taste flat and bland if seasoned with that same tare.

I typically employ a more-is-more approach to packing tare with umami-rich ingredients. It isn't very likely that you'll exceed the concentration levels past which you'll experience diminishing returns in flavor, and ingredients like kombu, katsuobushi, and shiitake mushrooms offer a world of flavors. I recommend adding these ingredients to almost any tare you make.

The technique for adding these ingredients to tare is essentially identical to making dashi. The primary difference is that for tare-making, the liquid you steep these ingredients in isn't always water, since tare need to have a high concentration of salt and flavor. For example, for a shoyu tare, it makes more sense to steep these ingredients in soy sauce, rather than making a dashi and then spiking it with enough soy sauce and salt to make it sufficiently salty/tasty. Otherwise, you make a tare as you would a dashi.

Cooked Tare and Raw Tare

Infusing tare with dried seafood brings up the question of whether or not to cook a tare. Although many tare are prepared by heating some or all the ingredients, that can have a detrimental effect on flavors, particularly volatile flavors and aromas that ingredients like miso and soy sauce have in quantity. I don't want to emphasize this fact *too* much; if you heat miso or soy sauce, their desirable aromas and flavors aren't obliterated entirely, they're simply muted. This effect is, again, temperature-dependent: the higher the cooking temperature, the fewer volatile flavors and aromas will remain.

The question of whether heating the tare results in a better-tasting bowl one way or another depends on the ingredients it contains and the preferences of whoever's doing the tasting. A tare made with a commercial soy sauce like Kikkoman won't be affected by heating as much as one made with artisanally produced aged soy sauce, simply because Kikkoman has less flavor and aroma; however, you may find that a fancy soy sauce may actually taste better to you when its flavors and aromas become muted. This is further offset by the fact that you can add a host of flavors and aromas to a cooked tare by infusing spices and other ingredients into it, and so the loss of volatile elements of miso or soy sauce may be an acceptable price to pay.

I advocate a hybrid approach, which relies less on sound science than on my propensity for frugality and for hedging my bets. If you want to infuse dried seafood and mushrooms in a liquid, the best way to do that is to heat the liquid; if you want to preserve the volatile compounds in your soy sauce and miso, the best way to do that is to avoid heating them. My solution is to simply do both, by heating a portion of the ingredients in question with dried seafood and mushrooms, then adding an equivalent volume of the uncooked ingredients.

There are, however, two drawbacks to this method. The first is that it can mean making far more shoyu tare than you'd need to season a single batch of soup stock, since you need a bare-minimum volume of soy sauce for infusing the flavors of dried seafood and mushrooms into it effectively; I've found that to be around a cup (240 ml). (A smaller volume requires that you cut your kombu into quite small pieces, which poses an inconvenience when it comes time to heat the liquid and pull out the kombu before adding the katsuobushi.) If you then add in an equivalent amount of soy sauce, you've got at least 2 cups (480 ml) of tare, and at about 30 ml of tare per bowl of ramen, that means enough for about 16 bowls of ramen; at about 350 ml of stock per bowl of ramen, that means you can season 5.5 liters of stock with that tare.

The second is that the method is fussy. If you can make a perfectly good tare simply by blending ingredients without cooking them, why go through the trouble? Alternatively, if you can make a perfectly good tare by blending all the ingredients, soaking kombu in them, and then bringing them to a simmer before removing the kombu and adding dried seafood to steep, without the inclusion of additional raw ingredients, why bother making a raw tare or adopting the two-step approach?

Again, the decision comes down to your own preferences. If ease and convenience are of paramount importance to you, a raw blended tare may make the most sense; if it seems ridiculous to you to add raw ingredients to a cooked tare for the slight improvement volatile aromas and flavors might provide, then skip the two-step approach. But if you want a tare infused with dried seafood that also contains some of the more volatile flavors and aromas that unheated soy sauce does, use the two-step approach.

Adding Other Flavors to Tare

With the basic components out of the way, there are various other flavors you can add to your tare, from a range of different sources. Garlic, ginger, onions, leeks, scallions, tomatoes, dried fruit, herbs, spices . . . all of these can be added to a tare, and all benefit from heating. For whole spices, that is especially true; toasting whole spices before adding them to a tare—well, toasting them before any use whatsoever—will make them more aromatic and flavorful, and I recommend doing so whenever you use them. Aromatic vegetables are flavorful when simply simmered, but they take on a different flavor profile when roasted or charred. Dried fruits like dried peppers, hot or mild, add their fruity complexity to tare, and, because their chili heat comes from the oil-soluble compound capsaicin, even the hottest peppers, when used to infuse something that is completely oil-free, like many tare, can be added simply for the flavor they provide, with none of their spiciness.

Seasoned Vinegars, Pastes, and Powders

While a tare is the primary seasoning for a bowl of ramen, you can add other seasonings. For ramen restaurants where a single broth is used for multiple kinds of ramen, these other seasonings help to differentiate the bowls from one another and offer cooks an opportunity to fine-tune their flavor profiles.

Many bowls of ramen benefit from a slight boost in acidity, and ramen shops will borrow from classical Japanese cuisine and use sweetened vinegar, or amazu, to add both sweetness and acidity to the bowl. Amazu can be added to any bowl of ramen, and I've found it is particularly useful for ramen made with emulsified stocks, as they contain a fair amount of fat. The vinegar helps offset the richness of the stock, and its sweetness helps to round out their funkier, sometimes more bitter flavors. Making sweetened vinegar is as simple as dissolving a pinch of sugar in it.

Rice vinegars are a natural fit for the overall flavor profile of most ramen, as they are made from rice wine and have a sweeter flavor profile than other vinegars. For a bowl of ramen with a decidedly more Chinese flavor profile, you could use any number of Chinese vinegars, like Chinkiang or red vinegar (which is sweetened). But other acids work, too: red or white wine, Champagne, or apple cider vinegar. Seasoned vinegars can also be steeped with dried seafood, or mixed with dashi, to add a little savoriness.

You can also add flavorful pastes to the bottom of a bowl of ramen. This includes pastes you can purchase, like miso, doubanjiang, XO sauce, and Thai curry paste, and those you can prepare yourself, such as the "dirty paste" (see Pork, Chicken, and Niboshi Shoyu, page 187) used by the renowned ramen chef Keizo Shimamoto to make his "dirty shoyu" ramen. A paste will have a chunky texture, whereas a tare will be liquid, which means that you'll need to evenly disperse the paste in the soup stock by using a whisk or an immersion blender.

Since seasoning pastes are relatively solid, they can be seared in oil in a hot pan before you add the soup stock. This is common practice for many kinds of miso ramen: some oil or fat, typically lard, will be heated in a wok, and then the paste-like miso tare will be added to the hot wok, and the soup stock poured into the wok. This gives the resulting ramen a seared flavor, and it blooms and disperses any oil-soluble flavors in the tare. The same method can be used with any other kind of paste.

Finally, you can add powdered ingredients directly to a bowl of ramen before adding the soup stock—anywhere from a pinch to a heaping tablespoon or two, depending on the flavor profile you want. The most common powders added to ramen are ground black or white pepper, which will add floral, spicy notes to the ramen; chili powders (ditto); and pulverized dried fish products, or gyofun. Gyofun adds a slight bitterness and an umami boost, but if it contains katsuobushi, it can sour the soup slightly.

reconstituted wakame
sliced scallions
blanched spinach
sous-vide pork shoulder chashu
sous-vide
chicken breast
braised pork belly chashu
slow-roasted fennel pork belly chashu
rolled braised pork belly chashu

4 TOPPINGS

Although I think a bowl of ramen needs nothing more than a scattering of thinly sliced scallions, there are a few toppings that are so popular that it would be silly to not to include recipes for them here: pork chashu, whether made from the shoulder or belly; soboro, or seasoned cooked ground meat mixtures; marinated soft- or hard-boiled eggs; blanched greens; and various other toppings you're undoubtedly familiar with if you've ever eaten a bowl of ramen in a restaurant.

There is one popular topping that I will not cover in this book: menma. This is because home cooks in the U.S. cannot easily purchase the specific kind of bamboo shoots required for making it. While you can buy boiled bamboo shoots in vacuum-sealed packs or in cans, menma is usually made from fermented, dehydrated bamboo shoots, which are sold dried, rehydrated, or rehydrated and preseasoned. The processes used determine the texture of the final product. The best menma has a crunchy texture, with little to no stringiness, and its light acidity and a measured hand with seasoning can elevate it to one of the most interesting elements of a bowl of ramen.

Some enterprising home ramen cooks have experimented with fermenting boiled bamboo shoots and drying them, mimicking the process used to make menma. I have included information about these cooks in the Resources section (page 309), if you're interested, but my suggestion for adding menma to your bowl of ramen is to find a ramen restaurant that serves menma you like and purchase some from them.

MEAT TOPPINGS

You can put any meat you like on top of a bowl of ramen, but I usually limit my meat toppings to the large category of sliced pork that falls under the term "chashu," with some exceptions. Chashu seems to me to be a natural fit for any kind of ramen, equally at home in a soup made with fish bones and meat or chicken, or a milky bowl of tonkotsu, or a serving of duck ramen. However, it can be nice to have a bit of pink duck breast sitting on top of a bowl of duck ramen, and a chicken ramen served with a slice of breast, or a couple slices of nicely cooked thigh meat, and a few wontons made with ground chicken is a delicious and impressive way to showcase the total utilization of a bird in a bowl.

The focus here is on pork and chicken, because these meats are more commonly used for topping ramen, and because the methods you use to cook pork and chicken can be applied to other meats with little to no alteration.

However, all animal flesh shares a few intrinsic characteristics, and understanding the makeup of different kinds of meat can help you to define your goals when making ramen toppings. Meat consists of muscle fibers, fat, and connective tissue. The proportions and types of each of these will determine how a given piece of meat will behave when cooked.

Connective Tissue

As explained earlier, connective tissue is primarily made up of collagen, which, when heated in the presence of water, converts to gelatin. Collagen is solid, insoluble in water, and, consequently, chewy; gelatin is liquid at slightly above room temperature, and it produces a sensation of juicy stickiness in the mouth. Cuts of meat with relatively large amounts of connective tissue, like pork shoulder and belly, are quite tough and unpleasant to eat unless the collagen they contain is converted to gelatin, which is accomplished by cooking them thoroughly.

Collagen begins converting to gelatin at around 130°F (54°C), but only very, very slowly; the rate of conversion increases rapidly up until the temperature hits 180°F (82°C). To make tough cuts of meat tender, you have to either cook them to an internal temperature above 180°F (82°C) or cook them at a low temperature, like 130°F (54°C), for 24 hours or longer.

Cuts of meat that contain very little connective tissue, like pork chops or steaks and chicken breasts, can be cooked at lower temperatures for brief periods of time, as collagen-to-gelatin conversion isn't a consideration.

Muscle

Muscles are bundles of muscle fibers. Alton Brown, in his seminal cooking series *Good Eats*, memorably used a bundle of plastic straws to demonstrate their structure, which I'll borrow here. As the muscle is used—to walk, or to run, to do any activity whatsoever—those individual fibers become larger and, thus, they're better able to accomplish whatever physical activity enlarged them in the first place. A pork tenderloin could be viewed as a bundle of very thin plastic straws, while a hunk of pork shoulder could be seen as a bundle of thicker plastic straws, like those that come with bubble tea.

If you think about cutting through a bundle of twelve very thin plastic straws or one of twelve thick straws (with the added assumption that the straws aren't hollow), it should be clear that cutting through the bundle of thicker straws would be harder than cutting through the one of very thin straws, whether with a knife or your teeth. (That difficulty is, in conjunction with the amount of connective tissue, what we are referring to when we call a piece of meat "tough.") Those fibers can be manipulated using several methods: applying heat, curing, or mechanically separating them by grinding, cutting, or slicing.

For tough cuts like belly and shoulder, it can be beneficial to cook them far past the point at which collagen converts to gelatin in order to break up or damage the thick muscle fibers they contain. As those fibers rise in temperature past 180°F (82°C), they begin to fracture, which makes them easier to slice through, and thus we perceive them as more tender. The differences are probably familiar to anyone who has ever roasted a pork butt: cook a butt to an internal temperature of 195°F (90°C), and it can be shredded into thin threads; cook it to higher temperatures, and it will fall apart with just a bit of pressure.

Salt also alters proteins, just as heat does, but at a slower rate, and the protein molecules unravel and then bond with one another to form a more compact structure. (This is also true of preparations where proteins are denatured with acid, like ceviche.) Salt-cured meats, that is, meats that have been left to sit in a brine, consequently become firmer the longer they're brined. Put a pork belly in brine, and in a week it will transform from a squishy, soft mass into a firm plank.

The structure and behavior of muscle fibers also heavily affect the way you should cut up your meat. This is important here, since much of the meat used for toppings is sliced off larger roasts. For the most tender meats, it's best to cut against the grain: if you think back to the bundle of straws, cutting against the grain simply means to cut perpendicularly through them, which would yield a flat perforated plane. If you instead cut with the grain, cutting the piece of meat so you are left with several straws bundled together, rather than a larger bundle of twelve straws, the slice of meat will be less difficult to bite into than the larger bundle, but it will still be significantly more difficult to bite through than the slice cut against the grain.

How to Make Chashu

"Chashu" is a Japanese loan word from the Chinese "char siu," which refers to roasted pork, typically pork shoulder or belly. In the context of ramen, chashu most often refers simply to sliced pork, as the cooking methods can vary considerably. Some chashu is boiled (or simmered), some is roasted, and some is braised, and each method can be combined with curing (before cooking) and/or marinating (before and after cooking), to season the meat more thoroughly. Cooked chashu can be sliced and placed on top of a bowl of ramen, or it can be torched, broiled, or grilled after slicing.

In the U.S, the chashu you'll find in most ramen bowls is made from pork belly; in Japan, it's far more common to find chashu made from pork shoulder. I prefer pork shoulder, because I like meat I can chew, and pork belly, particularly the way it's typically prepared in ramen restaurants in the U.S., has so much fat and is so tender that it essentially melts once you get it in your mouth. No matter what your preference, though, the way to cook pork belly and pork shoulder is basically the same.

You can boil them, pressure-cook them, roast them, or braise them. Belly and shoulder are tough cuts, so you want to cook them quite thoroughly, at least to an internal temperature of around 180°F (82°C), so that the collagen they contain is converted to gelatin. To guarantee that those slices of pork are tender, you want to cook either cut until the internal temperature hits about 190°F (32°C); to make them falling-apart tender, cook them to closer to 200°F (93°C).

If you exceed that temperature, the muscle proteins will become so damaged that it will be hard, if not impossible, to produce discrete slices of pork that hold their shape, even with thorough chilling.

You could also use a pork loin (or, I suppose, tenderloin) to make a kind of chashu, although it requires a different approach to cooking, because it is a lean cut with little intramuscular fat and connective tissue. Avoid cooking it beyond about 145°F (62°C), or it will become dry and unpalatable.

To season the pork, you have several options:

CURE THE MEAT WITH SALT OR A BRINE. Curing will alter the texture of the roast, the result depending on the length of the cure, and it will also season the interior, the degree to which the seasoning penetrates the center again depending on the length of the cure.

MARINATE THE MEAT BEFORE OR AFTER COOKING. While many people believe marination seasons the interior of the meat, that is false; the only seasonings that will penetrate more than a few millimeters into the meat are salt and sugar. However, that's not to discount the power of marination entirely; even a slice of chashu about 4 inches in diameter can have its flavor profile transformed by a strong marinade that seasoned just its outer periphery. Marinating cooked roasts is similarly effective, and it takes advantage of the fact that as meat cools, its muscle fibers relax, creating space for the marinade liquid to be absorbed.

COOK THE MEAT IN A HIGHLY SEASONED LIQUID ALONG WITH SOME AROMATIC VEGETABLES. The seasoning in the cooking liquid will similarly affect only the exterior of the meat, but, again, it can be very effective. Cooking the meat in a seasoned liquid has another advantage: the mingling of the meat, its juices, and the cooking liquid, along with evaporation, any contributions from Maillard browning and caramelization of sugars, and the countless reactions that take place as substances are heated at relatively high temperatures, will produce a flavor profile that is not achievable any other way.

SEASON THE MEAT AFTER IT HAS BEEN COOKED. This can be as simple as a sprinkling of salt, or it can be a glaze you apply to a slice of meat before broiling or torching it.

Tying and Shaping Roasts

Regardless of the method you use to cook it, it is helpful to tie up the roast for both practical and aesthetic purposes.

A pork belly is naturally a rectangular slab, but a pork shoulder is irregularly shaped. Yet both cuts can be easily transformed into rough cylinders with kitchen twine, and, once cooked, they will hold that shape and can be sliced crosswise to yield attractive rounds of chashu. The mechanism by which a formless blob of meat can be transformed into a solid cylinder, or any shape, really, has to do with the way proteins denature and become more compact during cooking. If pressed or otherwise forced into a specific shape, the proteins will conform to that shape and hold it after cooking. (This is applicable not only to pork and other red meats but also to poultry and fish.)

Beyond giving the roast an appealing presentation, tying it gives it a consistent shape that will promote even cooking. An uneven roast, with one side about 2 inches thick and the other side around 4 inches thick, will cook faster on the thinner side and more slowly on the thicker side.

Although tying can help even out the shape of a cut of meat, it helps to start with a relatively

LEFT TO RIGHT: Pork belly rolled vertically and horizontally, to yield rolled chashu with different diameters. Pork shoulder tied at 1-inch intervals with individual lengths of twine and pork shoulder tied more haphazardly with one very long length of twine.

evenly shaped cut of meat. If you buy a boneless pork shoulder roast from a butcher, they will already have taken its shape into consideration, and you will likely receive an evenly shaped block of meat. If you are cutting up a shoulder yourself, you want to try to cut out a hunk of meat that takes the rough form of a cylinder or rectangular prism.

The tying itself is straightforward, and you have several options. You can tie the roast at 1-inch intervals using foot-long lengths of kitchen twine, or use a single long piece of kitchen twine (about 4 feet long) to tie the roast, using a looping motion to secure the meat with just two knots. But the easiest way, I've found, is to simply wind a long piece of string around the roast from one end to the other to make a tight, compact shape and then securing the string with a single knot.

Remember that meat shrinks as it cooks. You want your roast to start out about 5 to 6 inches in diameter or, if you're cooking a slab of pork belly, about 5 to 6 inches wide.

With belly, you can roll it up either vertically or horizontally. Since belly is always thoroughly cooked, choosing which way to roll it has less to do with considerations about the direction of the grain—that is, the direction of the meat fibers—since cutting against the grain is less important than it is for tough cuts of meat that aren't cooked thoroughly, like medium-rare flank steak. But it's still a good idea to think about the direction of the grain; a slice of very well cooked pork belly will be exceedingly tender when sliced against the grain; it will be slightly more chewy if sliced with the grain.

It's best to season, marinate, or cure a roast before tying it, as tying is intended to reduce its surface area. Seasoning and marination are surface-level treatments, so a reduced surface area correlates to a reduction in flavor. Curing, while less dependent on surface area, is still more effective when the surface area is larger, and as curing firms up the meat, it makes it easier to tie the roast.

Chicken Toppings

You can use both chicken breasts and chicken legs to make chashu. Unlike the cuts of pork usually used to make chashu, chicken breasts and chicken legs are tender and significantly smaller. As a result, they cook for a much shorter time and at lower temperatures.

Chicken breasts are the most common chicken part used for sliced toppings. In part, this is because of their limited utility in stock-making. As discussed on pages 85–86, they contain little connective tissue, and thus don't provide the stock with much gelatin. It's also easy to cut cooked boneless breasts into neat slices for topping ramen.

The key to cooking chicken breasts, as with other lean meats, is to not overcook them. Determining whether something is over- or undercooked has to do not just with palatability but also with food safety.

The USDA recommends that chicken breasts be cooked to at least 165°F (73°C) to destroy harmful bacteria. The problem with this recommendation is that food safety is not just a matter of hitting target temperatures; it is also a matter of hitting specific temperatures for specific periods of time. If you cook a chicken breast to 150°F (65°C) and keep it at that temperature for about 3 minutes, you can be just as certain that those same bacteria are dead. At

CLOCKWISE FROM BOTTOM LEFT: Poached chicken breast, pan-seared chicken thigh, poached chicken meatballs, and pan-seared chicken breast.

the extreme end of low-temperature cooking, in a home kitchen you can conceivably hold a chicken breast at 135°F (57°C) for well over an hour and be reasonably assured you won't die from *E. coli* poisoning, but I don't recommend it.

If you cook a chicken breast to an internal temperature of 150°F (82°C), you can be reasonably assured that it is entirely food-safe regardless of the cooking method you choose, particularly if you use conventional means for cooking it: boiling, poaching, pan-searing, or roasting. If you use sous vide (see below for more on this) and leave the chicken breast in its 150°F (82°C) hot water bath for an hour and a half, you can be certain that it is safe to eat.

For chicken legs, since the goal in cooking them is to begin the process of converting the ample connective tissue they contain into gelatin, and to render the external and intramuscular fat, you want to achieve or even exceed a final internal temperature of 165°F (73°C).

Warmed-Over Flavor

All meats and fish are subject to a phenomenon known as "Warmed-Over Flavor," or WOF. If you've ever stuck a cold cooked chicken breast in the microwave and thought it smelled funny, you've experienced it. The rewarmed meat smells bad because cooked proteins facilitate an oxidation reaction in the polyunsaturated fatty acids it contains. This effect is most noticeable in poultry and fish—which is why warming up fish in the office microwave is such a faux pas.

This phenomenon presents a problem for ramen meat toppings, because they are typically prepared in advance, refrigerated, and then reheated before serving. Pork isn't as noticeably affected as chicken or fish, and chashu is usually prepared in a way that incorporates some of the common means of masking any off flavors: curing, marinating, or immersing the meat in a flavorful aromatic liquid after cooking. Another effective method for reducing WOF is limiting the meat's exposure to oxygen by wrapping it tightly in plastic wrap.

WOF presents a problem for chicken breasts used as a ramen topping, as they are often poached. So I like to cure the breasts, salting them lightly and letting them sit overnight (in the refrigerator) before cooking, and then I wrap them tightly in plastic wrap as soon as they cool to near room temperature after cooking. I may even submerge them in a light dashi, which will season them slightly and prevent WOF more effectively than even the tightest wrapping. But the best way to avoid WOF is to cook the chicken immediately before serving it. The next best method is to cook it sous vide (see pages 132–33).

Ground Meat Toppings

Ground meat toppings are a way to use parts of animals that are tough or less appealing, such as the tail portions of finfish or legs of chicken or other poultry. Tougher parts are ideally suited for ground meat preparations, since they contain a lot of intramuscular fat and connective tissue, which means they will be delicious and seemingly juicy even when cooked thoroughly, as the fat melts and the connective tissue becomes gelatinous. Ground leaner cuts of meat, like chicken breasts and pork loins and tenderloins, become chalky and dry when cooked.

You can purchase ground meat at any grocery store, but I recommend grinding or chopping your own meat. This way you can control what goes into the ground meat mixture (the meat, connective tissue, skin, and fat), and you can also use up any scraps left from cutting up whole chickens or pork shoulder roasts. Although you don't necessarily need a meat grinder to grind meat, it is effective and fun to use. But you can chop meat using a sharp, heavy knife or in a food processor.

Here are guidelines to observe for chopping or grinding up your meat and for working with ground meat:

CONTINUES ON PAGE 133 →

Sous Vide

Sous vide is a popular way of cooking meat toppings for ramen. The term translates to "under vacuum," and it refers to sealing ingredients in a plastic pouch after driving out as much air as possible and placing that pouch in a temperature-controlled water bath. Whatever ingredient is in the pouch is heated at a constant temperature until its internal temperature equalizes with the temperature of the surrounding water, at which point the ingredient can be removed or held at that temperature for however long is necessary.

Sous vide has one other main benefit, which has to do with the tenderness of the cooked meat. By using sous vide, you can hold a tough cut of meat like pork shoulder at 135°F (57°C) for 24 hours and produce meltingly tender, medium-rare chashu, and you can produce that medium-rare chashu in exactly the same way every time.

When using conventional cooking methods, tenderness can be seen as a function of the denaturation of proteins (via heat or salting) and the conversion of collagen to gelatin, but sous vide introduces another, trickier variable: enzymatic tenderization. Meat contains enzymes that break down proteins called proteases, which are instrumental in processes like dry-aging to improve the tenderness and flavor of meat, most often beef. One class of proteases, called cathepsins,* breaks down proteins at a much more rapid rate when heated to temperatures around 130°F (54°C), which is why low-temperature cooking methods like sous vide produce much more tender meat.

We typically view tenderness as a positive quality, but there is such a thing as "too tender," and sous vide offers anyone a way to test their own personal threshold for when a meat becomes so soft it crosses the Rubicon from delicious to off-putting.

If you want to take advantage of the consistency, convenience, and inimitable qualities of the results of sous-vide cooking, you need to observe a few rules to ensure that what you're cooking is safe to eat.

SEAL THE FOOD PROPERLY. Sous vide produces intensely flavored food by cooking it in a heated water bath without directly exposing it to the water, as it would be when poached. The ingredient is sealed in a plastic pouch, which prevents contact with the surrounding water as it allows the water to gently heat the ingredient *evenly*. For that to happen properly, the pouch must not contain any excess air, and it must be fully submerged in the bath. If any part of the ingredient rises above the level of the water line, this can lead to the unsubmerged portion being heated at temperatures that encourage the growth of harmful bacteria. And if there are air pockets in the pouch, it will float, so it is imperative to remove as much air as is possible from it.

To remove the air from the pouch, you can use a vacuum sealer. These devices are useful beyond sous-vide cooking, for storage. For a low-tech solution, place the ingredient in a zip-lock bag, submerge the bag in cold water to drive out all the air, seal the bag, and then remove it from the water.

* "Science: Why Sous Vide Is Perfect for Cooking Meat," *Cook's Illustrated*, June 25, 2018, https://www.americastestkitchen.com/cooksillustrated/articles/1140-science-why-sous-vide-is-perfect-for-cooking-meat.

ENSURE THAT THERE'S ENOUGH ROOM FOR THE FREE FLOW OF WATER AROUND YOUR SEALED FOOD. A water bath works by maintaining water at a constant temperature and *constantly circulating that water* around the food. That constant movement is crucial for maintaining the temperature of the bath and heating the food evenly—and safely. If you use too small a container of water for the bath, or the path of the circulating water is obstructed, you run the risk of creating pockets of unsafe temperatures.

AVOID COOKING MEATS BELOW 130°F (54°C). While you can cook a rare steak sous vide, you run into possible food safety issues if you hold a piece of meat in the temperature range of 120°F (48°C) to 130°F (54°C) for longer than a couple of hours. For ramen, where you're primarily going to be cooking pork and chicken or other poultry sous vide, you can avoid that temperature range entirely, because these meats are always cooked at higher temperatures.

COLD MEAT IS EASIER TO WORK WITH. Raw meat is soft and squishy even at refrigerator temperatures, which makes it harder to work with when you want to cut it into uniformly small or thin pieces. Freezing the meat briefly will help firm it up. Depending on the size of the piece of meat, this should take anywhere from 15 to 30 minutes.

WHEN YOU'RE GRINDING MEAT USING A MEAT GRINDER OR FOOD PROCESSOR, FREEZE THE MEAT PARTIALLY BEFORE RUNNING IT THROUGH THE MACHINE. Passing meat through a grinding plate or spinning it around the blades of a food processor creates a lot of friction, which in turn generates a significant amount of heat. If the meat starts at about refrigerator temperature, you run the risk of the friction heating up the meat and melting the intramuscular fat. This is called "smearing," and when you cook ground meat in which the fat has been partially melted, the result is denser and drier.

CUT YOUR MEAT INTO LONG THIN STRIPS. This applies to hand-mincing meat and running meat through a meat grinder; it is less important when using a food processor. For hand-mincing, using long thin strips of consistent size makes it easier to cut the meat into a fine dice, as you can line up the strips next to each other and cut them crosswise, particularly if you have partially frozen the strips of meat.

For grinding, long thin strips of meat help to reduce overall friction in the meat grinder. Pat LaFrieda, the celebrated butcher, notes in his book *Meat: Everything You Need to Know* that if you feed long strips of meat into a meat grinder, you do not need to freeze the meat, as the little fat that does melt helps to lubricate the grinder's parts, thus reducing friction and limiting smearing. I recommend you hedge your bets and both cut long strips *and* partially freeze them, which yields a nice grind.

IF USING A MEAT GRINDER, GRIND YOUR GROUND MEAT AGAIN. Double-grinding meat results in a more even distribution of the fat and meat and yields a more consistent grind without compacting the meat too much. Because the second grind also works the ground meat, it makes it stickier, which reduces the need for added binders and thus produces cooked meat with a lighter, more appealing texture.

IF USING A FOOD PROCESSOR, USE ONLY THE "PULSE" FUNCTION. A food processor is a powerful tool, and it can turn a hunk of meat into a puree in a matter of seconds. As a result, you don't want to just toss hunks of meat into the processor, turn it on, and let it rip. Instead, use the "pulse" function, and use it sparingly. If you haven't overloaded your food processor or put too-large hunks of meat into it, about ten pulses should be enough to reduce the meat to an acceptable grind.

KNOW WHEN TO ADD SALT. Adding salt to a ground meat mixture can profoundly and *quickly* affect the texture of the meat. Just as curing a large muscle or piece of muscle like a slab of pork belly or a pork shoulder roast will affect its texture and its ability to hold onto water, adding salt to ground meat achieves a similar effect, but because there is exponentially more surface area on ground meat than whole muscles, these effects will take place much more quickly.

When making sausages or meatballs, it's best to add the salt to the ground mixture and then either pass it again through the grinder or knead it with clean hands, which will help to distribute the salt evenly and draw out water and myosin, a protein that is soluble in salt solutions. Doing so will make the meat tackier and stickier, which means the meat mixture will stick together better. (This process is responsible for the characteristic springy texture of sausage meat.) But the longer the salt has to act on the meat fibers, and the more the salted meat is worked, the denser and bouncier and, ultimately, more rubbery it will be when cooked. (This is why you should never salt your hamburger patties until right before cooking.)

For dumplings, which are heavily salted, the meat is usually combined with a large proportion of vegetables, or soaked mung bean noodle threads, or minced cabbage, which will prevent the ground meat from bonding to itself and forming a dense mass.

For meatballs made without additional fillers, you can also simply salt and work the ground meat mixture right before cooking, which limits the amount of time the salt has to act on the meat proteins but still provides some of the benefits—like seasoning and making the exterior of the ground meat bits tacky, which will help keep the meatballs from falling apart.

Another method for adding salt to ground meat mixtures is to salt larger pieces of meat before grinding or chopping. Commonly used in sausage making, this has the benefit of evenly distributing salt and seasonings during the grinding process, obviating the need to mix your ground meat, so you run far less of a risk of overworking the meat and making dense sausages.

CHECK YOUR SEASONING. Before cooking any ground meat mixture, take a grape-size portion of the mixture and fry it in a pan until cooked through, or place that portion on a microwave-safe plate and microwave it on high for 15 seconds. With most ground meat mixtures—as with most ramen toppings in general—you want them to be a little saltier than you think is necessary, to compensate for it being submerged in the salty soup. Even what seems to be a perfectly seasoned meatball or wonton will taste bland when juxtaposed with highly seasoned soup.

Folding Wontons and Gyoza

There are many ways to fold dumplings and wontons, some beautiful and elegant, others straightforwardly utilitarian. As with most things, I tend to take a middle path. What's most important is that the filling be entirely contained by the wrapper—no tears or rips—and that you avoid creating any air pockets, which can cause the dumpling or wonton to burst during cooking.

Since you will almost always make far more gyoza or wontons at a time than you can reasonably eat, I recommend freezing whatever you won't use immediately. Place the formed dumplings in a single layer on sheet pans that have been dusted with cornstarch or lined with parchment paper, making sure they aren't touching, and freeze them until solid, about 3 hours. Transfer the dumplings to a zip-top freezer bag and stash them in the freezer until you're ready to cook them.

A sampling of dumpling shapes for wontons (top) and gyoza (bottom)

---

1. Place 2 to 3 teaspoons filling in the center of a gyoza skin. Dip a finger in water and lightly wet the edges of the skin.

2. Fold the skin over as if you were making a taco.

3. Cradling the skin in both hands, starting on one side and working your way to the other, use your index fingers to crimp the top edges of the gyoza skin.

4. Press the crimped top edge firmly against the flat bottom edge to seal.

mature leaf spinach

VEGETABLE TOPPINGS

Vegetables offer ramen cooks flavor possibilities otherwise impossible to include in ramen, like bitterness and a somewhat bland counterpoint to the heavily seasoned elements in the bowl.

The vegetables added raw to ramen are most often aromatics, typically from the genus allium, which includes onions, garlic, chives, shallots, and bunching onions like scallions and naga negi (Welsh onions). Rhizomes like ginger are also added raw. The flavors and aromas of these vegetables are "activated" by the heat of the soup stock and the oil in the bowl, which helps to release their water- and oil-soluble flavors, even as their rawness provides some freshness and crunch. The vegetables are typically finely cut or grated to increase their surface area, which in turn facilitates the dispersion of their flavor in the soup.

Other vegetables, like carrots and celery, or cruciferous vegetables such as cabbage and kale, or any vegetables that fall under the umbrella term of "greens" are not usually added raw. These vegetables can be sautéed, stir-fried, or braised, although in the context of ramen it is most common to see sturdy vegetables stir-fried, given ramen's roots in Chinese cuisine. Stir-frying hardy vegetables not only concentrates their flavor; it also produces a range of flavorful compounds due to Maillard reactions, caramelization, and, if done exceptionally well, the inimitable smokiness known as "wok hei."

Leafy greens and delicate vegetables like snap peas and asparagus are often briefly blanched in boiling water before being shocked in cold water to stop the cooking. Blanching and shocking ensures that these vegetables are barely cooked and vibrantly colored, preserving their texture, increasing their sweetness, and making them visually more appealing. For greens like spinach, blanching breaks down the cell walls of the plants sufficiently that you can express their excess water, which will concentrate their flavor.

Most vegetables can be fermented or pickled to improve their flavor and texture and increase their acidity. Similarly, cooked vegetables can be dressed or marinated to make them more flavorful and/or heighten their acidity.

How to Prepare Onions for Ramen

How you prepare raw onions for ramen is not solely a matter of aesthetics. The way an onion is sliced affects the way it is eaten as you sip your soup and slurp your noodles, and it can sometimes make or break a bowl of ramen.

While round onions can basically be cut horizontally or vertically, or some combination thereof, other alliums, like spring onions, scallions, leeks, and bunching onions, can be cut in a number of different ways, as you use not just the bulb but also the leaves of the plant. The way these different cuts interact with the soup produces vastly different eating experiences.

When you cut onions, they should be as dry as possible. If you rinse them prior to slicing, take the time to blot them dry with a kitchen towel; the resulting slices will be cleaner, with crisper edges.

It's a common practice to rinse cut onions in cold water, let them soak briefly in ice water, and then drain and pat them dry. Rinsing affects their flavor slightly, making them less pungent, but the process is primarily intended to improve their texture and appearance.

When vegetables are soaked in cold water, their cells absorb water through the process of osmosis. This is plainly evident if you soak wilted lettuce greens or a limp carrot in cold water for

A single naga negi sliced in a variety of ways

an hour; the greens no longer seem wilted, and the carrot becomes crisp again. That change is due to an increase in turgor pressure, or the amount of pressure exerted against the cell walls from inside the cells swollen with water.

When sliced onions are soaked in ice water, they will curl and arch in attractive ways, depending on how they were sliced. For example, lengths of naga negi that have been cut horizontally will look markedly different after soaking than lengths that have been cut vertically. The latter will curl and bend but retain a smooth, needle-like appearance, while horizontally cut long onions will have little clearly perceptible bends because of the grain of the onion's growth; these end up looking a little sparkly and jewel-like, or, less charitably, crinkly.

Sliced onions must be drained and patted dry before you add them to a bowl of ramen. Any excess water will not only dilute the broth but also drop the temperature.

SIMPLE SLICED ONIONS. Place the onion on your cutting board and slice it crosswise or on a slight bias. I like scallion slices that are as thin as you can get them, and this requires some good knife skills, as scallions are quite delicate and if sliced carelessly, can be crushed by the knife, particularly if it isn't sharp. You want to use the sharp edge to slice through the onion, which means you should apply more force to the forward (or backward) slicing motion than to bringing the blade down. Longer knives are useful here, as you can use more of the blade to cut through the onion. Use the knuckles of your nondominant hand, with your fingers curled into your fist to protect them, as a guide, sliding them back to adjust the thickness of the slices.

For very fine cuts, or for delicate alliums like chives, you can use **push-chopping** or **back-slicing**. Push-chopping is a Japanese cutting technique that's used with blades, often single-bevel, that have a flat cutting edge. You again use your nondominant hand as a guide, but instead of sliding the blade forward on its edge on the cutting board to execute a kind of rolling slicing motion, you push the blade forward and down repeatedly.

You can use any kind of knife for back-slicing, but it's easier to do with a Western-style blade with a slightly curved edge. You again use your knuckles as a guide, but you anchor the tip of the blade above whatever you're slicing and pull the knife back and up, keeping it on the cutting board for the duration.

SQUARE- OR DIAMOND-CUT/CONFETTI ONIONS. Cutting the bulb portion of scallions and naga negi into diminutive squares or diamonds yields a very attractive addition to the soup—they end up floating in the stock like confetti. Nearly every spoonful of soup will contain a scattering of them, and they provide both flavor and texture. To produce these cuts, you cut through the bulb end of the onion to divide it into quarters or eighths, but you do not cut completely through the onion greens—they will hold the cut white parts in place. Then you slice the white parts crosswise, adjusting the thickness of each slice to produce rectangular pieces of whatever size you'd like (you do want these pretty small). The remaining green parts can be sliced crosswise, or on a bias, or vertically. For large onions, like naga negi, and for *very* neat square cuts, split the onion in half vertically and work with three to four layers at a time, cutting them into equal thin lengths, then stacking those lengths and cutting them crosswise.

VERTICAL SLICES. The easiest way to cut long onions vertically is with a scallion shredder. It's a cylinder with an aperture at one end with blades inside it arranged like spokes of a wheel; you just push/pull the onion through the aperture, and long, thin cuts emerge from the other side. The same type of cut can be accomplished with a knife, but it's a fussy process.

I prefer to cut scallions into 1-inch lengths, then slice them so that they form rectangles, after which it's much easier to produce even lengths of vertically sliced onion leaves and/or bulb sections. This is particularly useful for larger long onions, like leeks and naga negi. These rectangles can also be sliced horizontally, which will yield lengths with a different texture than lengths of onion cut vertically.

Blanched Vegetables

You can use all kinds of blanched vegetables to top ramen, but the vegetable most often prepared this way is spinach. To blanch any vegetable, fill a large pot with salted water and bring it to a boil. Add your cleaned vegetables and then, for most vegetables, fish them out after 30 seconds to 1 minute; for sturdier greens, like yu choy or, say, spigarello, you should increase the blanching time by a minute or two. You want the vegetables to be easy to eat, meaning fully cooked but not turned to mush. Transfer the blanched vegetables to a bowl filled with cold water, preferably with ice, to "shock" them, or stop the cooking process. Shocking ensures that the vegetables won't overcook, and it also helps set their bright green color.

Once shocked, the vegetables should be thoroughly dried. For snap peas and asparagus, remove them from the water and pat dry (gently!) with a kitchen towel or paper towels. For leafy greens, scrunch them with your hands as you remove them from the water to express as much water as possible. The squished log of greens, neat or messy, can then be sliced into 1-inch lengths and placed as is, or after marinating/dressing, in the bowls of ramen; the vegetables do not need to be heated before adding them to the soup.

When blanching vegetables, it's important to salt the blanching water. The vegetable will absorb some of this salt and will taste better—sweeter, really—as a result. This is true even though the vegetable will be dunked in cold water to shock it. Don't believe me? Try blanching spinach in both salted water and unsalted water, shock them both, squeeze out the water, and taste them side by side; the spinach blanched in salted water will taste noticeably more like spinach. When salting blanching water, you want the concentration of salt to be at least 1% by weight, so for every liter of water, you want about 10 grams of salt (for every quart of water, that translates to about a tablespoon of Diamond Crystal kosher salt).

Blanched spinach is good on its own as a ramen topping, or you can dress it up with a vinaigrette. Sturdier green vegetables benefit from extra seasoning because they are more substantial and thus less able to soak up the seasoning from the soup. For these vegetables, dressing them like a salad or a Korean muchim, for which vegetables are massaged with a relatively strong seasoning, is a good idea. You can also take a Japanese approach and soak the blanched vegetables in a flavorful dashi for several hours or overnight. If you want a katsuobushi-forward gai lan preparation, use a dashi made from kombu and katsuobushi, seasoned simply with a little salt and sugar. If you want a soy-forward yu choy, use a dashi made with kombu seasoned heavily with soy sauce and a little mirin. The possibilities are endless.

Stir-Fried Vegetables

Stir-fried vegetables are a common topping for ramen-shop ramen, best exemplified by tanmen, a ramen that's topped with a stir-fry of cabbage, scallions, garlic, and sliced wood ear mushrooms.

For most home cooks, the main point of stir-frying is to brown the proteins and caramelize the sugars in whatever you're cooking *quickly*, before the food starts to steam. To accomplish this, cut your ingredients into uniformly sized bits, use as hot as pan as you can manage, and add only a small volume of ingredients at a time to the pan, the better to keep it at a high-enough temperature that the ingredients don't start to sweat and steam.

I often stir-fry vegetables for other meals and then use any leftovers as a ramen topping. Since stir-fried vegetables generally require a rounded flavor profile to taste good—sweetness, saltiness, and acidity to balance out their bitterness—leftovers are fine added as is to a bowl of ramen, as they'll stand up to the highly seasoned broth.

MARINATED EGGS (AJITSUKE TAMAGO)

Delicious, nutritious, and filling, eggs help to make a bowl of ramen a more complete meal. While the eggs added to ramen are often soft-boiled, with liquid yolks and firm whites (referred to in Japanese as a "hanjuku tamago," or half-cooked egg), there's no proscription against hard-boiled eggs. Most boiled eggs used in ramen are marinated in a flavorful liquid of some kind, and these are referred to as "ajitsuke tamago," which basically means "flavored eggs."

Many ramen shops in Japan offer raw eggs—often only the yolk, but sometimes whole—on the side or on top of ramen. And I've had bowls of ramen where the egg has been cooked in some other way: rolled or slivered omelets, poached eggs, or scrambled eggs with dashi, a riff on egg-drop soup where the egg is scrambled with starch and added to the hot broth to form ribbons and thicken the soup. Both soup ramen and soupless ramen are also sometimes served with onsen tamago, eggs cooked at the relatively low temperatures achieved by hot spring baths, which have a jelly-like exterior and a molten yolk. And while it's uncommon, there's no rule against serving ramen with a fried egg—or even a slice of quiche.

You can, of course, use other eggs, like duck eggs or quail eggs, prepared in any of the ways above.

For the most common egg preparations for ramen, the cooking is straightforward, and falls in line with most of the rest of ramen cookery. However, many people seem to find cooking eggs difficult, and some of that may be because eggs come in different sizes. "Large" eggs—eggs that weigh about 56 grams/2 ounces—are the recipe-writing standard, and all the recipes in this book, and the vast majority of the recipes published in the U.S., were developed and tested using large eggs. Therefore, I strongly suggest you only buy large eggs. If for whatever reason you do not want to do that, whether because you have your own chickens laying eggs in your backyard or you like a different size, be aware that you cannot use the eggs you have in most recipes without some adjustment. Through trial and error, you can figure out how to adapt recipes to the size of the eggs you have on hand.

For boiled eggs, the only adjustment you need to make is the length of the cooking time. However, even if you only purchase large eggs, you may need to adjust the cooking time. My "perfect" soft-boiled egg—slightly jammy yolk, softly set white—may not be anywhere close to yours; perhaps you like the yolk to be a little more runny, approaching a gel-like consistency, or you like your egg white to be quite firm.

There are many ways to cook a boiled egg.* I prefer to submerge cold eggs in boiling water and keep them moving for the first full minute they're in the water—this ensures that the yolk is centered. (This is a purely aesthetic concern.) I cook them for exactly 7 minutes and 10 seconds,

* My former colleague J. Kenji López-Alt has written not one, but two gigantic treatises on the best ways to boil and peel eggs, with hundreds, if not thousands, of tests done with hundreds of people involved, and I encourage anyone who is curious to read those treatises, if only to marvel at the scale and scope of the work: J. Kenji López-Alt, "How to Make Perfect Hard-Boiled Eggs," *Serious Eats*, September 30, 2023, https://www.seriouseats.com/the-secrets-to-peeling-hard-boiled-eggs; and López Alt, "How to Boil the Perfect Egg," *New York Times*, September 23, 2019, https://www.nytimes.com/2019/09/23/dining/how-to-hard-boil-eggs.html.

then shock them in ice water, mostly so I can move on to peeling (and marinating them if I'm doing so) as quickly as possible.

Once you have your peeled boiled eggs, to make an ajitsuke tamago, you submerge them in a flavorful liquid or cover them with a seasoning paste. How you season that liquid (or paste) depends primarily on the flavors you want to impart to the egg, as well as how long you plan on letting the eggs sit in that seasoning. Egg whites are porous, and they will absorb a lot of the flavor of whatever they're submerged in; if you let them sit for days in a concentrated solution of salt in the refrigerator, they will end up very salty.

Mike Satinover, the chef and founder of Akahoshi Ramen in Chicago, uses this fact to soak his boiled eggs in a relatively lightly seasoned brine for days at a time. He calls this an "equilibrium brine," which is a term borrowed from meat curing, and the idea is that the brine is prepared at the salt concentration you'd like the final product to achieve. The egg will eventually become as salty as its surrounding brine when the osmotic process brings the inside of the egg to an "equilibrium" with the surrounding liquid.

This is a smart way to prepare eggs, and it's especially useful for achieving consistent results, as after a few days, all the eggs will be seasoned identically from the center of the yolk to the exterior of the white. The only drawback is that it takes a day or two, and the prolonged exposure to the brine will alter the texture of both the white and the yolk—not in a way that's displeasing, but it is noticeable.

I use a slightly stronger brine, which seasons the egg more quickly; this produces well-seasoned eggs in about 12 hours. Leaving the eggs in the solution for longer than that, though, will dramatically alter the texture of the yolks and whites, but, again, not in an entirely displeasing way. Egg yolks will gradually turn jammy when exposed to highly concentrated brine for long, which is actually quite nice and more than makes up for a slight rubberiness in the whites.

For seasoning boiled eggs with miso, which doesn't readily form a solution in water, it's best to simply smear the paste over the egg. I add a bit of mirin to the paste to thin it, which makes it both more spreadable and sweeter. In order to minimize the amount of miso you use, I suggest smearing just enough of the thinned-out paste on the egg to cover it in a thin layer, then wrapping it in plastic wrap.

To slice the seasoned boiled eggs, use something very thin, such as (unflavored) dental floss, a cheese wire, or a segment of fishing line. A sharp knife will work, but it will mess with the way the yolk looks.

Onsen Eggs

I frequently use onsen eggs, eggs cooked at the relatively low temperature of a hot bath ("onsen" refers to the bathhouses located on hot springs), in soupless ramen, where their almost liquid character helps lubricate the noodles and temper the salinity of the tare (see page 285 for a recipe). It's best to use an immersion circulator for these, as the convenience, consistency, and results cannot be matched by conventional cooking methods. You can, of course, cook onsen eggs on the stovetop, but it's difficult to try to maintain the relatively low temperatures necessary to cook onsen eggs in a pot unless you use a large volume of water.

There's a range of temperatures at which you can cook an onsen egg, and each of these requires a slight adjustment in cooking time. I've settled on a time and temperature combination that was arrived at through testing by one of my former colleagues at *Serious Eats*, Daniel Gritzer: 167°F (75°C) for 13 minutes, followed by an ice bath. What I like about that temperature-and-time combination is, mostly, that it's quick, but it also produces a more solid onsen egg that holds its shape well when plopped on top of noodles.

halved ajitama
whole ajitama
onsen egg

⑤ NOODLES

Making alkaline wheat noodles presents a challenge for most home cooks. Unlike other alkaline wheat noodles, like hand-pulled lamian, ramen originated as a commercially manufactured product, and the formulas and methods required to produce it rely heavily on the use of powerful machinery.

The main way this has affected ramen is that the dough is relatively dry, which makes it hard to work. A dough used for making a loaf of bread may incorporate a quantity of water that's anywhere from 70% to 100% of the weight of flour, but ramen made using these machines uses an amount of water that's anywhere from 20% to 40% of the weight of flour. If you try to make a cohesive dough using the ratio of water to flour on the lower end of that spectrum by hand, it is difficult to impossible. However, if you mix the water and flour thoroughly, the crumbly mixture can be forced between powerful rollers to form a sheet of dough, which can then be manipulated (kneaded), thinned, and cut to produce snappy, springy noodles.

By using the rollers and/or cutters of a pasta machine, you can produce ramen that is like the kinds produced by noodle manufacturers simply by using a larger proportion of water to wheat.

With the right tools, making homemade ramen is simple enough; the recipes in this book have been designed with convenience in mind, and the method I have devised is intended to limit the stress your pasta rollers are put through (which means that the machine will be less likely to break). And one of the great pleasures of making ramen at home is experimentation, and one of its great rewards is that, with a little knowledge on your side, the results of those experiments by and large end up being delicious.

Wheat dough is a cohesive, viscoelastic paste made with ground wheat berries and water. What that means is when you mix flour with water, the resulting paste sticks to itself, forming a discrete whole, and that whole is both viscous—it deforms slowly when exposed to an external force—and elastic—it resists deformation and will return to its original shape once any external force that's been applied is removed. If you think of the process of making, for example, a simple flatbread dough with water, flour, and salt, you can get a clear idea of these three properties: The dry flour clumps together as you add water to it and mix, eventually forming a shaggy, blobby ball, which is the cohesive paste: the mixture of water and flour (and salt) sticks to itself, not to the bowl it's mixed in. If you hold that ball in your hand over a countertop and raise your hand, the dough will begin to flow in the direction of the countertop as gravity exerts its inexorable downward force, and the ball will stretch slowly, which illustrates the paste's viscosity. And if you let the dough fall and come to rest on the countertop, it will eventually retake the form of a shaggy, blobby ball, which illustrates the paste's elasticity.

If you continue to manipulate that dough through kneading, a series of chemical and physical reactions that alter these distinct properties will take place. For most doughs, including those for flatbreads, yeast-raised breads, and noodles, the dough must be kneaded until it becomes less viscous and more elastic. This produces a highly ordered and so-called "well-developed" gluten network, which is responsible for the chewy textures we value in breads and noodles. That gluten network also enhances the paste's ability to trap gas, which creates the airy texture we prize in yeast-raised breads and many pastries. However, for

35%-hydration noodles

semolina noodles

whole wheat noodles

40%-hydration noodles

instant ramen noodles

fresh frozen noodles

other dough applications, such as hand-pulled noodles, the dough must be kneaded more thoroughly, which eventually weakens some of the gluten network's bonds, reducing the dough's elasticity, enhancing its viscosity, and promoting extensibility—meaning it becomes easier to stretch.

How Wheat Gluten Works

Doughs made from wheat have a unique type of viscoelasticity, and that's because of gluten, a protein that naturally occurs in wheat, barley, and rye. Not all gluten proteins are the same, however, and the makeup of gluten proteins in flour will determine how a dough made from it behaves. Wheat gluten is composed primarily of glutenins and gliadins, and when mixed with water, these form a protein matrix, which you can think of as a very fine, densely packed web that can trap tiny molecules, like carbon dioxide and water. While the addition of water is crucial for the development of that protein matrix, the water isn't reacting with the gluten proteins, as gluten isn't soluble in water; the water provides a medium in which the glutenins and gliadins can immediately bond with one another, and the resulting web those bonds form in turn traps water molecules. "Developing" a dough's gluten refers to manipulating the protein matrix in ways that strengthen it, and that means providing the glutenins and gliadins ample time and opportunity to make more and more bonds with each other.

Harold McGee offers a good visual description of glutenins and gliadins,* likening them to lengths of tangled-up fishing twine. While both glutenins and gliadins are long proteins—some of the longest we know of—glutenins tend to take a more elongated shape, while gliadins tend to form "compact, ellipsoidal balls." The more linear glutenins are responsible for dough gluten's elasticity, as they readily bond with other glutenins along their lengths, and with themselves when they become folded over, which produces a rigid structure that resists deformation. The rounder, more self-contained gliadins are generally responsible for dough gluten's viscosity, as their compact structure makes them less likely to bond with other molecules, and they move freely in the protein matrix.

As soon as you mix water with wheat flour, the glutenins and gliadins begin linking up with one another, instantly forming the protein matrix with a random network of proteins. That matrix can then be "developed" using a couple different methods.

If left to sit, the protein matrix will continue to develop and strengthen, as protease enzymes in the flour begin consuming the proteins, breaking them up into shorter lengths, which in turn creates more opportunities for them to bond with each other. This process is known in bread-baking as an "autolyse," derived from the word "autolysis," which refers to the process by which cells or tissues are destroyed by their own enzymes. If left unchecked, those protease enzymes will obliterate the gliadins and glutenins, and the shaggy blob of dough will become a more liquid puddle. If it is allowed to work for a while and then stopped (by adding salt, which inhibits the proteolytic activity of the enzymes), an autolyse will yield a more extensible—that is, more easily stretched—dough because those longer protein chains have been shortened, and the dough will be easier to handle, yielding a better final texture in the bread.

Alternatively, the dough can be kneaded, which accomplishes mechanically what the enzymes accomplish chemically. When you fold a dough over itself repeatedly, you're encouraging the glutenins and gliadins to bond with one

* McGee, *On Food and Cooking*, p. 291.

another by literally pushing them into each other. As McGee describes it, "The constant movement and stress have the effect of forcing the long molecules into a more orderly pattern, lining up local groups of them in roughly the same direction." Continued kneading creates more bonds between the similarly oriented proteins, producing not only a stronger network but a more ordered one, all of which improves the elasticity of the dough.

Dough can become *too* elastic, which is why kneaded doughs of all kinds are often set aside, covered to prevent moisture loss, to rest for short periods of time. As the dough sits undisturbed, the gliadins gradually lose their hold on the glutenins and each other, leaving just the glutenins firmly bonded to one another. This is why a ball of well-kneaded dough resists losing its shape; press on it firmly, and the indentation will disappear, the dough bouncing back to form a smooth surface. However, if you let a ball of well-kneaded dough rest for 30 minutes and press on its surface to create an indentation, that indentation will remain.

Gluten in Noodles

The necessity of a well-developed gluten network in a yeast-raised bread is somewhat intuitive. When you slice open a loaf of bread, the bread's crumb structure—the network of holes surrounded by partially gelatinized starch—is a physical representation of the gluten network, and you can deduce from that how a durable, elastic scaffolding would be necessary to trap gas within the dough for long enough for the starch gel to solidify and maintain its shape. The same cannot be said of slicing a noodle in half and looking at its cross-section, which will look like, well, paste.

And yet the gluten network in a noodle is the same as that in bread and serves an identical function. The gluten network operates as a kind of skeleton for the starch and will give the noodles their shape, and it also contributes to "chewiness." What is chewiness? Chewiness in the context of gluten simply refers to the fact that it is insoluble in water because the bonds between the gliadin proteins are so strong and closely packed together that they don't allow water molecules to come between them. When you put a piece of a cooked noodle in your mouth and begin to chew, the gluten must be sheared or torn into small pieces to be digested, and we register this as a pleasant "chewiness." The better developed the gluten network in a noodle dough, the more ordered and compact the bonds between the gliadins and, consequently, the more chew.

Unlike bread bakers, though, noodle makers face a large obstacle in developing gluten: the low proportion of water used in ramen dough. The first issue this creates is that an autolyse is effectively impossible. Consequently, ramen makers cannot rely on the boost to gluten development that an autolyse provides. In bread making, salt is added after the autolyse, and it can then be evenly dispersed through mixing because of the higher water content. With ramen dough, it's imperative that you dissolve the salt (and the alkaline salts) in the water before mixing it with the flour to ensure even dispersal.

The low amount of water also makes kneading something of a challenge. Even a ramen dough made with a relatively large proportion of water, such as 40% of the flour's weight in water, will be so stiff as to make kneading very difficult. If you make the dough in a stand mixer fitted with the dough hook, the dough is more likely to crumble apart than to fold over itself, because there's barely enough water to make the dough cohesive without another type of mechanical assistance: i.e., powerful metal rollers that can turn the crumbly mixture into a cohesive sheet of dough.

The rollers on commercial ramen machines exert a lot of force on whatever passes between

Sodium carbonate (left) and potassium carbonate (right)

them. They can turn that pebbly, dry mixture of water and flour into a smooth sheet of dough instantly, smushing the pebbly bits together so forcibly that the gliadins and glutenins link up. Once a sheet of dough is formed, it's then rolled thinner and thinner, and then doubled over itself and passed through the rollers again, and the process is repeated several times. The result of this kneading process is that the gliadins and glutenins fall into an order that aligns with the direction the sheet is being rolled in, and as the sheet gets folded over and compressed, the gliadins form an ever more compact and ordered network that runs the length of the sheet of dough.

Home ramen cooks cannot rely on the rollers they use to produce a cohesive sheet of dough straight out of the gate, because the pasta rollers that are available for home use aren't powerful enough. However, using a bit of manual (or pedal!) assistance to form a loosely cohesive sheet of dough before starting to pass it through the rollers is effective: if you press the dry pebbly mixture into a sheet using your hands (or by stepping on it, using your entire body weight), the dough will be cohesive enough to survive passage through the pasta rollers easily.

Alkaline Salts (Kansui) and Gluten

Alkaline salts stiffen the gluten network by encouraging bonding between proteins, but different salts encourage slightly different behaviors. The two main alkaline salts used in ramen production are sodium carbonate (Na_2CO_3) and potassium carbonate (K_2CO_3), and they are usually used in combination. Solutions of water and these two salts are referred to in Japanese as "kansui."

The chemistry behind their effects is complex and still the subject of study. For home cooks, the main thing to understand is that sodium carbonate firms up the gluten network and contributes a slippery quality to the cooked noodles, and that potassium carbonate stiffens the gluten network, making it less extensible and more brittle, giving noodles a snappy quality. The different effects these salts have on noodle doughs can be plainly seen by simply making identical batches of noodles but subbing out one type of alkaline salt for the other, or using them in combination in different proportions. Noodles made with a higher proportion of sodium carbonate tend to be a little more crinkly than those made with a higher proportion of potassium carbonate. This suggests to me that sodium carbonate encourages glutenins to bond with gliadins, even as it firms up the bonds between gliadins, whereas potassium carbonate mostly strengthens the bonds between gliadins.

Alkaline salts have also been shown to improve the ability of the gluten network to hold onto water, which I think explains in part why it became so common to use so little water to make these noodles; it's simply easier to produce a workable dough with less water if alkaline salts are included in the mix.

However, alkaline salts don't just affect the way dough behaves; they also affect the color and flavor of the noodles. Alkaline salts react with flavonoids present in the flour to produce a yellowish pigment and almost sulfurous flavor, both of which set alkaline wheat noodles apart from nonalkaline wheat noodles.

Starch

Wheat flour typically contains anywhere from 8% to 16% of protein, of which glutenins and gliadins make up the majority; the remainder is mostly starch. If you look at the ingredient lists on instant ramen packages or on commercial fresh ramen, you'll often see tapioca starch there. When I first started making my own ramen noodles, the use of tapioca starch seemed entirely mysterious, even though I could see through my experimentation that adding a small amount of tapioca starch to the flour mix yielded noodles with a superior texture. They were lighter, yet seemingly more solid; they were chewier, but not in the way that noodles made with flours with higher protein content would be. These results seemed more mystifying because by adding tapioca starch I was effectively increasing the ratio of starch to protein in the flour mix, which should've resulted in *less* chew, as there was proportionally less gluten potential. If gluten potential (the protein content) of the flour and the development of the gluten network were the determining factors in the final texture of the noodles, why would adding more starch result in superior noodles?

The simple answer is that the type of starch you use has an enormous impact on the ease with which you can manipulate ramen dough, the way that dough behaves when it is cooked, and the final texture of the noodles, both when they're hot and when they've been chilled.

Starch consists of two kinds of molecules: amylopectin and amylose. Amylose is a linear molecule, while amylopectin is a branching, irregular molecule, and their molecular structures influence the way they behave when mixed and heated in the presence of water: Amylose is less soluble in water than amylopectin is. Thus, the relative proportions of these two molecules in a starch dictate its behavior. Starches derived from different grains and vegetables have markedly different proportions of these two molecules: grains like wheat, rice, and corn usually produce starches that are made up of upward of 20% amylose, whereas starches like those derived from root vegetables such as cassava or potatoes are likely to contain no more than 20% amylose.

The proportions of amylose and amylopectin aren't the only variables that determine the behavior of starches: the size of the starch granules also varies significantly among different starches. Starch granules are tightly packed and highly ordered combinations of amylose and amylopectin. The perimeter of a starch granule is more highly ordered, and the molecules in some parts can approach a crystalline degree of order, and this accounts for the resistance the starch granules have to being dissolved in water: water molecules have few opportunities to bond with the molecules that ring the granule. However, while the starch network is highly ordered, it isn't uniform, and just as there are areas where the order approaches a crystalline complexity, there are others that are more shapeless, and these more amorphous networks provide water with greater opportunities for bonding. When a starch granule is heated up in the presence of water, the less organized areas begin to absorb water, which breaks up the tightly packed organization of the molecules, and amylose and amylopectin begin to leak out of the granule even as more water is allowed in. The granule swells and swells as it absorbs water, eventually bursting, leaking out a large proportion of the less water-soluble amylose molecules and retaining a large proportion of the more water-soluble amylopectin molecules, at which point the granule forms a gel, a network of amylose and amylopectin with water molecules trapped within it.

The temperature at which starch granules burst is referred to as the gelatinization temperature, and granule size and the relative proportions of amylose and amylopectin determine the temperature range within which gelatinization will occur. For example, potato starch, with its large granules, has a gelatinization temperature range of 140° to 149°F (60° to 65°C), while wheat starch has a gelatinization temperature range of 124° to 140°F (51° to 60°C). Tapioca, which has relatively small granules, has a gelatinization temperature range of 153° to 158°F (67° to 70°C).

There is another way in which various kinds of starches differ from one another—the number of damaged-starch granules—but it has less to do with their inherent characteristics than with the methods used to produce them. This is an important consideration when choosing which wheat flour to use, as the milling processes for wheat, depending on their intensity, can produce vastly different damaged-starch values—the measure for grading the amount of damaged starch in flour. Milling grinds wheat kernels down to a powder, and the finer the grind, the more likely it is that the starch granules will be broken up under mechanical pressure. Undamaged-starch granules absorb up to 40% of their weight in water at room temperature without bursting, but damaged-starch molecules will absorb two or three times that amount.

If we look at the first two ways in which the differences in starch sources can affect noodle-making, the fact that ramen manufacturers typically include tapioca starch in their products can be understood.

The most obvious way that adding tapioca starch to a wheat flour dough alters its composition is that the proportion of amylose to amylopectin is changed, with the fraction of amylopectin increased, and this affects the texture of the noodles, making them firmer when cooked. This is because when a starch paste becomes gelatinized, the amylose leaks out, leaving the amylopectin behind in the gel. The more branching amylopectin molecules that remain, the more likely they are to form a more tightly bonded network to trap water, which results in a firmer gel.

The tapioca starch also raises the gelatinization temperature of the dough. As gelatinized starch granules are heated in water, they break up more and more, leaking more and more starch into the water; this is what accounts for the increase in viscosity in a pan sauce thickened with a starch slurry. Although the starch gelatinizes at below boiling temperature, you continue to boil the sauce to make it even thicker by releasing more and more starch molecules. For noodles, this gradual leaking of starch molecules into the cooking water weakens the starch gel, which results in blown-out, overcooked noodles that are very soft and unpalatable. Raising the gelatinization temperature of the dough means that the noodles will leak less starch into the cooking water.

Damaged-starch values have less to do with the use of alternative starches like tapioca starch and more to do with the type of flour you choose to begin with, and the primary effect is on the workability of the dough. But because of that effect, the damaged-starch values of a flour affect how much tapioca starch you can add to the mix, which will in turn affect the final noodles' texture and chemical properties. The wheat flours available at supermarkets in the U.S. all have similar damaged-starch values, but flours from other sources, such as small mills or foreign millers (East Asian flour blends tend to be ground finer), will have noticeably higher damaged-starch values. If you used an identical noodle formula to produce noodles with a mass-market American flour and with one from Japan, the dough made with Japanese flour will seem less dry, as the damaged starches it contains will absorb far more water than the damaged starches in the American flour. The ramen dough made with Japanese flour will be easier to work with, and it can also accommodate more adjunct starches in the flour mix while still producing a workable dough. For example, if you make a dough with a relatively large proportion of tapioca starch, say 20% of the total flour weight, and a moderate amount of water (say 40% of the total flour weight), and you use a flour with low damaged-starch values, it will be quite dry and chalky, and relatively difficult to form into a cohesive sheet that you can then knead. If you use the same proportion of tapioca and water with a flour that has relatively higher damaged-starch values, the dough will be supple and soft.

Damaged-starch values are, I think, one of the reasons why semolina can be used to make alkaline noodle doughs that are comparatively easy to work with, as durum wheat has larger, more rigid starch granules that are far more susceptible to damage during the milling process than other varieties of wheat.

Hydration

When speaking of doughs, the term "hydration" refers to the fraction of water used in the dough relative to its total weight of flour, and it is often expressed as a percentage. Referring to the quantity of a specific ingredient as a percentage of the total weight of flour is known as a "baker's percentage," and it is the governing convention used by bread and pastry bakers. Formulas expressed as baker's percentages are a convenient shorthand: cooks who understand the process for making a given baked good can take in at a glance the relative proportions of ingredients, and with a bit of simple math, they can apply those proportions to the quantities of ingredients they have on hand, or the quantity of the final product they'd like to make.

Many ramen makers have adopted baker's percentages for the same reasons. I use a modified baker's percentage when developing my own noodle recipes; instead of expressing the amounts of given ingredients as percentages of the flour amount, I express them as percentages of the *total dry mix*. For example, let's look at a noodle formula for a single portion of noodles that contains 90 g bread flour, 10 g tapioca starch, 1 g sodium carbonate, 1 g salt, and 40 g water. The amount of bread flour is 90% of the total flour mix (the weight of the bread flour plus the weight of the tapioca starch); the tapioca is 10% of the total flour mix; the sodium carbonate and salt are each 1% of the total flour mix; and the water is 40% of the total flour mix. If you use this formula in a table with one column for a true baker's percentage, another for my modified baker's percentage, and one for the weights of the ingredients in one portion of noodles, you can see the value of thinking about noodles in the modified way, as the percentage corresponds exactly to the gram amounts, and scaling up portions is a simple matter of multiplying whole numbers.

Ingredients	*Baker's percentage*	*Modified baker's percentage*	*Weight (grams) per serving*
Bread flour	100.0%	90%	90
Tapioca starch	11.1%	10%	10
Sodium carbonate	1.1%	1%	1
Salt	1.1%	1%	1
Water	44.4%	40%	40

This level of precision is important because there is so little water in ramen dough, and minor differences in the amount of water a dough contains can produce wildly different results. And yet, these formulas with their fancy percentages have a false aura of infallible accuracy, when they're merely aids for achieving a precise consistency, and it's important to understand that they do not necessarily guarantee success. They rely on understanding the processes by which the different ingredients can be combined and manipulated, and their efficacy is heavily dependent on the types and qualities of the ingredients a cook chooses to use. In short, context matters.

Let's consider another example. If a noodle manufacturer uses a dough formula that is based on 35% of the flour's weight in water, they might refer to that noodle as having 35% hydration. A home cook might think that if they use the same formula, their noodles will be identical. They mix up the formula and form a dough, run it through a pasta maker, and cut the dough into noodles, then compare their results with the noodle manufacturer's, only to find that their noodles are drastically different: looser, lighter, and soggier when cooked.

But take the same noodle formula and instead of having a home cook replicate it, assume that a different noodle manufacturer replicates it and then compare their results with the first manufacturer's noodles. In all likelihood, their noodles will be markedly different unless they use identical mixing, sheeting, resting, and cutting processes. And even if the two noodle manufacturers use identical processes, the noodles produced by a single formula might be drastically different, depending on the type of flour, how finely or coarsely that flour was ground, and the quality of the water.

It's common for both ramen makers and fans of ramen to refer to the hydration levels of noodles to distinguish them from one another. Someone might say of the noodles they make, "These are 35%-hydration noodles," and assume that the listener will understand what they mean—i.e., that they are relatively dry, or relatively wet, or fall well within the range of what would be considered typical noodles. Alternatively, they might say, "These are relatively high hydration noodles," and assume their listeners will understand that means the noodle has the qualities displayed by noodles with a larger proportion of water than is typical, and thus they are a little more crinkly, or feel lighter in the mouth. Of the two descriptors, the first has the illusion of accuracy, as it indicates that the maker has used 35% of the total flour weight in water to produce the noodle dough, although there's no information about whether or not starches or stabilizers have been added to it. So the second, even though it contains no numerical values and no information about additives, is the better descriptor, as it is more focused on the qualities of the noodles themselves, rather than on a precise point of contextless information about how the dough was produced.

For home cooks, I recommend hydration levels for ramen that fall within the range of 35% to 45% of the total weight of the flour mix—that is, according to my unorthodox baker's percentage—and that includes any added starches or stabilizers (like egg white powder). The context necessary to understand those hydration percentages is as follows: They apply to noodles made with commercial bread flour, and to noodles made with a pasta machine. If you happen to have a more powerful machine that rolls out sheets of dough, or if you use different kinds of flour—whether commercially available cake flour or all-purpose, or bread flours produced by small domestic mills or foreign millers—that range will change. A noodle made from a dough with 30% water using an industrial noodle machine will behave more like a noodle made with 40% water using a pasta machine.

Since ingredients, methods, and machinery can vary considerably, it's important to know not only how much water is added to a noodle dough but also the role water plays in doughs. As I explained earlier, water offers a medium through which gluten proteins can link up with one another and bond to form gluten networks (see page 146); water is absorbed by starch granules, and water forms a paste with damaged-starch molecules (see page 150). The combination of these processes can result in a cohesive dough that can be manipulated and kneaded to form strong gluten networks, but they can also produce a pile of pebbly bits of dough that won't come together into a cohesive dough.

In this context, "hydration" refers not only to the amount of water in a dough but also to the process of distributing the water among the disparate elements of the flour mix to produce a dough. Doughs can be insufficiently hydrated, or partially hydrated (in fact, all ramen doughs are only partially hydrated, given the low quantities of water involved; the amount of flour in their formulas could easily accommodate much more water). Since the amount of water used for ramen noodle doughs is so low, it's imperative that the flour mix be *evenly* hydrated, or it will be very difficult to produce a workable dough.

Mixing

This has profound implications for the way the ingredients for doughs should be mixed. Most cooks who have made pancakes or brownies understand that it's best to mix the dry ingredients separately from the wet ingredients and then combine them, for a more even dispersion of ingredients. The same is generally true for ramen doughs, except that the salt and alkaline salts should be dissolved completely in water instead of being added directly to the flour mix. However, you can't dump a solution of salts into a bowl of flour, mix, and expect a cohesive dough. Since there's so little water, the flour that's in immediate contact with the water will absorb most of it, forming a very wet dough, and the flour that does not make contact with the water will remain dry and powdery. If you then try to incorporate the dry, powdery flour into the wet dough, you will only be able to incorporate a small fraction, because there will simply be too little water to activate the gluten and dissolve the damaged starches in the remaining dry flour.

While a machine improves the speed and efficiency of the process, you can mix ramen dough by hand very easily. Whether you use a food processor, a stand mixer fitted with a paddle attachment, or a mixing bowl and your fingers, the principle is the same: you want to incorporate the alkaline salt solution into the flour mix evenly, and the best way to do that is *gradually*. With machines, that means turning them on to mix the dry ingredients thoroughly, then pouring a thin stream of the kansui solution into the dry mix in several stages, pausing the addition of the water to let the machine distribute whatever has already been added into the flour mix more completely. If you are mixing the dough by hand, you just have to make sure to add the water even more slowly, and you also consequently need to spend more time mixing after each addition, tossing the wetter pebbles of dough and breaking them up with your fingers to thoroughly distribute the water you've added.

The main difference between these mixing methods is the time each one takes; a food processor is very fast, hand mixing is much slower, and a stand mixer falls in the middle. There are minor differences in the behavior of the resulting doughs, particularly between doughs produced in a food processor and the two other methods, as the food processor's blades shear through the little balls of dough more forcefully than the stand mixer paddle or your hands. I use a stand mixer to mix dough, as it has the benefits of mechanical efficiency and speed on its side and it's easier to clean than a food processor.

Using a stand mixer does have one drawback: pouring the kansui into the flour while the paddle is spinning results in pockets of high moisture. For consistency's sake, I recommend stopping the mixer and using your hands to gather up a handful of pebbly dough, which you can then use to remove any wet bits of dough stuck on the paddle or against the side of the bowl; then you can run the mixer again to break up the clumps and distribute the water further.

Once it's properly mixed, depending on the hydration level of the dough and the flour you're using, ① **you'll have a fine or coarse pebbly mixture (for lower hydrations) or ② a mixture of larger pieces of dough (for higher hydrations)—both of which are referred to as a "soboro."*** The soboro must be formed into a single, cohesive dough so it can be run through and kneaded with pasta rollers. I've had the most success by forming the dough into a rough sheet before running it through the rollers, which reduces the amount of pressure exerted by the rollers on the dough and, conversely, the amount of pressure exerted on the rollers by the dough, making it less likely for your rollers to break or be knocked out of alignment.

To shape the dough, I use plastic wrap,† which helps to keep the soboro corralled and, once the dough has been formed into a rough sheet, helps to keep it from drying out. I lay out a sheet of plastic and transfer the soboro to the sheet. ③ ④ **I then use my hands, specifically the knuckles of the fist of my dominant hand, to compress the soboro firmly, using my other hand to assist with maintaining the shape.** ⑤ **The plastic wrap can be lifted up occasionally**

---

* "Soboro" is used to describe a lot of different things—ground meat preparations, streusel, etc.—that have a pebbly consistency.

† I understand that (over)use of plastics is a concern for many people, and while you could use plastic wrap alternatives, like beeswax wrap, they aren't as convenient. Here again, I'll note that even though the process of making noodles benefits from the use of plastic products, the amount of plastic you use is significantly lower than the amount used by noodle manufacturers to stock their products on grocery shelves.

to keep the soboro pebbles from being pushed away from the rest of the sheet. The goal is to create a cohesive, compressed sheet-like shape of dough that is no more than 1/4 inch thick, the thickness necessary to ensure that the pasta rollers aren't doing too much work to get the dough thin enough to pass through them. The compression also encourages the gluten molecules to bond with one another, promoting cohesion.

Resting

That cohesion is important because the dough is then wrapped and allowed to rest. This resting time accomplishes two things: it lets the gluten relax, which makes it easier to thin out the dough and roll through the rollers, and it encourages more complete hydration of the flour mix. The pebbles of dough will be very well hydrated in the center and less hydrated on the exterior. By compressing them, you are effectively creating millions of little hydrated dough sandwiches, and through the process of osmosis, the more hydrated interiors of all those pebbles will gradually give up water to the less hydrated exteriors, which in turn will encourage gluten bonding, which, turn and turn about, makes the dough more cohesive and easier to roll out and knead. As the dough rests, it gradually begins to look more hydrated; the surface becomes darker, smoother, and of a more consistent quality, with fewer and fewer light dry patches, and if you cut into the dough at various intervals, you will see a similar change. The gradual increase in hydration in the dough will continue as it's rolled out and kneaded, and even after the noodles have been cut and allowed to rest.

The success of this method relies heavily on how forcefully you can compress the dough. My upper body strength is pitiful, but for relatively higher hydration doughs (with the methods and materials I use, that means doughs with 40%

hydration or higher), simply by using my fist and some of my body weight, I can make a rough sheet of dough that, after resting for an hour, will easily pass through the pasta rollers. If you want to try your hand at making relatively drier doughs, like those in the 35%-hydration range, ⑥ **you can simply step on the wrapped dough repeatedly**, using the entire weight of your body to compress it.

Understandably, many people are put off by the idea of putting their feet anywhere near the food they're preparing. What I do is I wrap the formed dough tightly in plastic wrap, but not so tight that it will create air bubbles (which can pop, with pressure), then lay the sheet on a sheet pan. I place another sheet pan on top, put on a pair of clean socks, and step on the upper sheet pan, inching my body forward and back to step all over the dough underneath it.

⑦ **The result is a compact dough sheet.** After it has rested for about an hour, it should pass through pasta rollers set at the widest setting quite easily, and without falling apart into crumbly bits.

If for whatever reason your dough does break up into crumbly bits at that point, don't despair: you can still produce a workable sheet of dough if you cobble the bits together and run them repeatedly through the rollers, gradually forming a sheet. This can be a tedious process, but if you keep at it, you'll eventually form a sheet of dough that can be kneaded.

Kneading

Once the dough has rested, you can begin kneading it. The process is simple: First, using a knife or a bench scraper, cut the dough into as many equal planks as portions of noodles you want. Then take two portions, which you will be working with to produce a single sheet of dough, and cover the rest with plastic wrap to prevent them from drying out. This is imperative, as the dough is already dry; if it dries out any further, it will crumble when you try to knead it.

Set your rollers on the widest setting. (This is crucial, both to ensure that you successfully produce noodles and to be sure you won't break your rollers or knock them out of alignment.

⑧ **Again, the sheet should be no more than ¼ inch thick.**) Pass the first portion of dough through the rollers. Then pass the dough through the rollers at their second-widest setting. Then pass it through the rollers at their third-widest setting. ⑨ **The dough should still be a cohesive sheet, but it will look craggy, patchy, and rough around the edges; that is entirely normal.** Set it aside and repeat the process with the second portion of dough.

Stack the two portions of dough on each other. They may or may not have identical dimensions; it doesn't matter all that much. Press down firmly on the two sheets, up and down their lengths, to ensure that they stay aligned as they pass through the rollers. The rollers should be at their widest setting. Pass the stacked sheets of dough through the rollers, then pass the dough through the second-widest setting, the third-widest, and finally through the fourth-widest setting.

The dough should now be a legitimate sheet, although there will be streaking, or patchier areas of white, where the flour mix is insufficiently hydrated. Pat yourself on the back: the hardest part is over! Set the rollers once again to their widest setting, as now the kneading will begin in earnest.

In this context, kneading simply means folding the sheet crosswise in half over itself, running the folded dough through the rollers, compressing it into a thinner sheet, and then repeating the process until the gluten network is sufficiently developed, which can take anywhere from 3 to 6 or more iterations, depending on the dough.

There are a couple of annoying impediments to the process when using a pasta machine. First, as the dough sheet passes through the rollers, it will spread out, widening and lengthening as the dough is compressed. The sheet is limited from spreading horizontally by the width of the rollers, but when you fold the sheet over and press down on the seam, the seam will widen

⑧

⑨

⑩

significantly and will eventually exceed the width of the rollers. You can continue to feed the sheet through the rollers, but the excess must be accommodated for somehow. What typically happens is that the sheet will begin going through the rollers at odd angles, which will affect its uniformity and can produce a very lopsided sheet of dough, with one or both ends tapering to a triangular point. ⑩ **My solution is to cut off the corners of the seam using a bench scraper, resizing the width of the seam so it fits comfortably into the rollers. However, rather than squaring off the corners, I cut them off at a slight angle, as the corners will immediately widen as the sheet passes through the rollers.**

The second impediment to the process is the fact that most home pasta machines have uneven rollers, by which I mean that they will not thin out the sheets of dough to a uniform thickness. Because the gear that turns the rollers is located on one side of the machine, when a sheet of dough is passed through the rollers, the side that is closest to the gear will be thinner than the other side. But you can accommodate for this by endeavoring to pass the dough sheets through the rollers in the same way each time, so that the side of dough that passes closest to the gear the first time is the side that passes closest to that gear every time. This minimizes any problems you might have with the shape of the sheet. However, it's not essential to do this—you can still make noodles, but it's just more likely you'll produce irregularly shaped sheets of dough.

Noodle sheet after the third pass through the rollers, with visible patches of underhydrated dough

Of course, this means that every sheet of dough you produce will be lopsided in terms of the thickness across the sheet; typically, my noodle sheets end up with one side measuring about 1.3 mm on a digital caliper and the other measuring about 1 mm. This is barely noticeable, but it is noticeable, and there isn't a good solution for producing a more consistently sized batch of noodles.

The number of times you pass the dough through the rollers, and the degree to which a rest is needed during kneading, depends on the noodle formula you are using. A high-gluten, high-hydration formula, such as one made with commercial bread flour and about 40% water, will not have to go through the rollers many times; it is likely that three iterations will be more than sufficient. A dough with a lower amount of gluten potential but the same amount of water (let's say that 15% of the bread flour is replaced with other components such as starch and whole wheat flour) might need to be folded over and passed through the rollers two to three more times to be sure that the gluten network has developed. For noodles that have a lower degree of hydration, particularly those that contain dry ingredients other than high-protein flour, it helps to pause midway through the kneading process and let the dough sheet rest, covered, for 30 minutes to 1 hour. This allows the dough sheet to hydrate more evenly and completely.

There are visual and textural cues that can help guide your decisions. The most obvious visual cue indicating good gluten development is vertical striping. Faint lines that run the

Noodle sheet after the fourth pass through the rollers, with vertical striping indicating gluten development and some light patches of underhydrated dough

length of the dough sheet will start to become noticeable once the gluten begins developing. These lines are distinct from striping that occurs due to insufficient/uneven hydration, which is generally lighter colored and patchy. The striping stemming from hydration issues is both normal and easy to distinguish, as it simply looks like unmixed flour (or starch) on the surface of the sheet. If you can easily discern the vertical striping of gluten development, you can halt the kneading process (or, do what I do—knead the sheet one more time, *just in case*).

If the surface of the dough looks and feels rough, even after kneading it several times, that means the dough is still very dry. If the surface looks ragged, as if the layers are splitting slightly, this is an indication that it is dry, and compressing it is not helping it get any wetter. In that case, it's best to wrap the sheet in plastic and let it rest for 30 minutes to 1 hour. Then repeat the kneading process, and the sheet should start to look and feel more evenly hydrated; continue to knead the sheet until the vertical striping of good gluten development is apparent.

Wrap the sheet of dough again in plastic to rest for one final time before cutting. This rest allows the gluten to relax, any air that has been folded into the dough via the process of kneading to dissipate, and the dough to continue to hydrate before you cut it into noodles.

Cutting

First check again that the rollers are at their widest setting. Pass the dough sheet through them again, first folding it crosswise in half, pressing firmly down on the seam, and cutting off the corners of the seam, then pass it through successively narrower settings until it is the thickness you desire.

The main challenge of the thinning process is that as you pass it through the narrower settings, the sheet will become almost unmanageably long. Since the sheet will still be very robust at this point, there's little risk of tearing, but there is a risk of feeding the sheet unevenly through the rollers, in which case the sides of the sheet may start folding over themselves, and that will reduce the yield of usable noodles. Try to keep the dough sheet taut as it both enters and exits the rollers. If you are using a stand mixer's pasta attachment, this is relatively simple, as the attachment will be about two feet above the countertop, meaning gravity will pull the sheet down after it exits the rollers, so you can focus most of your attention on keeping the sheet taut as it enters them. (However, you don't want the sheet to fold over itself too much as it puddles on the counter; it helps to extend it a little along the counter.)

This is more of a challenge with a hand-cranked pasta machine, and it underlines the degree to which another pair of hands is helpful. If you don't have a friend to help you, it's still best to focus on keeping the sheet taut as it enters the rollers, and I do this by cranking with my dominant hand while resting my splayed-out other hand on top of the part of the sheet that is just about to go into the rollers. With a little

Cutting noodles by hand

pressure, you can create enough tension to keep the sheet taut as the rollers pull it through, and you can even direct the sheet of dough to the left or right, thus ensuring that it passes through the rollers evenly. Every so often you will need to stop rolling and spread out the sheet of dough on the other side of the rollers; quickly anchor the sheet where it's entering the rollers with your nondominant hand, and start cranking again. This will create small divots wherever you pause, but that effect will be mostly unnoticeable in the cooked noodles.

Once you have thinned the sheet to your desired thickness, it will be about 4 feet long. I cut it crosswise, using a pair of kitchen shears or a knife, into halves or thirds. From there, you have a couple of options for cutting the noodles. You can use the spaghetti cutter, which is standard on most pasta machines. You can also use other cutters, like the tagliatelle cutters that are part of most pasta machines, or cutters for specialty shapes that you can order from the manufacturer. Or you can, of course, cut the noodles by hand.

To cut the noodles using a pasta cutter, pass the sheet through it, keeping the end of the sheet that's being fed through it taut. When the noodles come out on the other side, gather them as neatly as you're able and dust them with some kind of native (i.e., unmodified) starch. You can use cornstarch, but I prefer potato starch. When cooked, cornstarch-coated noodles are a little slimier and more slippery than noodles coated in potato starch.

To cut the noodles by hand, dust the noodle sheet with starch, then fold it in half and then in half again, dusting each layer with starch. The starch will prevent the layers from fusing together as you slice through them. Place the folded sheet on a cutting board, square off the edges so they're lined up neatly, and steady the sheet with your nondominant hand, then curl those fingers into a claw and, using your knuckles as a guide, cut down firmly with a sharp, preferably long-bladed, knife. Try your best to cut noodles with consistent widths, but don't worry too much about it. Once cut, dust the noodles with a little more starch.

Gather or gently fold the starch-dusted noodles into bundles or nests of about 130 g (4½ ounces) each. Store in a resealable container or zip-top bag until ready to use.

Hand-cut tsukemen (left) and machine-cut tsukemen (right)

MASTER RECIPE: INSTRUCTIONS FOR HOMEMADE NOODLES

Every noodle recipe in this book gives you the base formula and the ingredient amounts to make a specific number of servings, along with a suggested thickness setting and suggested cook time.

Please be sure to press your initial dough to a thickness no greater than ¼ inch. Always check and double-check that the pasta rollers are set to the widest setting when you begin each iteration of the process. This will prevent damage to your rollers.

1. Combine the sodium carbonate, potassium carbonate, if using, salt, and water in a measuring cup or deli container and, using a spoon, stir gently to completely dissolve the dry ingredients, about 2 minutes. If necessary, break up any large clumps of salts with the tip of the spoon.

2. Combine the remaining dry ingredients (flours, starches, egg white powder) in the bowl of a stand mixer fitted with the paddle attachment or in the bowl of a food processor fitted with the steel blade (not the dough blade). Turn on the mixer to low, or turn on the food processor, and run until the mixture is thoroughly combined, about 1 minute for the stand mixer, 20 seconds for the food processor.

3. With the machine running, add the alkalized water one-third at a time in a slow, steady stream, allowing time after each addition for the liquid to be thoroughly incorporated (about 3 minutes for the stand mixer, 1 minute for the food processor). After the final addition, allow the machine to run for 2 minutes if using a stand mixer, 1 minute if using a food processor, then stop the machine. If using a stand mixer, using your hands, release any wet pockets of dough from the sides of the bowl and the beater or blade by rubbing it with some of the drier pebbly mixture in the bottom of the bowl. Turn the machine on again and let it run for another 1 to 2 minutes.

4. Lay a 3- to 4-foot-long sheet of plastic wrap on a work surface. Spread the dough mixture out evenly on the plastic wrap to form a rough rectangle (for 6 portions, the rectangle should be about 6 inches by 2 feet). Using your hands or fists, and using the plastic wrap to help corral any loose bits of dough, compress the dough into a single plank no more than ¼ inch (5 mm) thick. Wrap tightly in plastic wrap, using more wrap if necessary, and press the dough sheet so that there are no cracks on its surface or edges and it seems to be a cohesive whole.

5. Place the wrapped dough on a (clean) floor or a large sheet pan. Place a sheet pan on top of it and then stand on the sheet pan.

(Or, if it doesn't bother you, you can stand directly on the wrapped dough—wearing clean socks.) Shift your weight around and use it to compress the dough all over. Return the wrapped dough to your work surface and, using your hands, press down on it so there are no visible cracks. Let it rest for at least 1 hour, and up to 8 hours, at room temperature.

6. Set up a stand mixer fitted with a pasta-rolling attachment or a manual pasta-rolling machine.

7. Unwrap the sheet of dough and, using a bench scraper or knife, divide it evenly into as many portions as the recipe indicates. Wrap the portions completely in plastic to prevent them from drying out. If using a stand mixer, set the speed to medium. Check that the roller attachment is on its widest setting. You want to be extra careful that the setting is right; using a setting that's too thin for the dough can result in the rollers getting knocked out of alignment or breaking.

8. Feed one portion of the dough through the rollers, applying pressure to the dough to ensure it passes through evenly. Run the resulting sheet through the second-widest roller setting, and then the third-widest setting. Set it aside.

9. Repeat the rolling process with another portion of the dough.

10. Stack the 2 rolled sheets of dough on top of each other and press them firmly all along their length to encourage them to adhere to one another. Run the sheets together through the widest setting of the pasta roller, followed by the second-widest setting, the third-widest setting, and then the fourth-widest setting. Fold the dough sheet crosswise in half, making it half of its original length. Press down on the seam to flatten it, then run the sheet seam side first through the widest setting, followed by the second-widest, third-widest, and then the fourth-widest setting. The dough should feel cohesive and strong, not pebbly or grainy.

11. Fold the dough sheet crosswise in half again. Press down on the seam to flatten it and cut off both corners of the seam diagonally, so that the seam of the dough sheet fits easily into the rollers. Run the sheet seam side first through the widest setting of the pasta rollers, and then through the second-widest, third-widest, and fourth-widest setting. Fold it crosswise in half, press down on the seam, cut off the corners, and repeat the process. If this is done correctly, longitudinal lines will form in the sheet of dough, and the sheet itself will be smooth and pliable. If you do not see these lines, repeat the process until they appear—they are an indication that the gluten has been properly developed.

12. Fold the sheet over itself into a compact bundle and wrap it in plastic to prevent it from drying out. Repeat steps 8 through 11 with the remaining portions of dough. Let the dough rest for at least 30 minutes before proceeding.

13. *If you're working with a lower-hydration dough (35% to 39%)*: Repeat the kneading process once or twice with each portion of dough. Let rest for at least 30 minutes before proceeding.

CONTINUES →

14. Working with one dough portion at a time, unfold the bundle, fold the sheet crosswise in half, press down on the seam, and cut off the corners of the seam. Run the sheet seam side first through the widest setting of the rollers, and then through progressively narrower settings until it reaches the thickness indicated in the recipe.

15. Cut the sheets into halves or thirds, depending on your preference for the lengths of the noodles.

16. Run each cut sheet through the spaghetti-cutting attachment of your pasta machine. Dust the noodles with potato starch or cornstarch to prevent sticking, shake off excess starch, and fold the noodles into loose nests of about 130 grams each.

17. Place the noodles in a zip-top bag, seal it almost completely (so the noodles can dry slightly), and let rest at room temperature at least overnight, and up to 24 hours. Then seal the bag and place it in the refrigerator; the noodles can be used immediately but are at their best after 2 to 4 days in the fridge.

18. TO COOK THE NOODLES: Bring a large pot of unsalted water to a rolling boil over high heat. If using noodle baskets, add a single portion of noodles to each basket and plunge into the water, stirring the noodles rapidly with tongs or chopsticks to prevent them from sticking together. If not using noodle baskets, add the noodles one portion at a time directly to the boiling water and stir vigorously with tongs or chopsticks to prevent them from sticking together. Cook the noodles, stirring occasionally, for the time indicated in the recipe. (The exact cooking time will depend on your preference for doneness and the thickness of the noodles.) Drain the noodles thoroughly, shaking off as much excess water as possible, and add to hot ramen broth for serving.

Aging Noodles

Cut noodles can be used immediately, but they benefit immensely from aging, either at room temperature or in the refrigerator. Different noodle formulas require different aging periods to reach their "peak." If they are allowed to age past their peak, the quality starts to suffer, so it's best to use or freeze the noodles when they're at their peak.

Frozen fresh noodles are every bit as good as freshly made (and aged) ones. In fact, they are sometimes better than fresh noodles, as freezing results in changes in the gluten and starch networks, evident in the fact that frozen noodles are more translucent and glossier than nonfrozen noodles. The fact that noodles can be stored in the freezer for extended periods of time and even improve is one of the great arguments in favor of making your own ramen noodles.

Temomi

Temomi, or hand-massaged, noodles are noodles with a highly irregular texture. If most noodles are effectively long cylinders, massaging them will produce irregular surfaces and dimensions along their length. As discussed on pages 146–49, part of the point of developing a gluten network is to improve elasticity, or resistance to deformation; a noodle with a well-developed gluten network will barely be affected by a light "massage." You have to use a considerable amount of force, so I like to think a better translation is "hand-smushed." This may seem counterintuitive, even wrong, after you've spent quite a lot of time producing the noodles, and raw noodles seem like delicate things. But if you do just a gentle temomi, the noodles will in fact spring back to their original shape, particularly during cooking, and you'll notice very little difference between a massaged noodle and an un-massaged one.

Straight noodles

Temomi noodles

To smush the noodles, gather up a nest of noodles in both hands, squeeze it as hard as possible, and then immediately toss and pry apart the noodle strands. Repeat several times until the noodles are visibly crinkly and there are sections of flat planes along their length.

You can temomi any noodle, but it's best to use thicker ones. If you use thin noodles, the flat planes produced by the process can become too thin, so thin as to make the texture unpleasant, and some of the noodles will break up during cooking. Very thick noodles, like some hand-cut noodles, are incredibly fun to eat when they've been temomi'd.

Cooking Noodles

Cooking fresh ramen is straightforward: Use an ample quantity of boiling water, and boil the noodles until they have the desired texture. The water does not need to be salted, like pasta water, as the noodles contain salt and will take the rest of their seasoning from the soup, dipping sauce, or combination of tare and fat. To avoid diluting the soup, dipping sauce, or tare-fat combination, shake off as much of the water as possible when draining the noodles. (Don't use the noodle cooking water to build sauces or improve the emulsions of non-soup ramen dishes, as you might with pasta cooking water; it tastes funny.)

Everyone's tastes are different; some people prefer firmer textures, others like softer textures, and still others can get very, very particular about "perfect" noodle textures. The only way to figure out what you prefer is to try cooking the noodles for different intervals of time, and this is easy enough to do: Boil some water, cut up a few noodles into smaller lengths, and toss them into the water, then fish them out at set intervals: 1 minute, 1 minute and 30 seconds, etc.

If you know that a given fresh noodle reaches the texture you like after cooking for 2 minutes, but you temomi a batch of those noodles, you should slightly undercook them—about 1 minutes and 50 seconds—to account for the fact that they have very thin sections that will cook far faster than the thicker sections.

Since tsukemen noodles are cooked in boiling water and then shocked in cold water to halt the cooking, it's better to slightly overcook them. You want the starch network in the noodles to be more gelatinized. When the noodles are shocked, the gelatinized starch network retrogrades, which means the amylopectin molecules form a more organized, more compact network, and that produces a firmer gel. (This gel will be even firmer if there is a gel stabilizer like egg whites in the dough.) After the noodles are shocked, they need to be rinsed thoroughly in multiple changes of water to remove any exterior starch, which will make them stick to one another on the serving plate.

When cooking multiple portions of noodles, cook them either in individual batches, fishing them out with a spider strainer, or in separate noodle baskets: the starch on the exterior of the noodles makes them very difficult to separate into portions when cooked. For this reason, tsukemen is great for home cooks who want to serve ramen to many people simultaneously, as you don't need huge pots of water that can fit multiple noodle baskets. The noodles can be cooked en masse, strained, shocked, and rinsed, then portioned for serving.

How to Turn Any Stock-and-Tare Combination into Tsukemen

Every bowl of ramen in this book can be served as tsukemen with slight adjustments.

The method for constructing the soup is identical. However, there is one crucial difference, and that's the *quantity* of stock. Typically tsukemen will have about half to two-thirds the amount of stock as soup ramen, but the same amount (or more) of tare, which yields a more strongly seasoned soup. I call for using 200 ml of stock for tsukemen with the same amount of tare as you'd use for a full bowl of ramen, and if you only have a single 350-ml ladle, this can present a small problem. But it's perfectly acceptable to just eyeball the amount using your regular ladle.

Given how incredibly salty the soup is, you'll need to add sugar and vinegar in varying amounts, depending on the type of soup, to lessen its intensity. The amount of fat added to the soup also helps temper the salinity. For thicker emulsified soups, no extra fat is needed, but aromatic fats and oils can add another aromatic dimension. For thinner chintan broths, oil helps to coat the noodles *and* slightly insulate the soup, so it doesn't cool down drastically when you dip cold noodles into it.

In a good ramen restaurant, when you've finished the noodles, you will be given the option of adding "soup wari" to the remaining soup; this is a light soup stock that dilutes the broth enough that it will be pleasant to drink on its own. Since you took the time to make the stock from scratch, I recommend you also offer soup wari to yourself and anyone else you're making tsukemen for, but it's up to you.

There are two further considerations for serving tsukemen: the bowls you use and the method for cooking the noodles. Standard-size ramen bowls are too large for tsukemen. The larger surface area of the soup will mean it will cool down more rapidly than if it were served in a smaller bowl. I like to use miso soup bowls for tsukemen, but even rice bowls will do.

Any noodles can be prepared for tsukemen by plunging them into cold water after cooking and rinsing off all the surface starches. However, noodles cooked for soup ramen are often slightly undercooked to compensate for the fact that they will continue cooking in the hot broth. Noodles cooked for tsukemen should be slightly overcooked, which will gelatinize the starches more thoroughly, yielding a more pleasing gel once they've been thoroughly cooled after being rinsed in water.

Here is a basic formula for constructing tsukemen soup. The noodles can be cooked in advance, as they will not suffer from sitting in their serving dish for the 5 minutes it takes to construct the soup (provided you've *thoroughly* rinsed off their surface starches).

---

200 ml (about 1 cup) soup stock

2 tablespoons (30 ml) tare, or more to taste

2 tablespoons (30 ml) fat or oil

1 teaspoon (5 ml) amazu

Salt to taste

Vinegar to taste

HOW TO CONSTRUCT A BOWL OF RAMEN

Once you have all the elements of your bowl of ramen prepared—the stock, the tare, the aromatic oils, the noodles, the toppings, and the garnishes—you can put it together.

Every bowl of ramen can be tweaked according to personal preferences. If you have tare and oils and stock on hand, you can plate your ramen and then add tare or salt if you think it needs more seasoning, more oil if you think it needs a little richness, or more stock if you think the soup is overseasoned or too oily, or both. But ramen is unlike other noodle soups in that the seasoning of a served bowl should be dialed in when it is served and should not need any tweaking from the first sip of soup and first bite of noodles.

Standardizing portioning is helpful for achieving this goal. Ramen shops will typically use anywhere from 300 to 400 ml of stock for each bowl of soup, and the proportions of tare and aromatic oils are determined as a function of the volume of stock. How much stock is used is a matter of preference. For the recipes in this book, I settled on 350 ml stock for every bowl, the amount I like to drink in a single sitting. (I also think that amount of stock yields a nice-looking bowl of ramen, once the noodles and toppings have been added.)

Typically, tare constitutes one-tenth of the volume of the stock, and the same goes for the amount of aromatic oil and/or fat, and ramen shops use ladles of specific sizes to ensure consistency from one bowl to the next. For the recipes in this book, I fudge the 1:10 ratio a little bit and use two tablespoons of tare for every bowl of ramen, which amounts to 30 ml. Since my tare lie on the less salty end of the spectrum, the recipes in this book are a little undersalted to my taste, and I'll either scoop in a little extra tare or add a pinch of salt to each bowl.

Here is the process for constructing a bowl of ramen:

WARM THE SERVING BOWL. This step is optional, but a warm bowl will draw less heat from the boiling stock, and thus the ramen will stay hotter and consequently be more aromatic. You can pour hot water into the bowl and let it warm up while you cook the noodles; stash your serving bowl in an oven heated to its lowest temperature setting and then turned off, for about 15 minutes; or fill the bowl with water and stick it in a microwave on high for about 3 minutes. (Drain the bowl if necessary before proceeding.)

ADD THE TARE AND SOME OR ALL THE FAT, ALONG WITH ANY OTHER SEASONINGS. Adding tare and fat to the bowl before you ladle in the boiling stock ensures quick and even dispersion of the seasonings in the soup. (Thicker tare, like miso tare, will probably require a brief whisking, either with chopsticks or a whisk.) Other seasonings include the pinch of white pepper that should go in (almost) every bowl of ramen, any vinegars you might want to add, and seasoning pastes. I also like to add the sliced whites of scallions or naga negi (Welsh onions) to the bottom of the bowl, to let the heat wilt them a bit. If your fat is solid, like cold lard or refined coconut oil, it's best to add it to the bottom of the bowl, so that the hot stock can melt it. Pouring in the hot stock and lifting and folding the noodles will then disperse the fat in the soup, forming tiny globules. You can, alternatively, add liquid fats (hot animal fats and coconut oil, cold oils) to the surface of the liquid, after the noodles have been added, untangled, and folded, and the fat will form large slicks or pools, which can be attractive. Or . . . you can do a little of both.

ADD THE BOILING STOCK. Yes, you want the stock boiling. "But," I hear you say, "I just spent 10 hours not boiling the freaking stock!" That's true, but once it's been strained, the stock has very little particulate matter, and after chilling and defatting, it will contain very little fat. As a result, boiling will not affect its clarity all that much at this point, and you want the bowl of ramen to be as hot as possible when you serve it. So, get it to a boil and pour it into the bowl.

ADD THE THOROUGHLY DRAINED COOKED NOODLES. The hot bowl and boiling stock provide you with a little cushion of time, but once you add the noodles, it's best to work quickly, since they inevitably drop the temperature of the stock in the bowl, and cooked noodles sitting in hot broth will quickly get soggy and bloated. Using tongs or chopsticks, give the noodles a little lift and shake to untangle them slightly, making them easier to eat, and to help coat them in the broth. You can then, if you like, fold them over themselves neatly or swirl them in the bowl; both look attractive and give you a platform on which to perch your toppings.

ADD THE TOPPINGS. Arrange any toppings over the noodles, as messily or neatly as you like. Toppings can be added straight from the fridge, particularly if you've warmed the bowl and boiled the stock, and they won't affect the temperature of the soup much. If you're really loading up the bowl, though, it's best to warm at least some of the toppings; if I'm adding an egg, spinach, and pork, I'll at the very least broil or torch the pork to raise its temperature, which will also make the pork look, taste, and smell better.

ADD THE GARNISH. Add any delicate vegetables, like sliced scallions, and final toppings, like fried onions or cracklings, at the end. Garnishes also include any oils or fat you held off on adding to the bottom of the bowl. These could be as simple as a bit of lard you've reserved so it'll form an attractive pool of fat on top of the soup, or herb oils, oils infused with dried fish, or any oil with aromatic oomph, such as toasted sesame oil.

PLATING AND NOODLE FOLDS

If you've ever made ramen from scratch, the first time you did, the result was probably underwhelming. My guess is that first bowl of plated ramen didn't look all that photogenic.

And that's totally normal! I sometimes make ugly bowls of ramen, and I don't mind them at all, but then I also make *a lot* of ramen. It's only natural, though, to want the bowl of ramen to reflect the amount of care and attention you put into it.

To make the ramen look as if it has been composed, you need to practice. And the first thing you must practice is the noodle fold.

Ramen cooks spend a lot of time and energy thinking about folding noodles. I prefer a neat fold, but not so neat that every noodle is perfectly aligned, as if the cook had run a comb through them before adding them to the bowl (some ramen shops do this!).

Longer, thicker, straighter, and denser noodles are easier to manipulate after they've been cooked: length gives you room to work with, thick noodles and straight noodles are less likely to get tangled up with one another, and arranging denser noodles is easier because of the assist gravity provides as you lift them from the soup. If you are making your own noodles and noodle folding is important to you, you can adjust your formulas and methods to produce noodles that are easier to manipulate into crisp folds: cut them longer or thicker, use less water and more protein for denser noodles, or use less sodium carbonate for straighter noodles (see page 148). If you're working with store-bought fresh noodles or your noodles are superkinky or short or light, you'll be at a considerable disadvantage if a perfect noodle fold is your goal.

But even the crinkliest and shortest noodles can be manipulated into some semblance of organization, and they can serve as a scaffold to produce a ridiculously good-looking bowl of ramen with a little practice and creativity. I describe two basic noodle folds here that will work with any ramen noodles out there, store-bought or homemade. One uses chopsticks (you can also use long tweezers) to create a simple noodle fold, the other a pair of spring-loaded tongs to create a kind of noodle spiral or swirl.

Practice

With noodle folds, practice is essential. Although you can practice with cooked noodles in a bowl of hot water, doing so doesn't really mimic the way in which you'll be folding noodles you'll actually eat, because it doesn't account for the time constraints that exist when building a ramen bowl for service.

The first time constraint: You want to serve the ramen *hot*. A warmed bowl helps offer a buffer against the soup stock cooling down too much, but it's only a slight buffer. You need to get the noodles in the soup and folded *fast*.

The second time constraint: You want to serve the noodles fast. Fiddling with the noodle fold for 5 minutes means your noodles will be 5 minutes past prime eating time.

The third time constraint: the clarity of the soup: You've spent hours and hours carefully monitoring the temperature of your stock in order to produce a crystal-clear liquid (see page 68), and then you spend just 2 minutes futzing with the noodle fold, and all of a sudden your soup looks like mud. This has to do with the gelatin content of the stock, the fat you've added to the bowl, the starch that comes off the noodles and the noodle cooking water that still clings to them, and the agitation produced by fiddling with the noodles until they're perfectly folded.

The best way to avoid turning a clear stock cloudy is to fold or align the noodles *before* you slide them into the soup. There are several techniques, all of which require a fair amount of practice, that allow you to do that. But for most of us, myself included, the next best way is to simply try to fold the noodles as quickly as possible after they've been dunked into the soup. If you make ramen semiregularly, as I hope this book inspires you to do, you will be able to make a noodle fold or swirl that's neat enough by lifting the noodles only twice, after just a few times. Your soup will be clear (if it started out as such), the fat in the bowl will form relatively large globules that will glow like little pearls, and you'll have an ample platform for your toppings.

If you botch the first ten noodle-fold attempts you make, that's perfectly normal, even expected. And, ultimately, it doesn't *really* matter anyway; the soup and noodles should still taste great.

Practice is also important for the other elements of ramen-bowl styling: where and how you position such items as chashu slices, vegetables, chopped scallions, etc. A lot of ramen cooks will sketch out their bowls before plating, to give them a kind of mental guide to follow when the noodles come out of the boiling water and they want to get the bowl of ramen on the table fast. You can fiddle with the bowl endlessly as you plate it, but, as with noodle folding, every second you spend messing with stuff in the bowl is a second where the noodles are getting blown out and the soup is getting colder.

THE BASIC FOLD

This method produces a rectangular platform of folded noodles across the center of the bowl of ramen.

1. Add the cooked noodles to the hot soup.

2. Using chopsticks, quickly untangle the noodles.

3. Lift the noodles up and shake from side to side.

4. Using a forward motion, place noodles back in the bowl to form a rectangular platform.

5. Lift noodles from the front section of the bowl, sliding chopsticks under bend created by first fold.

6. Using a forward motion, place noodles back in the bowl to form a neater rectangular platform.

7. The platform can run across the bowl horizontally, vertically, or at an angle. You can fold the noodles to form a wide or narrow platform.

8. The folded-noodle platform, ready for toppings.

THE NOODLE SWIRL

This method gives you a circular platform with a little nest in the center for your toppings. This works best with long noodles, as you want the noodles to take up the entire surface of the bowl. This method requires absolutely no skill with chopsticks; you just need a pair of spring-loaded tongs.

1. Add noodles to hot soup and, using tongs, stir briefly to untangle them. Lift noodles high above the bowl.

2. In quick circular motion, drape noodles around edges of bowl to form a spiral.

FOLDING TSUKEMEN

Folding tsukemen is relatively easier, since you're working with cold, rinsed noodles, and you can fold them with your hands.

1. Lift the noodles up and, using your fingers, gently comb out any knots.

2. Raise the noodles high above the serving bowl.

3. Using your second hand as a guide, fold the noodles over neatly as you lower them into the bowl.

RECIPES

THIS chapter is divided into two sections: recipe sets and component recipes.

The **recipe sets** consist of recipes that are designed to go together, and each set starts with a formula and process for putting together a composed bowl of ramen, essentially a preparation checklist: how much stock you need, how much tare and fat, the kind of noodles, suggested toppings, etc.

The **component recipes** are for elements that can stand on their own (such as the fried pig's foot terrine or basic chicken stock) or that can be used in many bowls of ramen (like the ichiban dashi or rendered chicken fat).

Of course, every recipe in this book can be viewed as a "component" for a bowl of ramen. And while the recipes in the recipe sets have been extensively tested together and I recommend trying to make them in their entirety, you can mix and match components as you see fit. Do you have leftover tare from the Classic Shoyu recipe set? Use it in a basic chicken stock, pair it with any noodles you like, and top it with some stir-fried shimeji from the Vegan Chickpea Shoyu ramen—that's a great bowl of ramen. Do you have leftover shio tare? Combine it with any of the stock recipes and any aromatic fat, and you have a great soup that will work with literally any of the noodle recipes. Every one of the toppings—the various chashu recipes, the Spicy Soboro, the blanched spinach—can be used in any ramen, and every bowl of ramen can benefit immensely from a sprinkling of gyofun. The combinations are nearly endless.

RECIPE SETS

CLASSIC SHOYU

THIS BOWL OF RAMEN was inspired by the most basic method for making ramen, and the majority of the cooking takes place in one large pot. A stock made from chicken and pork is fortified by simmering cured chicken breasts and a pork shoulder roast that will be used for meat toppings in it. The tare is a straightforward infusion of kombu, katsuobushi, and shiitake in a mixture of soy sauce, mirin, fish sauce, and sake, although the sake is cooked until dry—"au sec"—to boil off the alcohol and concentrate and caramelize the sugars. The aromatic fat is rendered lard in which garlic and ginger have been fried.

The noodle dough has a relatively high hydration, which means it can be formed more readily than most and will be easy to sheet through pasta rollers. I add a little tapioca starch and powdered egg white to improve the starch gel of the noodles, and high-protein bread flour ensures that the gluten network will be sufficiently developed to produce a satisfying chew. The proportion of alkaline salts yields noodles that are slippery and light, a little curly, and with a slightly firm bite due to the potassium carbonate.

The stock recipe offers a clear demonstration of how maintaining a low simmering temperature can yield a clear stock along with nicely cooked meats for use as toppings. The stock uses a whole chicken, a pork shoulder roast, and ground pork. If you like, you can take the roast and the ground meat from a bone-in picnic shoulder (see page 94) or butt roast, and the remainder of that can be used to make a pork chintan (see page 270), or used as a roast (see page 281), which can then also be used to make a paitan for tsukemen (see page 272).

To round out the bowl, I suggest adding Blanched Spinach (page 290) and Super Simple Ajitama (page 284).

You also have the option of serving this ramen as a "double soup," that is, combining the stock with Dashi (page 269) in a ratio of 2 parts stock to 1 part dashi, which will yield a more aromatic and flavorful stock, but with less body. I recommend trying it both ways to see what you gain and what you lose by making a double soup.

RECIPE CONTINUES →

CLASSIC SHOYU

continued

For each serving of ramen, you need:

350 ml (1½ cups) Pork and Chicken Chintan (page 182)

1 serving 40%-Hydration Tapioca/Egg White Noodles (page 185)

2 tablespoons (30 ml) Shoyu Tare (page 184)

2 tablespoons (30 ml) Aromatic Lard (page 274)

⅛ teaspoon rice vinegar

Pinch of white pepper, or more to taste

Salt if needed

1 or 2 slices poached chicken breast (see page 182)

1 or 2 slices poached pork chashu (see page 182)

Other toppings as desired (optional)

Thinly sliced scallions or naga negi

1. Bring the noodle cooking water to a boil. Bring the soup stock to a simmer.

2. Add the noodles to the cooking water and set a timer for 2 minutes. Bring the stock to a boil.

3. Add the tare, lard, rice vinegar, and white pepper to a warmed serving bowl. Pour in the boiling stock. Taste and add salt if necessary.

4. Once the noodles are cooked, drain thoroughly and add to the bowl. Using chopsticks, loosen the noodles and fold them once or twice over themselves to distribute the seasonings and form a platform for the toppings.

5. Place the sliced chicken breast and pork chashu on top. Add other toppings as desired. Top with sliced scallions or naga negi and serve.

40%-hydration tapioca/egg white noodles
blanched spinach, naga negi
ajitama
poached chicken breast, poached pork chashu
Classic shoyu: pork and chicken chintan, shoyu tare, aromatic lard

PORK AND CHICKEN CHINTAN

YIELD: About 3 quarts (2.8 liters), plus pork and chicken for serving

SOAKING TIME: 12 hours

TOTAL COOK TIME: 10 hours

ACTIVE TIME: 1 hour

2 tablespoons plus 1 teaspoon (21 g) Diamond Crystal kosher salt, divided

1 tablespoon plus 2 teaspoons (25 g) sugar

One 2-pound (900 g) boneless pork shoulder roast

One 3- to 4-pound (1.3 to 1.8 kg) whole chicken, cut into 11 parts (drumsticks, thighs, breasts, tenders, wings, and back), divided

3¾ quarts (3.5 liters) water, divided

A 3-inch square of kombu (6 g), cut into 2-inch (5-cm) pieces

1 pound (450 g) ground pork

6 garlic cloves, peeled and crushed

A 1-inch piece of ginger, peeled and sliced

2 tablespoons (30 ml) soy sauce

2 teaspoons (10 ml) mirin

1 teaspoon (5 ml) fish sauce

1 medium onion, peeled and diced (2 cups/300 g)

¼ head Napa cabbage, roughly chopped (1 cup/222 g)

1. **The day before you make the stock:** Whisk 2 tablespoons (18 g) of the salt and the sugar in a small mixing bowl to thoroughly combine. Coat the pork roast with the salt-sugar mixture. Place the pork in a sealable container or zip-top bag and refrigerate for at least 6 hours, preferably overnight (12 hours).

2. Sprinkle the remaining 1 teaspoon (3 g) salt over the chicken breast halves. Place them in a sealable container or zip-top bag and refrigerate for at least 6 hours, preferably overnight (12 hours).

3. Combine the kombu and 1 cup (240 ml) of the cold water in a sealable container and refrigerate for at least 6 hours, preferably overnight (12 hours).

4. **The day you make the stock:** Place the remaining chicken parts in a large tall-sided pot, add the ground pork, garlic, and ginger, and cover with the remaining 3½ quarts (3.3 liters) cold water. Using your hands, break up the ground pork into small pieces; they should float in the water.

5. Bring the water to a simmer over high heat, taking care not to exceed 205°F (96°C). Reduce the heat to medium-low to low, to maintain a bare simmer, with the temperature hovering between 200° and 205°F (93° and 96°C), and cook for 10 hours.

6. Meanwhile, after the stock has been cooking for 4 hours, rinse the pork under cold running water to wash away the excess cure. Using kitchen twine, tie the roast using butcher's knots or at 1-inch intervals to give it a cylindrical shape. Gently submerge the roast completely in the simmering stock and cook until it is soft and giving when squeezed with tongs and an instant-read thermometer inserted into its center reads 190°F (87°C), 3 to 4 hours.

7. Using tongs, carefully remove the pork from the pot and place in a shallow baking dish or zip-top bag.

8. Stir together the soy sauce, mirin, and fish sauce in a small mixing bowl to thoroughly combine, and pour over the pork roast. If using a shallow baking dish, carefully turn the pork to coat; if using a zip-top bag, seal the bag and gently rotate the pork roast to coat. Let the pork cool to room temperature, about 1 hour, turning once or twice to distribute the seasoning, then refrigerate until completely chilled, at least 4 hours.

9. Rinse the chicken breasts under cold running water to wash away excess cure. Submerge the breasts in the simmering stock and cook until an instant-read thermometer inserted at a breast's thickest point reads 150°F (65°C), about 30 minutes. Gently transfer the chicken breasts to a plate and allow to cool to room temperature, about 30 minutes, then wrap tightly in plastic wrap and refrigerate until completely chilled, at least 1 hour.

10. Add the onion and cabbage to the simmering stock and cook for 30 minutes. Shut off the heat and add the soaked kombu, along with its soaking liquid. Using tongs or chopsticks, gently swish the kombu in the stock briefly to disperse any gooey stuff attached to it in the stock. Let the stock steep for 30 minutes.

11. Set a half sheet pan on a wire cooling rack and set a large metal mixing bowl on top of the pan. Strain the stock through a cheesecloth-lined fine-mesh strainer into the bowl; discard the solids. Let the stock cool to room temperature, about 1 hour.

12. Transfer the stock to sealable containers, cover, and refrigerate until completely chilled, about 4 hours. Remove any solidified fat that has risen to the surface before using the stock. The fat can be reserved for another use or discarded.

SHOYU TARE

YIELD: 3 cups (700 ml)

SOAKING TIME: 6 to 12 hours

TOTAL COOK TIME: 15 minutes

ACTIVE TIME: 20 minutes

- 2¼ cups (600 ml) koikuchi soy sauce, divided
- A 3-inch square of kombu (6 g), cut into several strips
- 3 or 4 dried shiitake mushrooms (4 g)
- 1 cup plus 2 tablespoons (300 ml) sake (junmai, dry)
- 0.2 ounce (6 g) katsuobushi
- ¼ cup (60 ml) fish sauce
- ¼ cup (60 ml) mirin
- 1 tablespoon (9 g) Diamond Crystal kosher salt

1. Combine 1 cup (240 ml) of the soy sauce with the kombu and shiitake in a sealable container. Seal the container and refrigerate for at least 6 hours, preferably overnight (12 hours).

2. Add the sake to a 2-quart saucepan and bring to a boil over medium-high heat. Cook until the alcohol has boiled off, the sake has reduced to about a tablespoon, and the bubbles that are forming in the liquid are quite large, 7 to 8 minutes.

3. Add the kombu, shiitake, and soy sauce mixture to the reduced sake and cook just until small bubbles begin to form around the edges of the liquid—the mixture should register 140° to 150°F (60° to 65°C) on an instant-read thermometer—about 2 minutes. Using tongs, remove the kombu; discard, or reserve for another use. Continue to cook until the mixture is barely simmering (it should be at about 185°F/85°C). Shut off the heat, add the katsuobushi, and let steep for 5 minutes, then pour the mixture through a fine-mesh strainer set in a small mixing bowl, pressing on the solids to extract as much liquid as possible (reserve the solids for another use or discard).

4. Add the remaining 1¼ cups (360 ml) soy sauce, the fish sauce, mirin, and salt to the liquid and stir until the salt dissolves. Transfer the tare to a sealable container and refrigerate until ready to use.

40%-HYDRATION TAPIOCA/EGG WHITE NOODLES

COOK TIME: 2 minutes
THICKNESS: 1.3 mm (setting #6 on KitchenAid, #7 on Marcato Atlas pasta machine)

Ingredients	*Baker's percentages*	*1 serving (grams)*	*6 servings (grams)*
Bread flour	100.0%	94	564
Tapioca starch	5.3%	5	30
Egg white powder	1.1%	1	6
Sodium carbonate	1.1%	1	6
Salt	1.1%	1	6
Potassium carbonate	0.5%	0.5	3
Water	42.6%	40	240

braised belly chashu,
naga negi
Pork, chicken, and niboshi shoyu:
tontorinibo chintan, nibo tare,
aromatic lard, nibo oil
35%-hydration tapioca noodle

PORK, CHICKEN, AND NIBOSHI SHOYU

THINK OF THIS BOWL as a starter niboshi ramen. Niboshi are infused into the stock, tare, and an aromatic oil. The tare is excellent in almost any stock for ramen, since it's packed with kombu, katsuobushi, oyster sauce, fish sauce, shiitake—a grab bag of glutamates, inosinates, and guanylates. The same is true of the niboshi oil, but if you are new to niboshi flavor, you may want to start off with a teaspoon or so.

A lot of people recommend gutting and deheading niboshi before making stock or tare with them, as the guts and head have a stronger, more bitter flavor. For a more refined niboshi flavor, you can use an equivalent weight of gutted and beheaded niboshi in any recipes that call for them. Gutting and deheading them is a simple, if slightly tedious process: Simply pinch off the heads and the dark stuff around the belly with your fingers. You can save the heads and bellies for use in nibo oil and "Dirty Paste" (see page 287).

Since niboshi produces a strong flavor profile, it helps to have a thick stock, so I include a pig's foot along with a whole chicken to increase the concentration of gelatin. This stock should form an almost opaque gel when chilled; it should clear once heated. The pig's foot can be removed from the stock and turned into a terrine (see page 292); the instructions in this recipe call for wrapping the foot in cheesecloth to facilitate removing it in one piece for that purpose.

I call for firm, relatively low-hydration noodles for this bowl; be sure to read the noodle sheeting instructions (see page 162) carefully, as these are actually the most difficult noodles to make in the book.

Suggested toppings are: Braised Belly Chashu (page 277) or Pork Shoulder Chashu (page 282), Pork Wontons (page 288), Blanched Spinach (page 290), and Super Simple Ajitama (page 284).

This is a trickier bowl to construct than the Classic Shoyu (page 179) because it calls for wontons. Time the wonton cooking so they're done right after the noodles. (A noodle basket is handy for this: drop the noodles into the basket and add them to the boiling water along with the wontons, which you can scatter around the pot. By the time you drain the noodles and add them to the ramen, the wontons will be cooked and ready to go.) You could also boil the wontons first and transfer them, along with a cup of the boiling water, to a bowl to stay warm. This is not ideal, but it's convenient, and they'll survive (this is how I make my lunches); drain them before using.

RECIPE CONTINUES →

PORK, CHICKEN, AND NIBOSHI SHOYU

continued

For each bowl of ramen, you need:

350 ml (1½ cups) Tontorinibo Stock (page 189)

1 serving 35%-Hydration Tapioca Noodles (page 192)

3 or 4 Pork Wontons (page 288)

2 tablespoons (30 ml) Nibo Tare (page 190)

1 tablespoon plus 1 teaspoon (20 ml) Aromatic Lard (page 274)

⅛ teaspoon (0.4 g) Diamond Crystal kosher salt, or more to taste

Pinch of white pepper

2 teaspoons (10 ml) Nibo Oil (page 191)

Splash of toasted sesame oil

Thinly sliced scallions or naga negi

1. Bring the noodle cooking water to a boil. Bring the soup stock to a simmer.

2. Add the wontons and noodles to the boiling water and set a timer for 2 minutes. Bring the stock to a boil.

3. Add the tare, lard, salt, and white pepper to a warmed serving bowl. Pour in the boiling stock. Taste and add more salt if necessary.

4. Once the noodles are cooked, drain thoroughly and add to the bowl. Using chopsticks, loosen the noodles and fold them once or twice over themselves to distribute the soup seasoning and form a platform for the toppings.

5. Top the noodles with any desired toppings, along with the drained cooked wontons. Add the nibo oil and splash of toasted sesame oil, drizzling them around the perimeter of the bowl. Top with sliced scallions or naga negi and serve.

TONTORINIBO STOCK

YIELD: About 2½ quarts (2.3 liters)

SOAKING: 6 to 12 hours

TOTAL COOK TIME (PRESSURE COOKER): 3 hours, plus time for coming to pressure/depressurizing

TOTAL COOK TIME (STOVETOP): 8 hours

ACTIVE TIME: 15 minutes

1 ounce (30 g) niboshi

One 3-inch square piece of kombu (6 g)

3 quarts plus ½ cup (2.9 liters) water, divided

One 3- to 4-pound (1.8 kg to 2.3 kg) whole chicken, cut into parts

1 small (about 1 pound/450 g) pig's foot, scrubbed clean and any hair singed or shaved off

A 3-inch piece of ginger, peeled, divided

1 head garlic, separated into cloves (about 14) and peeled, plus 5 garlic cloves, peeled, divided

1 large onion, peeled and roughly chopped

10 scallions, cut into 2-inch lengths

4 leaves Napa cabbage

1. **The day before you make the stock:** Combine the kombu and niboshi with 2 cups (480 ml) water in a sealable container and refrigerate for at least 6 hours, preferably overnight (12 hours).

2. **The day you make the stock:** Wrap the pig's foot in several layers of cheesecloth and tie tightly with kitchen twine at 2-inch intervals.

3. Add the chicken to a pressure cooker or stockpot, along with a 1-inch piece of the ginger and the cloves from the head of garlic. Put the wrapped pig's foot on top.

4. Add the remaining 10½ cups (2.5 liters) water to the cooker. Do not exceed the maximum fill line. If using a stockpot, you may need to add water to cover the contents.

5. **If using a pressure cooker:** Seal the lid and bring to high pressure. (If using a stovetop pressure cooker, bring it to pressure over medium-high heat.) Cook at pressure for 2 hours, then turn off the heat and allow the pressure cooker to depressurize naturally. Remove the lid and set aside.

6. **If using a stockpot:** Bring the contents of the pot to a boil over high heat, then reduce the heat to low/medium-low to maintain a weak simmer, with small bubbles regularly rising to the surface of the liquid (about 206°F/96°C), and cook for 7 hours.

7. Remove the pig's foot and reserve for another use, such as the terrine (page 292), or discard. Add the remaining ginger and garlic cloves, along with the onion and scallions, to the pot. Layer the cabbage leaves over the top and cook for 30 minutes. Turn off the heat.

8. Add the kombu and soaking liquid to the pot. Using tongs or chopsticks, gently swish the kombu through the hot stock. Let steep for 30 minutes.

9. Set a half sheet pan on a wire cooling rack and set a large metal mixing bowl on top of the pan. Strain the stock through a cheesecloth-lined fine-mesh strainer into the bowl; discard the solids. Let cool to room temperature, about 1 hour, then transfer the stock to sealable storage containers and refrigerate until completely chilled, at least 4 hours.

10. Spoon the solidified fat off the top of the stock and reserve for another use or discard.

NIBO TARE

YIELD: About 1¾ cups (400 ml)

SOAKING TIME: 6 to 12 hours

TOTAL COOK TIME: 10 minutes

ACTIVE TIME: 15 minutes

- 1½ cups (350 ml) koikuchi soy sauce, divided
- 0.35 ounce (10 g) niboshi
- A 3-inch square of kombu (6 g)
- 1 dried shiitake mushroom (3 g)
- 1 cup (240 ml) sake
- 0.2 ounce (6 g) katsuobushi
- 2 tablespoons (30 ml) mirin
- 2 tablespoons (30 ml) fish sauce
- 3 tablespoons (27 g) Diamond Crystal kosher salt
- 1 tablespoon plus 1 teaspoon (20 ml) oyster sauce
- 1 tablespoon (10 g) sugar

1. Combine 1 cup (240 ml) of the soy sauce, the niboshi, kombu, and shiitake in a resealable container and refrigerate for at least 6 hours, preferably overnight (12 hours).

2. Turn on your hood vent if you have one. Add the sake to a small saucepan and bring to a boil over high heat. Reduce the heat to medium-high and, using a long match or a kitchen lighter, carefully ignite the area above the boiling liquid, and cook until the flame dies down completely, 1 to 2 minutes.

3. Shake the container of soy sauce mixture several times, then transfer it to the saucepan. Cook until faint bubbles start to form around the edges of the pan (140° to 150°F/60° to 65°C), about 3 minutes. Remove the kombu; reserve for another use or discard.

4. Continue heating the mixture until it is steaming hot and bubbles have formed all around the edges of the pan (185°F/85°C). Shut off the heat, add the katsuobushi, and let the mixture steep for 3 minutes.

5. Strain the mixture into a small metal mixing bowl. Add the remaining ½ cup (110 ml) soy sauce, the mirin, fish sauce, salt, oyster sauce, and sugar and stir until the salt is dissolved, about 1 minute. Transfer to a sealable container and refrigerate until ready to use.

NIBO OIL

YIELD: About 1½ cups (350 ml)

TOTAL COOK TIME: 10 minutes

ACTIVE TIME: 15 minutes

1⅔ cups (400 ml) neutral oil

1 ounce (30 g) niboshi, torn by hand or clipped with scissors into small pieces

3 bunches scallions (180 g), thinly sliced

1. Combine the oil and niboshi in a 3-quart saucier and heat over medium-high heat until it registers 300°F (148°C) on an instant-read thermometer.

2. Add the scallions a handful at a time, pausing if the oil begins to foam up precipitously. Cook until the scallions smell sweet and just start to take on a brown color, about 8 minutes.

3. Pour the oil through a fine-mesh strainer into a medium metal mixing bowl. (If desired, reserve the solids for Dirty Paste, page 287.) Let the oil cool to room temperature, then transfer to a sealable container and refrigerate.

35%-HYDRATION TAPIOCA NOODLES

COOK TIME: 1 minute 50 seconds
THICKNESS: 1.3 mm (setting #6 on KitchenAid; #7 on Marcato Atlas pasta machine)

Ingredients	*Baker's percentages*	*1 serving (grams)*	*6 servings (grams)*
Bread flour	100.0%	95	570
Tapioca starch	5.3%	5	30
Potassium carbonate	1.1%	1	6
Salt	1.1%	1	6
Sodium carbonate	0.5%	0.5	3
Water	36.8%	35	210

DUCK SHOYU

THE GOAL WITH THIS RECIPE SET is to demonstrate near-total utilization of a whole duck.* The carcass, neck, and thighs are used for the stock; the skin and large pieces of fat are rendered down for the aromatic fat; the breasts and thighs are used for the toppings. The skin can be crisped up after it's been rendered and used as a kind of crunchy garnish for the ramen—or you can do what I do and eat it while sitting on the couch at 11 p.m.

You need a whole Pekin duck. You can buy Pekin ducks at any large Chinese grocery store, and these will likely be sold with head and feet attached (throw them in the stockpot too). You can sometimes find frozen Pekin ducks at the grocery store.

The tare is unorthodox, because it contains whole dried spices and Chinkiang vinegar. This flavor profile is heavily indebted to Chinese-style noodle soups.

For the fat component, I use the gently rendered duck fat, with no added flavors, and two herb oils (you can use one or both of the oils, or skip them entirely). Using lower temperatures to render the fat gives it just a few "brown," roasted flavor notes, and consequently, it tastes "clean." The herb oils are very aromatic, so a little has a big impact. The two oils work well in ramen made with emulsified stocks, such as Tori Paitan (page 223), particularly when paired with the Roasted Fennel Pollen Belly Chashu (page 277); their fresh aroma helps lighten the heaviness of stocks that have a lot of fat.

The noodles contain a small amount of whole wheat flour, which speckles them in an appealing way; tapioca starch; and egg white to improve the chew of the starch gel.

The suggested toppings for this bowl are sous-vide duck breasts and duck wontons made with the duck's thigh meat. The breasts are transformed through salt, pressure, and time into cylinders that, when sliced, are attractive and easy to eat. A duck breast has an artery that runs through its center; either remove the artery or express any liquid it contains by pushing down and out. If you are unfamiliar with sous vide, see page 132.

You need ground duck thighs for the wontons, which will be difficult to find unless you grind them yourself. To do so, refer to the instructions for grinding meat (page 133).

* The liver and heart aren't used here, but I've included a recipe for them on page 295.

RECIPE CONTINUES →

DUCK SHOYU

continued

For each bowl of ramen, you need:

350 ml (1½ cups) Duck Stock (page 196)

1 serving 40%-Hydration Noodles with Whole Wheat and Tapioca (page 203)

3 Duck Wontons (page 197)

2 tablespoons (30 ml) Duck Tare (page 198)

2 tablespoons (30 ml) Duck Fat (page 199)

Pinch of white pepper

Salt if needed

2 slices Sous-Vide Duck Breast (page 200)

Other toppings as desired

¼ teaspoon Marjoram Oil or Thyme Oil page 201, or a combination (optional)

Thinly sliced scallions or naga negi

Duck Fat Cracklings (page 202)

As with any ramen, you can make this as a double soup by combining the duck stock with an Ichiban Dashi (page 269), which will yield a more aromatic soup that has less body. If you'd like to try it, use a ratio of 1 part ichiban dashi to 4 parts duck stock, as the duck stock has a relatively low amount of gelatin.

Recommended additional toppings include Blanched Spinach (page 290), Charred Scallion Whites (page 291), and Super Simple Ajitama (page 284).

1. Bring the noodle cooking water to a boil. Bring the soup stock to a simmer.

2. Add the noodles and wontons to the cooking water and set a timer for 2 minutes. Bring the stock to a boil.

3. Add the tare, duck fat, and white pepper to a warmed serving bowl. Pour in the boiling stock. Taste and add salt if necessary.

4. Drain the cooked noodles thoroughly and add to the bowl. Using chopsticks, loosen the noodles and fold them once or twice over themselves to distribute the soup seasoning and form a platform for the toppings.

5. Top with the duck breast, wontons, and any other toppings. If using herb oil, sprinkle it (them) around the perimeter of the bowl. Top with sliced scallions or naga negi and the duck cracklings and serve.

charred scallion whites, blanched spinach
Duck shoyu: duck chintan, duck shoyu tare, duck fat, marjoram oil, thyme oil
duck wontons
40%-hydration whole wheat-tapioca noodles
sous-vide duck breast, duck cracklings

DUCK STOCK

YIELD: About 2.6 quarts (2.5 liters)

SOAKING TIME: 6 to 12 hours

TOTAL COOK TIME: About 9 hours

ACTIVE TIME: 15 minutes

A 3-inch square of kombu (6 g), cut into 2 to 4 pieces

2 dried shiitake mushrooms (about 4 g)

2.9 quarts (2.7 liters) water, divided

Carcass, neck, wings, and skinless drumsticks from 1 whole Pekin duck

A 2-inch piece of ginger, peeled and sliced

6 garlic cloves, peeled and smashed

8 scallions

1. **For the kombu dashi:** Combine 1 cup (240 ml) of the water, the kombu, and dried shiitake in a sealable container. Refrigerate for at least 6 hours, preferably overnight (12 hours).

2. **For the duck stock:** Combine the duck parts, the remaining 10½ cups (2.5 liters) water, ginger, garlic, and scallions in a stockpot or tall-sided pot and bring to a boil over high heat, about 15 minutes. Reduce the heat to a low simmer (about 205°F/96°C) and cook, without skimming, for 8 hours. Turn off the heat.

3. Remove the kombu dashi from the refrigerator, give the container a vigorous shake, and pour the contents into the stockpot. Using tongs or chopsticks, gently swish the kombu leaves through the stock several times. Let the stock steep for 30 minutes.

4. Set a half sheet pan on a wire cooling rack and and set a large metal mixing bowl on top of the sheet pan. Strain the stock through a cheesecloth-lined fine-mesh strainer into the bowl; discard the solids. Let the stock cool for 1 hour, then transfer to sealable storage containers and refrigerate until chilled, at least 4 hours.

5. Once the stock has chilled, use a clean spoon to scrape off any fat that has congealed on the surface; discard, or reserve for use in an aromatic fat.

DUCK WONTONS

YIELD: About 40 wontons

TOTAL COOK TIME: 3 to 5 minutes

ACTIVE TIME: 1 hour

2 boneless, skinless duck thighs from a whole Pekin duck, ground or minced (about 130 g)

3 scallions (30 g), thinly sliced

1 teaspoon (5 ml) Duck Tare (page 198)

1 teaspoon (3 g) Diamond Crystal kosher salt

½ teaspoon (1.5 g) sugar

Pinch of white pepper

Cornstarch for dusting

About 40 wonton skins

1. In a medium mixing bowl, combine the ground duck, scallions, tare, salt, sugar, and white pepper and, using clean hands, mix thoroughly, about 2 minutes.

2. Place a grape-sized ball of the meat mixture on a plate and microwave for 15 seconds on high, or fry in a small nonstick pan over medium heat, turning once, until cooked through, about 2 minutes. Taste and adjust the seasoning if necessary; it should be a little saltier than you'd like.

3. Cover the mixture and refrigerate for at least 6 hours, preferably overnight (12 hours). Alternatively, you can proceed immediately to step 4.

4. Set up your wonton-shaping station: Dust a half sheet pan with a layer of cornstarch; fill a small ramekin with cold water; and set out your wonton skins and the filling. If you have refrigerated the filling, use a spoon to give it a good stir.

5. Place a teaspoon of filling in the center of a wonton skin, wet its edges with water, and fold it into a wonton, making sure to incorporate as little air as possible. Press the edges together to seal. Place the wonton on the prepared sheet pan and turn to coat with starch. Repeat with the remaining wonton skins and filling.

6. Transfer the sheet pan to the freezer and freeze until the wontons are frozen solid, about 4 hours. Transfer the wontons to a zip-top freezer bag and freeze until ready to use.

7. To cook the wontons, bring a large pot of water to a boil over high heat. Add the wontons and cook until the skins are fully tender and the filling is cooked through, 3 to 5 minutes. Drain the wontons before adding to the ramen.

DUCK TARE

YIELD: About 2½ cups (600 ml)

SOAKING TIME: 6 to 12 hours

TOTAL COOK TIME: 20 minutes

ACTIVE TIME: 20 minutes

1⅔ cups (400 ml) soy sauce, divided

1 dried shiitake mushroom (4 g)

A 4-inch square of kombu (8 g)

1 star anise pod

1 black cardamom pod

5 dried chilies (such as er jing tiao)

1 tablespoon (3 g) Sichuan peppercorns

½ teaspoon (1.5 g) white peppercorns

½ teaspoon (1.5 g) black peppercorns

1 cup (240 ml) sake

3 garlic cloves, peeled, crushed, and sliced

A 1-inch piece of ginger, peeled and sliced

1 bay leaf

3 tablespoons (45 ml) Chinkiang black vinegar

0.2 ounce (6 g) katsuobushi

2 tablespoons (30 ml) mirin

1 tablespoon plus 1 teaspoon (20 ml) oyster sauce

2 teaspoons (10 ml) fish sauce

1 tablespoon plus 2 teaspoons (15 g) Diamond Crystal kosher salt

1 tablespoon (10 g) sugar

1. Combine 1 cup (240 ml) of the soy sauce, the kombu, and shiitake in a sealable container. Refrigerate for at least 6 hours, preferably overnight (12 hours).

2. When you are ready to make the tare, heat the star anise, black cardamom, dried chilies, Sichuan peppercorns, white peppercorns, and black peppercorns in a small skillet over medium heat, tossing constantly, until quite fragrant, about 5 minutes. If the spices seem like they are threatening to burn at any time, lower the heat. Set aside.

3. In a small saucepan, combine the sake, garlic, and ginger and bring the mixture to a boil over high heat. Lower the heat to medium-high to maintain a steady boil and, using a kitchen lighter or a long match, carefully ignite the air just above the boiling sake and continue to boil until the flame goes out, about 2 minutes.

4. Add the toasted spices, bay leaf, and black vinegar to the pan and heat to a simmer. Lower the heat to medium-low and simmer for 5 minutes.

5. Remove the soy sauce mixture from the refrigerator and give the container a vigorous shake, then pour the mixture into the saucepan. Using tongs or chopsticks, swish the kombu leaves around in the liquid. Heat the liquid until small bubbles form on the surface (140° to 150°F/60° to 65°C), then remove the kombu; reserve for another use or discard.

6. Continue heating the liquid until small bubbles form around the edges of the pan (about 185°F/85°C). Add the katsuobushi, pushing down on the flakes to ensure they're submerged, and shut off the heat. Let the mixture steep for 5 minutes.

7. Pour the mixture through a fine-mesh sieve into a small mixing bowl; discard the solids. While the mixture is still hot, add the remaining ⅔ cup (160 ml) soy sauce, the mirin, oyster sauce, fish sauce, salt, and sugar and stir until the salt and sugar are dissolved. Let cool, then transfer to a sealable container and refrigerate until ready to use.

DUCK FAT

YIELD: About 1 cup (240 ml)

TOTAL COOK TIME: 3 hours

ACTIVE TIME: 10 minutes

Fat and skin from 1 whole Pekin duck, cut into 1-inch pieces

1 cup (240 ml) water

1. Combine the fat and skin and water in a saucepan, bring to a boil over high heat, and cook until the skin pieces begin to fry and the water has mostly evaporated, about 12 minutes.

2. Reduce the heat to low; the fat should register 210°F (98°C) on an instant-read thermometer. Cook until most of the fat has been rendered from the skin, about 3 hours.

3. Pour the fat and skin into a fine-mesh sieve set in a medium metal bowl; reserve the skin for making cracklings. Allow the fat to cool slightly, then transfer to a sealable container. Let cool to room temperature before refrigerating.

Microwave Method

TOTAL COOK TIME: 45 minutes

ACTIVE TIME: 10 minutes

1. Place the fat and skin in a microwave-safe bowl (no need to add any water). Microwave at 30% power for 30 minutes.

2. Using a fork, stir the fat and skin; if it has formed a relatively solid mass, flip that over. Microwave at 30% power for another 15 minutes. Pour the fat through a fine-mesh sieve into a medium metal bowl; discard the solids or reserve for another use. Allow the fat to cool slightly, then transfer to a sealable container. Let cool to room temperature; refrigerate until ready to use.

SOUS-VIDE DUCK BREASTS

YIELD: 2 cooked duck breasts

CURING TIME: 40 minutes to 12 hours

TOTAL COOK TIME: 3 hours

ACTIVE TIME: 15 minutes

1 teaspoon (3 g) salt

2 duck breast halves from a whole Pekin duck, skin and fat removed, central artery removed from each breast or expressed, and breasts trimmed to relatively rectangular pieces (about 283 g total)

1. Sprinkle the salt evenly all over the breast halves. Refrigerate for at least 40 minutes, or cover and refrigerate overnight.

2. Set up a hot water bath with an immersion circulator and set the temperature to 140°F (60°C).

3. Lay a sheet of plastic wrap or a length of cheesecloth about 18 inches long by 12 inches wide on a work surface. Lay one duck breast skin side down across the bottom of the plastic wrap or cheesecloth and roll it up in the wrap or cloth to form a cylinder. Place your nondominant hand flat on the work surface to anchor the wrap or cloth and, using your dominant hand, roll the cylinder forward while simultaneously pulling the wrap or cloth taut, which will tighten the rolled breast.

4. Then roll the breast forward slightly to fully encase it in the wrap or cheesecloth. Gather up and twist the wrap/cheesecloth at either end of the cylinder in opposite directions to form a more compact cylinder. Gripping each end tightly at the base of the cylinder, roll the cylinder against the work surface in a forward motion several times, which will tighten the cylinder further. Secure the twisted ends with kitchen twine.

5. Repeat with the second breast half.

6. Place the wrapped breasts in a zip-top bag or vacuum-sealable bag and seal using the water displacement method or a vacuum sealer.

7. Place the bagged breasts in the hot water bath, making sure they are completely submerged and there is ample room for water to circulate around them. Cook for 2 hours.

8. Prepare an ice water bath. Transfer the bag to the ice bath and let the duck cool completely. Then remove the bag from the ice bath, pat dry with a kitchen towel, and refrigerate until ready to use.

9. To serve, remove the breasts from the bag and unwrap. Slice into ¼- to ½-inch-wide rounds and place on top of bowls of ramen. Alternatively, arrange the slices on a sheet pan and use a broiler or a kitchen torch to warm and lightly char the surface.

MARJORAM OIL

YIELD: Scant 1 cup (240 ml)

TOTAL COOK TIME: 4 minutes

ACTIVE TIME: 4 minutes

1 cup (240 ml) neutral oil

A large bunch of marjoram (50 g), stems and all, roughly chopped if particularly long

1. Place the oil in a saucepan and heat over medium-high heat until it registers 300°F (148°C) on an instant-read thermometer.

2. Add the marjoram a handful at a time, to ensure the oil doesn't boil over. Once all the marjoram has been added, stir, shut off the heat, and let sit for 2 minutes.

3. Transfer the mixture to a high-speed blender and blend on high until the herbs and stems are completely pulverized, about 2 minutes. Strain the oil through a cheesecloth-lined fine-mesh sieve into a small metal mixing bowl; discard the solids. Let cool to room temperature.

4. Transfer the oil to a sealable container and refrigerate until ready to use.

THYME OIL

YIELD: A little less than ½ cup (120 ml)

TOTAL COOK TIME: 5 minutes

ACTIVE TIME: 5 minutes

½ cup (120 ml) neutral oil oil

A large bunch thyme (28 g), stems and all

1. Place the oil in a saucepan and heat over medium-high heat until it registers 300°F (148°C) on an instant-read thermometer.

2. Add the thyme a handful at a time, to ensure the oil doesn't boil over. Once all the thyme has been added, stir, shut off the heat, and let sit for 2 minutes.

3. Transfer the mixture to a high-speed blender and blend on high until the herbs and stems are completely pulverized, about 2 minutes. Strain the oil through a cheesecloth-lined fine-mesh sieve into a small metal mixing bowl; discard the solids. Let cool to room temperature.

4. Transfer the oil to a sealable container and refrigerate until ready to use.

DUCK FAT CRACKLINGS

YIELD: About ½ cup

TOTAL COOK TIME: 30 minutes

ACTIVE TIME: 10 minutes

2 teaspoons neutral oil or duck fat

Skin pieces left from rendering duck fat

Salt to taste

1. Adjust a rack to the middle position and preheat the oven to 400°F (200°C). Grease a quarter sheet pan lightly with the oil or duck fat, using your hands to spread it evenly. Spread the duck skin pieces out on the sheet and place it in the oven. Bake until the skin bits are very crispy, about 30 minutes, scraping up the pieces and turning them over with a slotted turner once halfway through cooking.

2. Remove the cracklings from the oven and immediately season with salt, then transfer to a plate lined with paper towels. The cracklings can be further seasoned with any spice mix you like: za'atar, shichimi togarashi, chaat masala, and so on.

40%-HYDRATION WHOLE WHEAT/TAPIOCA NOODLES

COOK TIME: 2 minutes
THICKNESS: 1.3 mm (setting #6 on KitchenAid, #7 on Marcato Atlas pasta machine)

Ingredients	*Baker's percentages*	*1 serving (grams)*	*6 servings (grams)*
Bread flour	100.0%	78	468
Whole wheat flour	12.8%	10	60
Tapioca starch	12.8%	10	60
Egg white powder	2.6%	2	12
Salt	1.3%	1	6
Potassium carbonate	0.6%	0.5	3
Sodium carbonate	0.6%	0.5	3
Water	51.3%	40	240

seared salt-cured sea bass fillet, naga negi
black sea bass chintan,
usukuchi shoyu tare,
ginger-scallion oil
wakame
38%-hydration
tapioca noodles
fish tail meatballs

FRESH FISH SHOYU

IF YOU REGULARLY PURCHASE (or catch) whole roundfish and fillet them yourself, this recipe set should be straightforward—and welcome: it's a great way to use fish carcasses.

Buy the freshest whole fish possible, and ask your fishmonger to fillet and gut it if you don't want to do that yourself. If your best bet for getting a whole fish is by ordering it online, you will need to fillet it (see page 103 for instructions). You can use the fish fillets as toppings for this ramen or for another meal.

The tare is meant to be light, in both color and flavor. Since it is relatively simple, using high-quality soy sauce is important (see page 56).

The bright ginger-scallion oil is particularly good with fish stock. Refined coconut oil has a thicker mouthfeel than neutral plant-derived oils.

The noodles are thin, slippery, and light enough to match the lightness of the stock, tare, and oil.

For each bowl of ramen, you need:

350 ml (1½ cups) Fresh Fish Stock (page 206)

1 serving 38%-Hydration Tapioca Noodles (page 211)

2 tablespoons (30 ml) Usukuchi Shoyu Tare (page 207)

1 tablespoon (30 ml) Aromatic Lard (page 274)

Pinch of white pepper

Salt if needed

2 slices Seared Salt-Cured Fish Fillets (page 209)

2 Fish Tail Meatballs (page 210)

Wakame (page 296)

1 tablespoon (30 ml) Ginger-Scallion Oil (page 208)

Thinly sliced scallions or naga negi

1. Bring the noodle cooking water to a boil. Bring the soup stock to a simmer.

2. Add the noodles to the cooking water and set a timer for 1 minute 30 seconds. Bring the stock to a boil.

3. Add the tare, lard, and white pepper to a warmed serving bowl. Pour in the boiling stock. Taste and add salt if necessary.

4. Once the noodles are cooked, drain thoroughly and add to the bowl. Using chopsticks, loosen the noodles and fold them once or twice over themselves to distribute the seasoning and form a platform for the toppings.

5. Top the noodles with the seared fish, meatballs, and wakame. Drizzle the ginger scallion oil around the perimeter of the bowl. Top with sliced scallions or naga negi and serve.

FRESH FISH STOCK

YIELD: About 2 quarts (1.9 liters)

SOAKING TIME: 6 to 12 hours

TOTAL COOK TIME: 2 hours

ACTIVE TIME: 10 minutes

2¼ quarts (2.1 liters) water, divided

A 2-inch square of kombu (2 g)

Carcasses from 2 medium black sea bass or red snapper (about 2 pounds; 900 g), with the skin and other trimmings from filleting

4 scallions, cut into 2-inch lengths

A 2-inch piece of ginger, peeled and sliced into coins

1 garlic clove, peeled and smashed

1. **For the kombu dashi:** In a sealable container, combine 1 cup (240 ml) of the water and the kombu. Refrigerate for at least 6 hours, preferably overnight (12 hours).

2. **For the stock:** Remove the dashi from the refrigerator, give the container a vigorous shake, and pour the dashi into a medium metal mixing bowl. Remove the kombu; reserve for another use or discard. Add the remaining 2 quarts (1.9 liters) water, the fish carcasses and trimmings, scallions, ginger, and garlic to the bowl, making sure the carcasses are completely submerged; if necessary, snap the spines and press the carcasses down to submerge them.

3. In a 3-quart saucier or saucepan, bring about 1½ quarts (1.4 liters) water to a boil over high heat. Place the bowl with the stock ingredients over the pan, making sure that the bottom of the bowl is not touching the boiling water, and cover the bowl with a tight-fitting lid. Cook until steam begins to escape from under the lid, about 15 minutes; the stock liquid should read exactly 206°F (97°C) on an instant-read thermometer.

4. Reduce the heat to medium-low and cook undisturbed for 2 hours. Using oven mitts, remove the bowl from the saucier and let the stock cool slightly, about 15 minutes.

5. Set a half sheet pan on a wire cooling rack and set a large metal mixing bowl on top of the sheet pan. Strain the stock through a cheesecloth-lined fine-mesh sieve into the bowl; discard the solids. Allow the stock to cool to room temperature, about 1 hour, then transfer to sealable storage containers and refrigerate until ready to use.

USUKUCHI SHOYU TARE

YIELD: About 2 cups (480 ml)

SOAKING TIME: 6 to 12 hours

TOTAL COOK TIME: 10 minutes

ACTIVE TIME: 10 minutes

1⅓ cups (300 ml) koikuchi soy sauce, divided

⅔ cup (160 ml) usukuchi soy sauce

1 dried shiitake mushroom (3 g)

A 2-inch square of kombu (2 g)

½ cup (120 ml) sake

0.2 ounce (6 g) katsuobushi

3 tablespoons plus 1 teaspoon (50 ml) mirin

2 tablespoons plus 2 teaspoons (40 ml) fish sauce

1 tablespoon plus 2 teaspoons (15 g) Diamond Crystal kosher salt

1. Combine ⅓ cup (60 ml) of the koikuchi soy sauce, the usukuchi, shiitake, and kombu in a sealable container. Refrigerate for at least 6 hours, preferably overnight (12 hours).

2. In a small saucepan, bring the sake to boil over medium-high heat. Turn on the oven vent and, using a long match or kitchen lighter, carefully ignite the area above the boiling sake. Cook until the flames die out, about 2 minutes.

3. Remove the container with the soy sauce mixture from the refrigerator and give it a vigorous shake. Add the contents to the saucepan and cook until small bubbles begin to form on the surface (140° to 150°F/60° to 65°C). Remove and discard the kombu and continue cooking until small bubbles form around the edges of the pan (about 185°F/85°C), about 1 minute. Add the katsuobushi, shut off the heat, and let steep for 3 minutes.

4. Strain the tare through a cheesecloth-lined fine-mesh sieve into a small metal mixing bowl. Add the remaining 1 cup (240 ml) koikuchi soy sauce, the mirin, fish sauce, and salt, and stir until the salt is dissolved. Transfer to a sealable container and refrigerate until ready to use.

GINGER-SCALLION OIL

YIELD: 1 cup (240 ml)

TOTAL COOK TIME: 8 minutes

ACTIVE TIME: 8 minutes

1 cup (240 ml) refined coconut oil

A 6-inch piece of ginger, grated

1 bunch scallions, finely sliced

1. Combine the coconut oil, ginger, and scallions in a 2-quart saucepan and heat over medium-high heat, stirring occasionally, until the mixture begins to sizzle, about 3 minutes. Then, stirring constantly, cook until the ginger and garlic start to take on color, about 5 minutes.

2. Pour the mixture through a fine-mesh strainer set over a small mixing bowl; the fried ginger and scallions can be reserved for another use or discarded. Let the oil cool to room temperature, then transfer to a sealable container. Store in the refrigerator or freezer until ready to use.

SEARED SALT-CURED FISH FILLETS

YIELD: 4 to 8 servings as a ramen topping, 4 servings as part of a larger meal with rice

CURING TIME: 6 to 24 hours

TOTAL COOK TIME: 7 minutes

ACTIVE TIME: 15 minutes

4 skin-on fillets of black sea bass or red snapper, pinbones removed, final 2 to 3 inches of tail meat removed and reserved for Fish Tail Meatballs (below) (about 12 ounces; 350 g)

2 teaspoons (6 g) Diamond Crystal kosher salt

1 tablespoon (15 ml) neutral oil

1. With a sharp knife, score the skin on each fish fillet several times using parallel, crosswise cuts; try not to pierce the flesh.

2. Place the fillets flesh side up on a half sheet pan in a single layer. Sprinkle half the salt evenly over the flesh. Flip the fillets over and sprinkle evenly with the remaining salt.

3. Wrap the sheet pan in plastic wrap and refrigerate for at least 6 hours, and up to 24 hours (the fillets will be noticeably saltier if left to cure for longer than 6 hours).

4. Heat the oil in a 10-inch cast-iron skillet over medium heat until shimmering. Place one fillet skin side down in the hot oil and immediately press down gently but firmly on it, to ensure that the skin is in full contact with the surface of the pan and to prevent the skin from curling, for at least 30 seconds and up to 1 minute. Repeat with a second fillet. Cook undisturbed until the skin is crisp and the fillets are mostly cooked through (the flesh side will be pale save for a raw area right at the top), about 5 minutes. Using a fish spatula, carefully turn the fillets over and cook for about 30 seconds. Remove the fillets to a plate, skin side up, and repeat with the remaining 2 fillets.

5. If using the fish for ramen, using a sharp knife, slice the fillets crosswise into 1-inch-wide pieces and place atop ramen. If eating the fillets as part of a larger meal, serve immediately, skin side up.

NOTE: The cured fillets can also be broiled or grilled using similar cooking times; the skin will be less crisp.

FISH TAIL MEATBALLS

YIELD: 4 servings as a ramen topping

TOTAL COOK TIME: 1 hour

ACTIVE TIME: 15 minutes

Reserved tail portions from the black sea bass or red snapper fillets (from page 209), skin removed (about 6½ ounces; 200 g)

2 teaspoons (6 g) Diamond Crystal kosher salt, divided

2 scallions, white parts finely minced, green parts reserved for another use or discarded

1 garlic clove, minced

½ teaspoon koikuchi soy sauce

1½ cups (360 ml) Fresh Fish Stock (page 206), Niban Dashi (page 269), or water for poaching

1. Place the fish on a quarter sheet pan or a plate and sprinkle evenly with 1 teaspoon of the salt. Refrigerate for at least 45 minutes (or cover the fish with plastic wrap and refrigerate overnight).

2. Remove the fish from the refrigerator and slice each piece crosswise into ¼-inch-wide strips. Line up as many strips as you can comfortably manage and slice them crosswise as thin as possible; repeat with the remaining fish. Gather the diced fish together and, using a rocking motion with the knife, finely chop (larger pieces will yield a more tender meatball, smaller pieces will yield a denser meatball).

3. In a small mixing bowl, combine the fish with the scallions, garlic, the remaining 1 teaspoon salt, and the soy sauce. Using clean hands, thoroughly mix the ingredients until the mixture becomes slightly tacky, about 1 minute.

4. Bring the stock, dashi, or water to a boil over high heat in a small saucepan; reduce the heat to medium to maintain a steady simmer. Using wet hands, compress the fish mixture into meatballs about 1 inch in diameter and drop into the simmering liquid, working in batches if necessary to avoid overcrowding the pan. Cook until the meatballs turn white and float, 2 to 3 minutes. Using tongs or a fine-mesh skimmer spoon, remove the meatballs to a plate and reserve until ready to use.

NOTE: The stock or dashi can be strained after poaching the meatballs and used to make ramen or for another purpose (it will be slightly cloudy).

38%-HYDRATION TAPIOCA NOODLES

COOK TIME: 1 minute 30 seconds
THICKNESS: 1 mm (setting #7 on KitchenAid; #8 on Marcato Atlas pasta machine)

Ingredients	*Baker's percentages*	*1 serving (grams)*	*6 servings (grams)*
Bread flour	100.0%	97	582
Tapioca starch	3.1%	3	18
Salt	1%	1	6
Sodium carbonate	1%	1	6
Potassium carbonate	0.3%	0.33	2
Water	39.2%	38	228

stir-fried lacinato kale, naga negi

ajitama

pan-roasted chicken thigh

semolina noodles

pan-roasted chicken breast,
chicken meatballs

roasted chicken chintan, blended
shoyu tare, aromatic chicken fat

ROASTED CHICKEN SHOYU

THE INSPIRATION FOR THIS bowl of ramen was the all-chicken ramen that's become fashionable in Japan in the last decade, a style that, in the United States among ramen heads, is referred to as "New Wave Shoyu Ramen." This name was coined by Mike Satinover, the chef and owner of Akahoshi Ramen in Chicago.

This is a roasted chicken version, and I deviate from the bare simplicity of the style by adding a turkey wing for body and an almost unplaceable gamy depth to the soup. Since this is a Western-style soup stock, I deglaze the roasting pan with wine so that all those tasty brown bits aren't wasted. I don't add a lot of vegetables, just garlic for sweetness and that mouth-filling sensation that may or may not be real: kokumi (see page 110).

The tare for this is very simple. There are no dried seafood elements. It relies instead solely on soy sauce, tamari, and mirin for its glutamates and the poultry parts and fish sauce for inosinates, and it forgoes guanylate entirely. The quality of the soy sauce you use will be important. I also add dark soy sauce for extra complexity.

Instead of roasting the whole chicken for the stock, I remove the breasts and legs for use as toppings. The breasts can be pan-roasted or cooked sous vide (pan-roasting is my recommendation and instructions are included with this set; for sous-vide instructions, see page 283). Pan-roasting will work best with smaller boneless chicken breasts, about 7 ounces (200 g) each. (Larger, thicker breasts will be difficult to cook evenly on the stovetop.) I separate the legs into thighs and drumsticks. The thighs are scored to the bone on the fleshy side to facilitate even cooking and then they, too, are pan-roasted. The legs are skinned, deboned, and the meat chopped up or ground and turned into meatballs, which are poached; the skin from the legs can just be thrown into the stockpot.

The pan-roasted breasts and thighs are at their best when served within 30 minutes of preparation (see pages 18–19).

For the fat, this bowl should use only chicken fat, either plain or infused with ginger and garlic (see page 274). The fat harvested from on top of the chilled broth will not be sufficient for the number of bowls the stock can make; you will need to supplement it with more chicken fat, either purchased from a butcher or rendered yourself. (For instructions for rendering chicken fat, see page 275.)

RECIPE CONTINUES →

ROASTED CHICKEN SHOYU *continued*

For each bowl of ramen, you need:

350 ml (1½ cups) Roasted Chicken Stock (page 215)

1 serving Semolina Noodles (page 222)

2 tablespoons (30 ml) Blended Shoyu Tare (page 216) or more to taste

2 tablespoons (30 ml) Aromatic Chicken Fat (page 220) or plain chicken fat (page 275)

½ teaspoon Amazu (page 298), or more to taste

Pinch of white pepper, or to taste

Pinch of black pepper, or to taste

Salt if necessary

1 or 2 slices Pan-Roasted Chicken Breasts (page 217)

1 or 2 slices Pan-Roasted Chicken Thighs (page 218)

1 or 2 Chicken Meatballs (page 219)

Stir-Fried Lacinato Kale (page 221)

Thinly sliced scallions or naga negi

The noodles are made from semolina, a hard durum wheat flour often used for pasta, and in the recipe here, it forms a soft dough that feels more like fresh pasta dough than the typical alkaline noodle dough. It requires a little more kneading through the machine to properly develop the gluten network, but, prepared correctly, the noodles have a wonderfully bouncy texture.

To round out the bowl, I add kale that's been stir-fried and charred in a wok. Kale has an assertive flavor, heightened by the fish sauce and garlic, which allows it to stand out in an assertively flavored soup.

Recommended additional topping: Super Simple Ajitama (page 284).

1. Bring the noodle cooking water to a boil. Bring the soup stock to a simmer.

2. Add the noodles to the cooking water and set a timer for 2 minutes. Bring the stock to a boil.

3. Add the tare, fat, amazu, and white and black pepper to a warmed serving bowl. Pour in the boiling stock. Taste and add salt and/or more tare or amazu if necessary.

4. Once the noodles are cooked, drain thoroughly and add to the bowl. Using chopsticks, loosen the noodles and fold them once or twice over themselves to distribute the seasonings and form a platform for the toppings.

5. Place the chicken breast, chicken thigh, meatballs, and kale on top. Top with sliced scallions or naga negi and serve.

ROASTED CHICKEN STOCK

YIELD: About 2 quarts (1.9 liters)

TOTAL COOK TIME (PRESSURE COOKER): 2 hours 45 minutes, plus time for coming to pressure/depressurizing

TOTAL COOK TIME (STOVETOP): 8 hours 15 minutes

ACTIVE TIME: 15 minutes

1 chicken carcass, along with its neck, leg bones, and any trimmings and skin (about 1 pound; 450 grams)

1 tablespoon neutral oil or chicken fat

½ cup (120 ml) dry white wine, sake, or water

1 whole turkey wing (about 1 pound; 450 grams), separated at the joints to yield a wingtip, a flat, and a drumette

2 heads garlic, separated into cloves and peeled

2½ quarts (2.3 liters) water

1. Preheat the oven to 400°F (200°C). Place the chicken carcass, neck, and leg bones on a half sheet pan. Pour the oil evenly over the chicken parts and, using your hands, rub it all over them.

2. Place the sheet pan in the oven and roast, turning the chicken parts once, until they are deeply brown all over, about 1 hour.

3. Using tongs, transfer the chicken parts to a stockpot or a pressure cooker. Pour the rendered fat from the sheet pan into a small bowl; reserve for another use or discard. Set the sheet pan over two burners, turn the burners on to medium-high heat, and add the wine, sake, or water to the pan. Using a wooden spoon, and holding onto the hot sheet with a pot holder or oven mitt, carefully scrape up the brown bits sticking to the pan. Pour the liquid into the stockpot, and add the turkey wing and garlic cloves. Add water; if using a pressure cooker, do not exceed the maximum fill line.

4. If using a pressure cooker: Seal the pressure cooker lid and bring it up to pressure. Cook for 1 hour and 30 minutes. Let it depressurize naturally. Open the lid away from you, allowing the steam to escape. Set the lid aside.

5. If using a stockpot: Bring the liquid to a boil over high heat. Reduce the heat to medium-low to maintain a bare simmer (about 205°F/96°C) and cook for 6 hours.

6. Set a half sheet pan on a wire cooling rack and set a large metal mixing bowl on top of the pan. Strain the stock through a cheesecloth-lined fine-mesh sieve into the bowl. Let cool to room temperature, about 1 hour. Transfer to sealable containers and refrigerate until chilled, at least 4 hours.

7. Spoon off the solid fat that has risen to the top of the stock; reserve for another use or discard. Refrigerate until ready for use.

BLENDED SHOYU TARE

YIELD: 2 cups (480 ml)

ACTIVE TIME: 5 minutes

1 cup (240 ml) koikuchi soy sauce

½ cup (120 ml) tamari

⅓ cup (80 ml) mirin

1 tablespoon plus 2 teaspoons (25 ml) Chinese dark soy sauce

1 tablespoon (15 ml) fish sauce

2 tablespoons (18 g) Diamond Crystal kosher salt

Combine all the ingredients in a small bowl and whisk together until salt dissolves. Refrigerate in a sealable container.

PAN-ROASTED CHICKEN BREASTS

YIELD: 2 cooked chicken breasts

CURING TIME (OPTIONAL): 6 to 12 hours

TOTAL COOK TIME: 22 minutes

ACTIVE TIME: 15 minutes

2 skin-on, boneless chicken breast halves (about 14 ounces; 400 g)

1 teaspoon (3 g) Diamond Crystal kosher salt

1 tablespoon (15 ml) neutral oil or chicken fat

¼ teaspoon mayonnaise (optional)

1. Place the chicken breasts on a quarter sheet pan and sprinkle the salt evenly on both sides. Turn the chicken breasts skin side up and refrigerate, uncovered, for at least 6 hours, preferably overnight (12 hours). Alternatively, you can proceed immediately to step 2.

2. Heat a large cast-iron skillet over medium heat. Add the oil and swirl to coat the pan. If using, rub a thin layer of mayonnaise over the skin of both chicken breasts (mayonnaise encourages browning . . . and it's delicious). Place the breasts skin side down in the pan and place a cooking weight (see page 45) on top of them. Cook, without disturbing them, until the skin is well browned and crisp, about 6 minutes.

3. Carefully remove the weight and, using tongs, flip the breasts over. Lower the heat to medium-low and continue to cook until an instant-read thermometer inserted into the thickest part of a breast registers 150°F (65°C), about 6 minutes. Transfer the breasts to a plate, skin side up, and let rest for at least 10 minutes, then slice and serve.

PAN-ROASTED CHICKEN THIGHS

YIELD: 2 cooked chicken thighs

CURING TIME: 6 to 12 hours

TOTAL COOK TIME: 19 minutes

ACTIVE TIME: 10 minutes

- 2 skin-on chicken thighs (about 12 ounces; 340 g), butterflied to reveal the central bone on the flesh side (see page 80)
- ½ teaspoon (1.5 g) Diamond Crystal kosher salt
- 1 tablespoon (15 ml) neutral oil or chicken fat
- ¼ teaspoon mayonnaise (optional)

1. Place the chicken thighs on a quarter sheet pan and sprinkle evenly on both sides with the salt. Turn the thighs skin side up and refrigerate, uncovered, for at least 6 hours, preferably overnight (12 hours). Alternatively, you can proceed immediately to step 2.

2. Heat a large cast-iron skillet over medium heat. Add the oil and swirl to coat the pan. If using, rub a thin layer of mayonnaise over the skin of both chicken thighs. Place the thighs skin side down in the pan and place a cooking weight on top of them. Cook, without disturbing them, until the skin is well browned and crisp, about 6 minutes.

3. Carefully remove the weight and, using tongs, flip the thighs over. Lower the heat to medium-low and continue to cook until an instant-read thermometer inserted into the thickest part of a thigh registers 160°F (71°C), about 3 minutes. Transfer the thighs to a plate, skin side up, and let rest for at least 10 minutes. Remove the central bone from each thigh, then slice them crosswise and serve.

CHICKEN MEATBALLS

YIELD: About 10 meatballs

TOTAL COOK TIME: 30 minutes

ACTIVE TIME: 10 minutes

2 boneless, skinless chicken drumsticks (6 ounces; 170 g)

4 scallions, white parts minced, green parts thinly sliced

A ½-inch piece of ginger, grated

1 garlic clove, minced

1 teaspoon (5 ml) Blended Shoyu Tare (page 216)

1 teaspoon (3 g) Diamond Crystal kosher salt

½ teaspoon (1.5 g) sugar

Pinch of white pepper

1½ cups (360 ml) Roasted Chicken Stock (page 215), Niban Dashi (page 269), or water

1. Place the drumsticks on an eighth sheet pan or plate and freeze until firm but not frozen, about 10 minutes.

2. Remove the drumsticks from the freezer and, using a sharp knife, slice them crosswise into ½-inch-wide strips.

3. If using a meat grinder: Grind the meat through the coarsest plate, then run the ground meat through the grinder again.

4. If using a food processor: Cut the chicken strips into ½-inch cubes, return to the sheet pan or plate, arranged in a single layer, and freeze until firmed up but not frozen, about 5 minutes. Place the chicken in the food processor and pulse (do not process) until a coarse-ground texture is achieved, about 10 times.

5. If mincing by hand: Return the chicken strips to the sheet pan or plate, arranged in a single layer, and freeze until firm but not frozen, about 5 minutes. Group together as many strips as you can reasonably manage and slice them crosswise as thin as possible; repeat with the remaining strips. Gather the pieces of chicken into an even pile and, using a rocking motion with your knife, mince the chicken to a coarse ground-meat texture.

6. Combine the chicken with the remaining ingredients and, using clean hands, mix thoroughly until the mixture becomes tacky, 1 to 2 minutes. Set aside.

7. Bring the stock, dashi, or water to a boil in a 2-quart saucepan over high heat, then reduce the heat to medium to maintain a steady simmer. Form the meat mixture into balls about 1 inch in diameter and, working in two batches, drop them into the simmering water. Cook until the meatballs are entirely pale on the exterior, float, and are cooked; an instant-read thermometer inserted into the center of a meatball should read 150°F (65°). Using tongs, chopsticks, or a fine-mesh skimmer spoon, remove the meatballs and serve immediately.

AROMATIC CHICKEN FAT

YIELD: About 1½ cups (360 ml)

TOTAL COOK TIME: 1 hour

ACTIVE TIME: 5 minutes

- 2 cups (480 ml) rendered chicken fat (page 275)
- 1 white onion, three-quarters roughly chopped, one-quarter minced, divided
- 2 heads garlic, separated into cloves, peeled, and smashed, plus 2 garlic cloves, peeled and minced, divided

1. Combine the chicken fat, chopped onion, and whole garlic cloves in a 2-quart saucepan and heat over medium-high heat until the vegetables start bubbling. Reduce the heat to medium-low (an instant-read thermometer inserted into the oil should read about 210°F/98°C) and cook, stirring occasionally, for 45 minutes.

2. Increase the heat to medium and cook until the vegetables begin to fry and take on a bit of color (the temperature of the oil should rise above 212°F/100°C). Add the minced garlic and onion and cook, stirring frequently, until they begin to take on a golden coloring.

3. Set a half sheet pan on a wire cooling rack and set a medium metal mixing bowl on top of the pan. Strain the fat through a cheesecloth-lined fine-mesh sieve into the bowl. Allow to cool to room temperature, about 1 hour, then transfer to a sealable container and refrigerate.

STIR-FRIED LACINATO KALE

YIELD: 4 servings

TOTAL COOK TIME: 5 minutes

ACTIVE TIME: 5 minutes

1 tablespoon (15 ml) neutral oil, lard, Aromatic Chicken Fat (page 220), or regular chicken fat (page 275)

1 bunch lacinato kale, tougher lower ribs removed, leaves sliced crosswise into 1-inch-wide strips

1 garlic clove, sliced

2 teaspoons (10 ml) fish sauce

Black pepper to taste

Juice of half a lemon

1. Heat a carbon steel wok or 12-inch cast-iron pan over high heat until smoking. Add the oil or fat, swirl to coat the pan, and immediately add the kale. Toss the kale to coat it in the hot oil and then, using a wok spatula, spread out the kale for maximum contact between it and the pan, Cook, undisturbed, until you start to smell the kale charring, 1 to 2 minutes.

2. Toss the kale, spread out once again, and cook, undisturbed, for another 1 to 2 minutes. The kale should be dark green and charred in spots.

3. Add the garlic, toss to distribute it, and cook until fragrant, about 30 seconds. Pour in the fish sauce around the edges of the pan (it should sizzle) and toss the kale and garlic thoroughly to coat. Turn off the heat. Season the kale with pepper and the lemon juice, stir to combine, and transfer to a plate.

SEMOLINA RAMEN

COOK TIME: 2 minutes
THICKNESS: 1.5 mm (setting #5 on KitchenAid, #6 on Marcato Atlas pasta machine)

Ingredients	*Baker's percentages*	*1 serving (grams)*	*8 servings (grams)*
Semolina flour	100.0%	100	800
Salt	1.0%	1	8
Potassium carbonate	0.8%	0.75	6
Sodium carbonate	0.8%	0.75	6
Water	45.0%	45	360

TORI PAITAN

THIS IS AN EMULSIFIED chicken stock-based ramen. An emulsified stock is more labor-intensive than a clear stock because it requires blending the bones with an immersion blender and passing the chicken stock/bone sludge through a fine-mesh sieve, pressing on the solids rather forcefully to express as much liquid as possible. I add a potato to release its starch into the stock, which will assist with the emulsification process, and then I steep vegetables and kombu in the stock before straining.

The stock will "break" as it sits in the refrigerator, separating into three distinct layers: a sludgy bottom layer with sediment, a middle milky layer of stock, and a cap of fat. You can re-emulsify the stock by transferring it to a pot and boiling it briefly. To make a stronger emulsion, stick an immersion blender into the hot stock and pulse several times. For an even stronger emulsion that will look pale and milky, transfer 2 cups (480 ml) of the hot stock to a countertop blender and blend on high for a minute, then pour the blended stock back into the pot and stir it in: you will immediately see the stock lighten in color. (Whichever method you use, the stock will separate again if left to sit undisturbed.)

Recommended toppings: Roasted Fennel Pollen Belly Chashu (page 279), Thyme Oil (page 201), and Super Simple Ajitama (page 284).

RECIPE CONTINUES →

TORI PAITAN

continued

For each bowl of ramen, you need:

350 ml (1½ cups) Tori Paitan Stock (page 226)

1 serving 35%-Hydration Tapioca Noodles (page 192)

2 tablespoons (30 ml) shoyu tare (any one will do), or more to taste

1 tablespoon (15 ml) Aromatic Chicken Fat (page 220)

½ teaspoon Amazu (page 298), or more to taste

Pinch of white pepper, or to taste

Salt if necessary

Other toppings as desired (see headnote)

Thinly sliced scallions or naga negi

1. Bring the noodle cooking water to a boil. Bring the soup stock to a simmer.

2. Add the noodles to the cooking water and set the timer for 2 minutes. Bring the stock to a boil.

3. Add the tare, fat, amazu, and white pepper to a warmed serving bowl. Pour in the boiling stock. Taste and add salt if necessary and/or more tare or amazu.

4. Once the noodles are cooked, drain thoroughly and add to the bowl. Using chopsticks, loosen the noodles and fold them once or twice over themselves to distribute the seasonings and form a platform for the toppings.

5. Add toppings as desired. Top with sliced scallions or naga negi and serve.

ajitama
Tori paitan shoyu: chicken paitan, shoyu tare, aromatic chicken fat, thyme oil, amazu
naga negi
35%-hydration noodles
roasted fennel pollen belly chashu

TORI PAITAN STOCK

YIELD: About 2 quarts (1.9 liters)

SOAKING TIME: 6 to 12 hours

TOTAL COOK TIME (PRESSURE COOKER): 3 hours, plus time for coming to pressure/depressurizing

TOTAL COOK TIME (STOVETOP): 9 hours

ACTIVE TIME: 30 minutes

A 5-inch square of kombu (10 g)

2¾ quarts (2.5 liters) water, divided

One 3- to 4-pound (1.3 to 1.8 kg) whole chicken, cut into 11 parts (drumsticks, thighs, breasts, tenders, wings, and back)

1 head garlic, separated into cloves and peeled

A 2-inch piece of ginger, peeled

1 russet potato, peeled and cut into 2-inch pieces

1 carrot, peeled and diced

1 white onion, peeled and diced

2 leeks, cleaned and thinly sliced

1 bunch scallions (6 to 9), thinly sliced

1. **For the dashi:** Combine the kombu and ½ cup (120 ml) of the water in a sealable container and refrigerate for at least 6 hours, preferably overnight (12 hours).

2. **When ready to make the stock:** Combine the chicken, garlic, ginger, potato, and the remaining 10½ cups (2.4 liters) water in a pressure cooker or stockpot.

3. **If using a pressure cooker:** Seal the pressure cooker lid, bring it up to pressure, and cook for 2 hours. Let it depressurize naturally. Open the lid away from you, allowing the steam to escape; set the lid aside.

4. **If using a stockpot:** Bring to a boil over high heat, cover, reduce the heat to low to maintain a steady simmer (about 210°F/99°C), and cook for 8 hours.

5. Using an immersion blender, pulse the stock 7 to 10 times to break up the chicken bones, Then blend it briefly to emulsify it slightly, about 1 minute.

6. Add the carrot, onion, leeks, and scallions to the stock and bring to a simmer. Shut off the heat and let the stock steep for 15 minutes.

7. Remove the dashi from the refrigerator and give the container a vigorous shake. Add the dashi to the stock and, using tongs or chopsticks, swish the kombu through the water several times. Let stand for 15 minutes, then remove the kombu; reserve for another use or discard.

8. Working in batches, strain the stock through a fine-mesh sieve into a large metal mixing bowl, pushing down on the solids to extract as much liquid as possible; discard the solids.

9. Set a half sheet pan on a wire cooling rack and set a second large metal mixing bowl on top of the pan. Strain the stock through a cheesecloth-lined strainer into the bowl. Allow to cool to room temperature, then transfer to sealable containers and refrigerate.

SHIO TANMEN

A GOOD SHIO TANMEN is challenging to make, particularly if you, like me, avoid using MSG (see page 115). As a result, the base stock must be very flavorful. Theoretically, it should need nothing more than salt to produce a decent bowl of noodle soup, so the kaleidoscope of flavors that make ramen taste good—the synergistic relationships between the glutamic, inosinic, and guanylic acids; the compounds produced by fermentation and Maillard browning; the long-cooked flavors of allium; etc.—must all be present in the stock before any seasoning is added in the form of tare, pastes, or fat.

The roasted pork and dried clam stock that serves as the base for the next three bowls of ramen is an example of one that's packed with flavor, from dried scallops, dried clams, and the Maillard browning of the roasted pork shanks.

My inspiration was a shio tanmen served at Hokuto, a mom-and-pop shop steps away from my grandmother's house in Fukushima Prefecture. Topped with a garlicky and lardy stir-fry of cabbage, bean sprouts, and wood ear mushrooms, it features hand-cut, hand-massaged noodles. To mimic them, I call for cutting the high-hydration noodles wide and thick—by hand or with a machine—so you can scrunch them together, producing noodles with a lot of textural complexity.

For some visual indication that there are clams in the soup, and because I love clams, I also call for marinated steamed clams as a topping. You can prepare the clams a day in advance, but hold on to the steaming broth; you can add a tablespoon or two of it to each bowl for extra clam flavor.

RECIPE CONTINUES →

SHIO TANMEN

continued

For each bowl of shio tanmen, you need:

350 ml (1½ cups) Roasted Pork and Dried Clam Stock (page 230)

1 serving 45%-Hydration Noodles (page 235), massaged (see page 165)

2 tablespoons (30 ml) Shio Tare (page 232)

2 tablespoons (30 ml) Aromatic Lard (page 274)

2 tablespoons (30 ml) clam broth reserved from Marinated Clams (page 233; optional)

Pinch of white pepper

Salt if necessary

1 scallion, thinly sliced

1 or 2 tongs-grips' worth of Stir-Fried Cabbage, Bean Sprouts, and Wood Ear Mushrooms (page 234)

2 or 3 Marinated Clams (page 233)

Rice vinegar for serving

1. Bring the noodle cooking water to a boil. Bring the soup stock to a simmer.

2. Add the noodles to the cooking water and set the timer for 2 minutes 30 seconds. Bring the stock to a boil.

3. Add the tare, lard, the reserved clam broth, if using, white pepper, and scallions to a warmed serving bowl. Pour in the boiling stock. Taste and add salt if necessary.

4. Once the noodles are cooked, drain thoroughly and add to the bowl. Using chopsticks, loosen the noodles and fold them once or twice over themselves to distribute the seasonings and form a platform for the toppings.

5. Top with stir-fried cabbage and arrange the clams along the perimeter of the bowl. Serve rice vinegar alongside.

Shio tanmen: pork and
clam chintan, shio tare,
aromatic lard
stir-fried cabbage
marinated clams
45%-hydration temomi
noodles, naga negi
milk-braised pork shoulder chashu

ROASTED PORK AND DRIED CLAM STOCK

YIELD: About 3 quarts (2.8 liters)

SOAKING TIME: 6 to 12 hours

TOTAL COOK TIME (PRESSURE COOKER): 6 hours 30 minutes, plus time for coming to pressure/depressurizing

TOTAL COOK TIME (STOVETOP): 11 hours 30 minutes

ACTIVE TIME: 30 minutes

3½ quarts (3.4 liters) water, divided

A 6-inch square of kombu (12 g)

½ cup (45 g) dried clams

¼ cup (28 g) dried scallops

2 dried shiitake (4 g)

2½ pounds (1.1 kg) pork shanks, cut into 2-inch sections

1 tablespoon (15 ml) neutral oil

½ cup (120 ml) sake or water

One 1-pound (450 g) pig's foot, cleaned

1 pound (450 g) ground pork

2 heads garlic cloves, peeled, half roughly chopped, half left whole

1 white onion, halved and peeled

A 6-inch piece of ginger, peeled, half sliced into thick coins, half roughly chopped

1 bay leaf

2 leeks, white parts only, cleaned and thinly sliced

1 small carrot, halved and sliced into thin half-moons

6 leaves Napa cabbage

1. **For the dashi:** Combine 2 cups (480 ml) of the water, the kombu, dried clams, dried scallops, and shiitake in a sealable container. Refrigerate for at least 6 hours, preferably overnight (12 hours).

2. **When ready to make the stock:** Preheat the oven to 400°F (200°C). Pat the pork shanks dry and place them on a half sheet pan. Drizzle with the oil and, using your hands, rub the oil all over the pork. Cook until the pork is evenly browned all over, about 1 hour and 30 minutes. Remove from the oven.

3. Using tongs, transfer the pork shanks to a pressure cooker or stockpot. Pour any rendered fat on the sheet pan into a heatproof bowl; reserve for another use or discard. Place the sheet pan over two burners, turn the burners on to medium-high heat, and add the sake or water. Using a wooden spoon, and holding onto the hot sheet pan with a pot holder or oven mitt, carefully scrape up any brown bits sticking to the pan. Pour the liquid into the pressure cooker or stockpot and add the pig's foot, ground pork, whole garlic cloves, onion, the ginger coins, and bay leaf. Add the remaining 3 quarts (2.9 liters) water; if using a pressure cooker, do not exceed the maximum fill line.

4. **If using a pressure cooker:** Using a wooden spoon, stir the contents of the pot to break up the ground pork, and try your best to push all the solid material below the surface of the water, taking care that the water does not exceed the max fill line. Seal the pressure cooker and bring up to pressure; if using a stovetop pressure cooker, bring it up to pressure over medium-high heat—using high heat can scorch the pork bones—then reduce the heat to medium-low to maintain the pressure without causing excessive venting. Cook for 2 hours, then shut off the heat and allow the pressure cooker to depressurize naturally. Open the lid of the pressure cooker and allow the steam to escape away from you; set the lid aside.

5. If using a stockpot: Bring the water to a boil over medium-high heat, then reduce the heat to medium-low to maintain a bare simmer (about 205°F/96°C), with small bubbles steadily rising to the surface. Cook for 8 hours, then turn off the heat.

6. Remove the dashi from the refrigerator and give the container a vigorous shake. Add the dashi to the pot. Using tongs or chopsticks, swish the kombu through the liquid several times, then reserve for another use or discard.

7. Add the leeks, carrot, chopped garlic, and chopped ginger and lay the cabbage leaves over the surface of the stock. Bring the stock back up to a simmer over medium-high heat, then turn off the heat and let the stock steep for 30 minutes.

8. Set a half sheet pan on a wire cooling rack and set a large metal mixing bowl on top of the pan. Strain the stock through a cheesecloth-lined fine-mesh sieve into the bowl; discard the solids. Let the stock cool to room temperature, about 1 hour, then transfer to storage containers and refrigerate until chilled.

9. Spoon off the layer of solid fat that has risen to the surface of the stock; reserve for another use or discard. Refrigerate the stock until ready to use.

SHIO TARE

YIELD: About 2 cups (240 ml)

SOAKING TIME: 6 to 12 hours

TOTAL COOK TIME: 10 minutes

ACTIVE TIME: 10 minutes

1½ cups (360 ml) water

A 5-inch square of kombu (10 g)

0.35 ounce (10 g) niboshi

0.17 ounce (5 g) dried scallops

2 dried shiitake mushrooms (6 g)

¾ cup (180 ml) sake

3 garlic cloves, peeled and thinly sliced

A ½-inch piece of ginger, thinly sliced

0.5 ounces (15 g) katsuobushi

¼ cup plus 1 tablespoon (45 g) Diamond Crystal kosher salt

1 tablespoon (9 g) sugar

2 teaspoons (6 g) black salt (see page 57)

⅔ cup (160 ml) mirin

⅓ cup (80 ml) shiro shoyu

1. Combine the water, kombu, niboshi, dried scallops, and shiitake in a sealable container and refrigerate for at least 6 hours, preferably overnight (12 hours).

2. In a small saucepan, combine the sake, garlic, and ginger and bring to a boil over medium-high heat. Turn on the vent and, using a long match or kitchen lighter, carefully ignite the area above the boiling sake; cook until the flames die out, about 2 minutes. Continue cooking until the sake has reduced to about 1 tablespoon and the bubbles forming in the liquid are quite large, 5 to 6 minutes.

3. Remove the container of dashi from the refrigerator and give it a vigorous shake. Add the dashi to the saucepan and heat over medium-high heat until small bubbles form on the surface (140° to 150°F/60° to 65°C). Remove the kombu; reserve for another use or discard. Continue cooking until the tare is barely simmering (it should be at about 185°F/85°C). Add the katsuobushi and let steep for 30 seconds.

4. Strain the tare through a cheesecloth-lined fine-mesh strainer into a bowl, pressing firmly on the solids to extract as much liquid as possible. Add the kosher salt, sugar, and black salt and whisk to dissolve. Add the mirin and shiro shoyu and stir to combine.

5. Transfer the tare to a sealable container and refrigerate until ready to use.

MARINATED CLAMS

YIELD: 24 marinated clams; 4 servings

TOTAL COOK TIME: 5 minutes

ACTIVE TIME: 5 minutes

2 garlic cloves, peeled and minced, divided

1 scallion, green parts sliced, white parts minced

2 teaspoons (10 ml) rice vinegar

1 teaspoon (5 ml) olive oil

1 teaspoon (5 ml) toasted sesame oil

1 teaspoon (5 ml) usukuchi soy sauce

½ teaspoon (1.5 g) sugar

2 dozen littleneck clams

1 tablespoon (15 ml) neutral oil

A 1-inch piece of ginger, grated

½ cup (120 ml) sake

1. Combine half the garlic, the scallions, rice vinegar, olive oil, sesame oil, soy sauce, and sugar in a small mixing bowl and stir to thoroughly combine; set aside.

2. Rinse the clams under cold running water to remove any grit. Check the clams to make sure none have died; they should all smell like a sea breeze, not low tide. Discard any that smell funny.

3. Heat the oil in a 3-quart saucepan over medium-high heat until shimmering. Add the remaining garlic and the ginger and cook, stirring constantly, until fragrant, 30 seconds. Add the sake and clams, cover, and cook just until all the clams have opened, about 5 minutes. Remove from the heat and let cool slightly.

4. When they are cool enough to handle, remove the clams from the shells; discard the shells. The broth can be discarded; or, if you plan to use it in ramen, strain it through a cheesecloth-lined fine-mesh strainer into a small mixing bowl; discard the solids. Add the clams to the marinade and stir to coat.

5. Cover the clams and refrigerate until ready to use; stir before using. The clam broth can be refrigerated for up to 1 day for use in ramen.

STIR-FRIED CABBAGE, BEAN SPROUTS, AND WOOD EAR MUSHROOMS

YIELD: 2 to 4 servings

TOTAL COOK TIME: 40 minutes

ACTIVE TIME: 15 minutes

4 dried wood ear mushrooms

3 tablespoons (45 ml) lard or neutral oil, divided

1 pound (450 g) Napa cabbage (half a head), cored and chopped into 1- to 1½-inch square pieces

5 garlic cloves, peeled and sliced

2 teaspoons (10 ml) soy sauce

Black pepper to taste

6 ounces mung bean sprouts

Salt to taste

1. Place the mushrooms in a small mixing bowl and cover with boiling water by 1 inch. Let stand until hydrated, about 30 minutes.

2. Remove the mushrooms from the soaking liquid and cut them into thin strips using a knife or scissors. Set aside.

3. Heat half of the lard or oil in a carbon steel wok or 12-inch cast-iron skillet over high heat until smoking. Add half the cabbage and toss to coat it in the fat, then, using a wok spatula or tongs, spread the cabbage out in an even layer in the pan. Cook, without stirring, until the cabbage is charred in spots, about 2 minutes. Toss the cabbage again, spread it out again, and cook without stirring for another 2 minutes, or until the cabbage is soft and charred. Transfer to a plate and set aside.

4. Repeat the charring process with the remaining lard and cabbage. Toss the garlic with the cabbage and cook until the garlic is fragrant, about 30 seconds. Add the sliced mushrooms along with the reserved cabbage and toss to combine. Cook, tossing frequently, for another 3 minutes.

5. Pour in the soy sauce around the edges of the pan and toss the vegetables to distribute it. Season with black pepper.

6. Add the mung bean sprouts and cook, tossing frequently, until they are just starting to wilt, about 3 minutes. Season with salt to taste. Serve immediately.

THICK 45%-HYDRATION NOODLES FOR TEMOMI

COOK TIME: 2 minutes 30 seconds
THICKNESS: If cutting by hand or with fettuccine cutters: 1.3 mm (setting #6 on KitchenAid; #7 on Marcato Atlas pasta machine); if cutting with spaghetti cutters: 1.5 mm (#5 on KitchenAid; #6 on Marcato Atlas)

Ingredients	*Baker's percentages*	*1 serving (grams)*	*6 servings (grams)*
Bread flour	100.0%	85	510
Whole wheat flour	11.8%	10	60
Tapioca starch	5.9%	5	30
Sodium carbonate	1.6%	1.33	8
Salt	1.2%	1	6
Potassium carbonate	0.6%	0.5	3
Water	52.9%	45	270

TO TEMOMI THE NOODLES, SEE PAGE 165.

milk-braised chashu, naga negi
45%-hydration noodles
ajitama
Negi shoyu: pork and clam chintan, saishikomi shoyu tare, seabura

NEGI SHOYU WITH SEABURA

THIS BOWL USES A simple shoyu tare to complement the flavors in the stock, the same roasted pork and dried clam stock used in the Shio Tanmen (page 230), although it would benefit immensely from making a double soup. Because the concentration of gelatin in the stock is relatively high, a 1:1 ratio of dashi to stock will yield a sufficiently thick soup with all the aromatic and flavor benefits of dashi.

Instead of aromatic lard or oil, this calls for seabura, or boiled pork backfat (page 241).

Scallions or, even better, naga negi, pair exceptionally well with pork fat, so this bowl also provides an opportunity to showcase a negi ramen, or ramen topped with an extravagant amount of sliced long onions.

This recipe set also includes a milk-braised chashu, a riff on Marcella Hazan's famous milk-braised pork, which demonstrates that you can use unorthodox braising liquids for chashu with excellent results.

For each bowl of ramen, you need:

2 to 3 slices Milk-Braised Chashu (page 239) or other chashu, chopped

5 scallions or half a naga negi, thinly sliced on a bias

350 ml (1½ cups) Roasted Pork and Dried Clam Stock (page 230) or a combination of stock and dashi (see headnote)

1 serving Thick 45%-Hydration Noodles for Temomi (page 235)

2 tablespoons (30 ml) Saishikomi Shoyu Tare (page 238) or more to taste

2 tablespoons (30 ml) Seabura (page 241) or more to taste

Pinch of white pepper, or to taste

Salt if necessary

1. Combine the chopped chashu and scallions or naga negi in a small mixing bowl and toss to mix.

2. Bring the noodle cooking water to a boil. Bring the soup stock to a simmer.

3. Add the noodles to the cooking water and set the timer for 2 minutes. Bring the stock to a boil.

4. Add the tare, seabura, and white pepper to a warmed serving bowl. Pour in the boiling stock. Taste and add salt if necessary and/or more tare or seabura.

5. Once the noodles are cooked, drain thoroughly and add to the bowl. Using chopsticks, loosen the noodles and fold them once or twice over themselves to distribute the seasonings and form a platform for the topping.

6. Top the ramen with the scallion and chashu mixture. Using a kitchen torch, char the topping until aromatic and slightly singed, about 1 minute. Serve immediately.

SAISHIKOMI SHOYU TARE

YIELD: About 2 cups (480 ml)

SOAKING TIME: 6 to 12 hours

TOTAL COOK TIME: 10 minutes

ACTIVE TIME: 10 minutes

1 cup (240 ml) koikuchi soy sauce

A 2-inch square of kombu (4 g)

1 cup (240 ml) sake

¼ cup (80 ml) mirin

1 cup (240 ml) saishikomi soy sauce

1. Combine the koikuchi and kombu in a sealable container and refrigerate for at least 6 hours, preferably overnight (12 hours).

2. Bring the sake to a boil in a saucepan over medium-high heat and cook until the alcohol has boiled off, the sake has reduced to about 1 tablespoon, and the bubbles forming in the liquid are large, 7 to 8 minutes.

3. Remove the soy sauce mixture from the fridge, give the container a vigorous shake, and add it to the saucepan. Continue to heat the mixture until small bubbles appear on the surface (140° to 150°F/60° to 65°C). Remove the kombu; reserve for another use or discard.

4. Add the mirin and saishikomi shoyu and stir to combine. Transfer the tare to a sealable container and refrigerate until ready to use.

MILK-BRAISED CHASHU

YIELD: About 10 servings

CURING TIME: 5 days

TOTAL COOK TIME: 3 hours

ACTIVE TIME: 30 minutes

*For the cure:**

One 2-pound (900 g) boneless pork shoulder roast

1 tablespoon plus 1 teaspoon (11 g) Diamond Crystal kosher salt

1 tablespoon plus 1 teaspoon (11 g) sugar

For the braise:

2½ cups (360 ml) whole milk

1 cup (240 ml) sake

1 white onion, peeled and quartered

A 2-inch piece of ginger, peeled and sliced into coins

6 garlic cloves, peeled and smashed

1 bay leaf

1. Combine the salt and sugar in a small bowl and mix thoroughly. Place the pork roast on a quarter sheet pan or large cutting board. Sprinkle half the salt and sugar cure evenly over the top of the pork and gently press it into the flesh. Flip the roast over, sprinkle the remaining cure evenly over it, and gently press it into the flesh. Gather up the excess cure and gently press it onto the sides of the pork roast.

2. Transfer the pork roast to a zip-top bag. Scrape any cure remaining on the work surface into the bag. Work most of the air out of the bag and seal it. Refrigerate, turning the pork over every other day, for 5 days.

3. Adjust a rack to the middle position and preheat the oven to 300°F (150°C). Take the roast out of the bag and pat it dry. Tie the roast at 2-inch intervals with kitchen twine to give it an even cylindrical shape.

4. Combine the milk, sake, onion, ginger, garlic, and bay leaf in a 5-quart Dutch oven or other heavy ovenproof pot with a lid and add the pork; the liquid should come at least halfway up the sides of the roast. Bring the contents of the pot to a boil over high heat, cover partially, and place in the oven.

5. Braise the pork for 2½ to 3 hours, taking the pot out of the oven and turning the roast over once every hour, until pork is fully tender throughout and an instant-read thermometer inserted into the center reads between 190° and 195°F (87° and 90°C). Transfer the pork to a plate and let cool to room temperature; discard the braising liquid.

6. Wrap the pork tightly in plastic wrap, place in a zip-top bag, and refrigerate until completely chilled, at least 6 hours, preferably overnight (12 hours).

RECIPE CONTINUES →

---

* 11 g is 1.25% of the weight of a 2-pound (900 g) pork shoulder roast. If you are using a roast that is not exactly 2 pounds, weigh it in grams and use 1.25% of that weight in both salt and sugar for the cure.

MILK-BRAISED CHASHU
continued

7. To serve, cut the chashu into ¼-inch-thick slices and use as a topping as is. Alternatively, warm the slices and brown them before serving: Place them in a single layer on a half sheet pan. If using a broiler, place the pan under the preheated broiler set on high and cook until the chashu is warm and slightly charred, 2 to 3 minutes. If using a kitchen torch, place the sheet pan on a heatproof surface and run the torch over the chashu until warmed through and charred in spots, 1 to 2 minutes. Serve immediately.

SEABURA (BOILED AND CHOPPED PORK BACKFAT)

YIELD: 2 cups (500 ml)

TOTAL COOK TIME: 2 hours 15 minutes

ACTIVE TIME: 15 minutes

2 pounds (900 g) pork backfat, cut into 3-by-2-inch slabs

1. Fill a large pot with water and bring to a boil over high heat. Add the backfat and cook until the pieces feel wobbly and soft when squeezed with tongs, about 2 hours.

2. Place a fine-mesh sieve over a large metal mixing bowl. Working with one piece of backfat at a time, place it in the sieve and, using the back of a ladle, smush the backfat through the sieve. Transfer the sieved backfat to a sealable container and refrigerate.

3. Alternatively, place the backfat on a cutting board and, using a sharp knife, cut each piece into ¼-inch-wide slices, then cut the slices crosswise as thin as you're able. Run your knife in a rocking motion over the backfat to mince it further. Using a bench scraper, transfer the chopped backfat to a sealable container and refrigerate.

stir-fried cabbage,
naga negi
45%-hydration
temomi noodles
ajitama
braised belly chashu
pork and clam chintan,
rendered lard, miso tare

MISO

MISO RAMEN HAS THE distinction of being one of the few styles of ramen for which it's common for the tare to be seared in fat in a wok, after which the soup is made in the wok and poured into a bowl. You can make a miso ramen simply by whisking the tare into boiling stock in a bowl, but using the wok blooms the aromatics' oil-soluble flavors and adds depth of flavor. Try it both ways to see how the flavor is affected by the searing step; since I prefer it, I call for it here.

This tare is made with Chinese fermented black beans, a salty and umami-rich seasoning common in stir-fries, and shoyu tare to provide savory oomph. The shoyu tare functions as a huge dose of liquid salinity, and any extra flavors, like dried fish or mushrooms, are a bonus.

Recommended toppings: Milk-Braised Chashu (page 239), Spicy Soboro (page 249), Super Simple Ajitama (page 284), Stir-Fried Cabbage, Bean Sprouts, and Wood Ear Mushrooms (page 234), Blanched Spinach (page 290), and/or nori.

For each bowl of ramen, you need:

350 ml (1½ cups) Roasted Pork and Dried Clam Stock (page 230)

2 tablespoons rendered lard (see pages 59 and 111–12)

3 scallions, sliced

1 garlic clove, minced

2 tablespoons Miso Tare (page 244)

Salt if needed

Pinch of white pepper, or more to taste

1 serving Thick 45%-Hydration Noodles for Temomi (page 235)

Toppings as desired (see headnote)

1. Bring the noodle cooking water to a boil. Bring the soup stock to a simmer.

2. Meanwhile, heat the lard in a carbon steel wok over high heat until smoking. Add half the scallions and all the garlic, followed by the miso tare, and cook, stirring constantly, until the mixture is aromatic, about 1 minute.

3. Add the stock to the wok, stir, and bring to a boil.

4. Add the noodles to the cooking water and set the timer for 2 minutes.

5. Pour the contents of the wok into a warmed serving bowl. Taste for seasoning and add salt if necessary and white pepper to taste.

6. Once the noodles are cooked, drain thoroughly and add to the bowl. Using chopsticks, loosen the noodles and fold them once or twice over themselves to form a platform for the toppings.

7. Add any desired toppings, then sprinkle the ramen with the remaining scallions. Serve immediately.

MISO TARE

YIELD: About 2 cups (480 ml)

TOTAL COOK TIME: 25 minutes

ACTIVE TIME: 15 minutes

1 cup (240 ml) sake

6 garlic cloves, peeled and grated

A 1-inch piece of ginger, peeled and grated

1 cup (275 g) red miso, divided

½ cup (135 g) white miso

½ cup mirin (120 ml)

½ cup (120 ml) shoyu tare (any will do)

1 tablespoon (14 g) fermented black beans (douchi), chopped

1 tablespoon (9 g) sugar

¼ cup (60 ml) roasted sesame paste

1. Combine the sake, garlic, and ginger in a 3-quart saucepan and bring to a boil over high heat. Cook until the alcohol has boiled off, the sake has reduced to about 1 tablespoon, and the bubbles forming in the liquid are quite large, 7 to 8 minutes.

2. Add half the red miso, the white miso, mirin, shoyu tare, black beans, sugar, and sesame paste and, using a flexible spatula, mix thoroughly. Reduce the heat to medium/medium-low and cook, stirring frequently to prevent scorching, until some of the liquid has evaporated and the mixture takes on a paste-like consistency, about 15 minutes.

3. Stir in the remainder of the red miso. Transfer the tare to a sealable container and refrigerate until ready to use.

TANTANMEN

TANTANMEN IS A DESCENDANT of dan dan noodles, the Sichuan dish in which wheat noodles are dressed with a spicy, tingly preparation of ground meat, zhacai (a pickled tuber), Sichuan peppercorns, and a chili oil made from dried chilies. Dan dan noodles are most commonly served without soup, but there are variations served in soup. Tantanmen can be thought of as one such variation.

For the soboro, or ground meat mixture, rather than Sichuan peppercorns, I choose to use less tingly Sansho peppercorns, which I like for their "green," floral, citrusy aroma. (You can, of course, substitute Sichuan peppercorns.)

I use a straightforward Sichuan-style chili oil. You can use a store-bought chili oil or chili oil–like product such as chili crisp, but it is simple to make and, provided you purchase fresh dried chilies, yours will almost certainly be more flavorful. Any dried chili works; the spiciness level will vary accordingly. Pour the hot oil into the ground chili mixture in an extremely well-ventilated space, preferably outside; you do not want to breathe in the fumes or be trapped in your house waiting for what is essentially tear gas to dissipate. The oil is bolstered by the hongyou doubanjiang, or red oil doubanjiang, which is savory, spicy, and adds a lot of color to the bowl.

The spicy soboro is designed for tantanmen, but it can be used as a topping for any ramen. It would also be delicious served with white rice, pickles, and stir-fried greens. Zhacai is a pickled tuber that is often sold as "preserved Chinese vegetable." Substitute with yacai, which is a pickled mustard green stem, or, in a pinch, takana zuke, which is Japanese pickled mustard greens and stems. All add acidity, funk, and salt to the mix.

Nira, also referred to as Chinese chives or garlic chives, have a unique, garlicky-sweet flavor when cooked. They're essential for this dish, but if you cannot find them, you can substitute an equal amount of scallions; the flavor will be different but still pretty tasty.

Recommended toppings: Super Simple Ajitama (page 284) and Blanched Spinach (page 290).

RECIPE CONTINUES →

TANTANMEN

continued

For each bowl of tantanmen, you need:

350 ml (1½ cups) Roasted Pork and Dried Clam Stock (page 230)

1 serving Thick 45%-Hydration Noodles for Temomi (page 235)

1 tablespoon (15 ml) shoyu tare (any will do), or more to taste

1 tablespoon (15 ml) rendered lard (see pages 59 and 111–12)

2 teaspoons (10 ml) hongyou doubanjiang (red oil doubanjiang) or doubanjiang, or more to taste

2 tablespoons (30 ml) roasted sesame paste

1 teaspoon (5 ml) rice vinegar, or more to taste

¼ cup Spicy Soboro (page 249)

1 tablespoon (15 ml) Chili Oil (page 248)

Other toppings as desired

Sliced scallions or naga negi for serving

1. Bring the noodle cooking water to a boil. Bring the soup stock to a simmer.

2. Add the noodles to the cooking water and set the timer for 2 minutes. Bring the stock to a boil.

3. Combine the tare, lard, doubanjiang, sesame paste, and rice vinegar in a warmed serving bowl. Pour the boiling stock into the bowl. Using a small whisk or chopsticks, stir to distribute the seasonings. Taste for seasoning and add more tare, doubanjiang, and/or vinegar if necessary.

4. Once the noodles are cooked, drain thoroughly and add to the bowl. Using chopsticks, loosen the noodles and fold them once or twice over themselves to distribute the seasonings and form a platform for the toppings.

5. Top the noodles with the spicy soboro. Pour the chili oil around the perimeter of the bowl. Add other toppings, if using, then top everything with sliced scallions or naga negi and serve.

45%-hydration
noodles, naga negi
spicy soboro
pork and clam chintan, shoyu tare,
roasted sesame paste, doubanjiang,
rendered lard, chili oil

CHILI OIL

YIELD: About 2 cups (480 ml)

TOTAL COOK TIME: 45 minutes

ACTIVE TIME: 20 minutes

2 ounces (56 g; about 2 cups packed) dried er jing tiao chilies or other spicy dried chilies

1 tablespoon (3 g) Sichuan peppercorns

3 star anise pods

2 whole cloves

2 cups (480 ml) neutral oil

3 scallions, roughly chopped

2 small shallots, peeled and roughly chopped

3 garlic cloves, peeled and smashed

A 3-inch piece of ginger, sliced

1. Toast the chilies in a 10-inch cast-iron skillet or a carbon steel wok over medium heat, stirring frequently, until aromatic and slightly darker in color, about 3 minutes. Set aside to cool to room temperature.

2. Meanwhile, toast the Sichuan peppercorns, star anise, and cloves in the same pan until very fragrant but not burnt, about 2 minutes. Transfer the spices to a small saucepan.

3. Grind the chilies to a coarse powder using a mortar and pestle or a spice grinder. Transfer the powder to a medium metal bowl set on a quarter sheet pan.

4. Add the oil to the saucepan of spices, along with the scallions, shallots, garlic, and ginger. Heat over medium-high heat until the vegetables start sizzling, about 5 minutes, then cook, stirring occasionally, until the vegetables start to take on color, about 7 minutes. Using a fine-mesh skimmer spoon, remove all the solids from the saucepan and discard; alternatively, strain the oil through a fine-mesh sieve into a medium metal bowl, then return the oil to the saucepan.

5. Heat the oil until it reads 350°F on an instant-read thermometer. Shut off the heat.

6. Place the sheet pan with the bowl of chili powder on a heat-proof surface in a well-ventilated place. Grab a long-handled spoon or some other implement for stirring the oil and take the saucepan of hot oil over to the sheet pan. Keeping your face well away from the bowl of ground chilies, carefully pour the oil into it. Stir the oil with the spoon to expose all the chili powder to the hot oil. Let cool to room temperature, then transfer the chili oil to a sealable container and refrigerate.

SPICY SOBORO

YIELD: 4 to 6 servings as a topping for ramen, 3 to 4 servings as part of a meal

TOTAL COOK TIME: 20 minutes

ACTIVE TIME: 10 minutes

- 1 teaspoon (1.3 g) sansho peppercorns
- ½ teaspoon (1.5 g) white peppercorns
- 3 tablespoons (45 ml) neutral oil
- 1 pound (450 g) ground pork
- 4 garlic cloves, peeled and minced
- A 2-inch piece of ginger, peeled and minced
- 2 tablespoons (30 ml) doubanjiang
- 2 ounces (57 g) zhacai (pickled mustard stem), chopped
- 6 nira (2 ounces; 57 g), thinly sliced
- 4 scallions, thinly sliced
- 2 tablespoons (30 ml) sake
- 2 tablespoons (30 ml) soy sauce
- 1 tablespoon plus 1 teaspoon (20 ml) mirin
- 2 tablespoons (30 ml) toasted sesame oil

1. Toast the sansho and white peppercorns in a carbon steel wok over medium-high heat until fragrant, about 1 minute. Set aside to cool.

2. Grind the peppercorns to a fine powder using a mortar and pestle or a spice grinder.

3. Heat the oil in the wok over high heat until smoking. Add the pork and cook, using a wok spatula to break it up into small pebbles. Then continue to cook until the pork is completely gray, 1 to 2 minutes.

4. Add the garlic, ginger, and ground peppercorns and cook until the mixture is fragrant, about 30 seconds. Add the doubanjiang and cook, stirring constantly, until it is thoroughly distributed and fragrant, about 2 minutes. Add the zhacai, nira, and scallions and cook, stirring constantly, until the vegetables are softened, about 2 minutes.

5. Add the sake and cook, stirring constantly, until the alcohol cooks off and any bits stuck on the bottom of the pan have been released, about 2 minutes.

6. Add the soy sauce and mirin and cook, stirring constantly, until the liquid has mostly evaporated. Turn off the heat.

7. Stir in the sesame oil, transfer the soboro to a storage container, and let cool to room temperature. Refrigerate until ready to use.

crispy fried
scallions
38%-hydration noodles,
charred scallion whites
stir-fried shimeji mushrooms,
naga negi
chickpea broth, vegan shoyu tare, naga negi oil

VEGAN CHICKPEA SHOYU

MAKING A GOOD VEGAN ramen is challenging, since ramen cooks typically rely on a range of animal products: fish sauce, dried fish, meaty bones, and so on, but not out of reach. By using flavorful and aromatic products like tomato paste, smoked chilies, and dried spices, you can turn a bean broth—in this case, chickpea broth—into a soup that is as tasty as one packed with meat and dried fish. To make up for the relative lack of body a bean broth has, use all the suggested accompaniments for the bowl of ramen, particularly the fried onion bits, as they help to give the soup texture.

For more depth of flavor, I add morita chilies and black cardamom to the cooking liquid, which lend it a little smokiness, as well as charred ginger and onion, in the manner of pho, and roasted button mushrooms, for some brown notes from the Maillard reactions. (If you are sensitive to spiciness, I suggest seeding the chili.) I give you the option of making a clear broth or a paitan, by blending cooked chickpeas into the broth. If you choose to use the paitan version, the soup will need slightly more seasoning to account for the pulverized chickpeas.

While any shoyu tare that doesn't contain dried fish elements will be vegan, the tare for this bowl is designed for use in a stock that has no gelatin or inosinic acid. It will work well with nonvegan stocks too.

Just as with meat-based stocks, the broth can be used for other styles of ramen, such as miso (page 243) and tantanmen (page 245). To make the miso ramen vegan, simply use the vegan shoyu tare from this recipe. To make the tantanmen vegan, substitute crumbled tofu or plant-based "meat" for the pork in the soboro.

Instead of trying to mimic chashu, I chose a simple shimeji mushroom stir-fry. Shimeji are diminutive thin mushrooms with a mild flavor, but you can use other mushrooms, such as oyster mushrooms or shiitake, provided you cut them into similar sizes as the shimeji; the cooking time will be slightly longer. When serving this mushroom stir-fry with rice, I like to toss in a handful of daikon radish sprouts right at the end.

Recommended toppings: Blanched Spinach (page 290) and karashi takana (spicy pickled mustard leaves).

RECIPE CONTINUES →

VEGAN CHICKPEA SHOYU

continued

For each bowl of ramen, you need:

350 ml (1½ cups) Chickpea Broth (page 253)

2 tablespoons (30 ml) Vegan Shoyu Tare (page 255) or more to taste

2 tablespoons (30 ml) Naga Negi Oil (page 286)

Pinch of white pepper, or to taste

Salt if needed

1 serving 38%-Hydration Noodles (page 257)

¼ cup Stir-Fried Shimeji Mushrooms (page 256)

2 Charred Scallion Whites (page 291)

Fried Naga Negi (page 286)

Other toppings as desired

Sliced scallions or naga negi for serving

Toasted sesame oil for drizzling

1. Bring the noodle cooking water to a boil. Bring the soup stock to a simmer.

2. Add the noodles to the cooking water and set the timer for 1 minute 15 seconds. Bring the stock to a boil.

3. Add the tare, oil, and white pepper to a warmed serving bowl. Pour in the boiling stock. Taste and add salt or more tare if necessary.

4. Once the noodles are cooked, drain thoroughly and add them to the bowl. Using chopsticks, loosen the noodles and fold them once or twice over themselves to distribute the seasonings and form a platform for the toppings.

5. Add the shimeji mushrooms, charred scallions, and fried naga negi/scallions, along with any other toppings you'd like. Garnish with sliced scallions or naga negi and drizzle with sesame oil. Serve immediately.

CHICKPEA BROTH

YIELD: About 3 quarts (3 liters)

SOAKING TIME: 6 to 12 hours

TOTAL COOK TIME (PRESSURE COOKER): 1 hour 30 minutes, plus time for coming to pressure/depressurizing

TOTAL COOK TIME (STOVETOP): 2 hours 30 minutes

ACTIVE TIME: 45 minutes

31/4 quarts (3.1 liters) water, divided

A 6-inch square of kombu (12 g)

2 dried shiitake mushrooms (6 g)

3 morita chilies (12 g), snipped in half

1 pound (450 g) dried chickpeas

1 tablespoon (9 g) Diamond Crystal kosher salt

2 heads garlic

2 large white onions, peeled and halved

A 6-inch piece of ginger, halved

1 carrot, peeled

3 ribs celery

2 black cardamom pods

1 bay leaf

1 tablespoon (30 ml) tomato paste

2 tablespoons (30 ml) neutral oil

8 ounces (225 g) button mushrooms, quartered

1. **For the dashi:** Combine 3 cups (710 ml) of the water, the kombu, shiitake, and morita chilies in a sealable container and refrigerate for at least 6 hours, preferably overnight (12 hours).

2. Combine the chickpeas and salt in a medium metal mixing bowl and cover with 1 inch of boiling water. Let soak for at least 6 hours.

3. **When ready to make the broth:** Drain the chickpeas and add them to a stockpot or a pressure cooker, along with 1 head of garlic, 1 onion, the carrot, celery, cardamom pods, bay leaf, tomato paste, and 1 tablespoon (15 ml) of the oil. Remove the dashi from the refrigerator, give the container a vigorous shake, and add to the pot. Add the remaining 2½ quarts (2.4 liters) water and heat until small bubbles start to form around the kombu (about 140° to 150°F/60° to 65°C), about 15 minutes. Using tongs or chopsticks, swish the kombu through the mixture several times, then remove it; reserve for another use or discard. Continue heating the liquid until it reaches a bare simmer (about 200°F/93°C); remove the shiitake and discard.

4. **If using a pressure cooker:** Seal the pressure cooker, bring it up to pressure, and cook for 10 minutes. Allow the pressure cooker to depressurize naturally.

5. **If using a stockpot:** Cook until the chickpeas are completely soft, about 2 hours.

6. While the chickpea broth cooks, preheat the broiler on high. Place the halved onion and halved ginger on a quarter sheet pan and cook, turning them once, until they are thoroughly charred, about 10 minutes for the onion and 15 minutes for the ginger. Remove and set aside.

7. Adjust a rack to the middle position and preheat the oven to 400°F (200°C). Place the mushrooms in a mixing bowl, add the remaining tablespoon of oil, and toss to coat the mushrooms. Spread the mushrooms in a single layer on a quarter sheet pan and roast in the oven until the mushrooms release their liquid, about 15 minutes. Take the pan out of the oven. Pour the liquid into a small bowl and reserve it. Return the mushrooms to the oven and cook until thoroughly browned, about 30 minutes. Remove from the oven and set aside.

RECIPE CONTINUES →

CHICKPEA BROTH

continued

8. When the chickpeas are cooked, add the remaining head of garlic, the charred ginger and onion, mushroom liquid, and roasted mushrooms to the pot and bring the liquid back up to a simmer. Cook for 30 minutes.

9. Set a half sheet pan on a wire cooling rack and set a large metal mixing bowl on top of the pan. Using a slotted spoon, remove the black cardamom, bay leaf, and vegetables from the broth, leaving the chickpeas behind. Strain the broth through a fine-mesh sieve into the large bowl; reserve the chickpeas.

10. To make a "paitan" chickpea stock: Transfer 2 cups (280 ml) of the chickpeas and 2 cups (280 ml) of the broth to a countertop blender and blend on high until the chickpeas are completely pulverized, about 3 minutes. Transfer the contents of the blender back to the remaining chickpea broth and stir to combine.

11. Let the broth cool to room temperature, then transfer to sealable containers and refrigerate.

VEGAN SHOYU TARE

YIELD: 2 cups (480 ml)

SOAKING TIME: 6 to 12 hours

TOTAL COOK TIME: 15 minutes

ACTIVE TIME: 10 minutes

- 1⅓ cups (300 ml) koikuchi soy sauce, divided
- 4 dried morita chilies (14 g), snipped in half
- 4 sun-dried tomatoes, snipped in half
- A 2-inch square of kombu (4 g)
- 3 dried shiitake mushrooms (6 g)
- ½ white onion, peeled and grated
- 10 Charred Scallion Whites (page 291)
- 1 garlic clove, minced
- A 1-inch piece of ginger, sliced
- 1 cup (240 ml) sake
- ¼ cup (60 ml) tamari
- 3 tablespoons (45 ml) mirin
- 1 tablespoon plus 1 teaspoon (12 g) Diamond Crystal kosher salt

1. Combine ⅔ cup (180 ml) of the soy sauce, the chilies, sun-dried tomatoes, kombu, and shiitake in a sealable container and refrigerate for at least 6 hours, preferably overnight (12 hours).

2. In a small saucepan, combine the grated onion, scallions, garlic, ginger, and sake, bring to a boil over high heat, and cook until the alcohol has boiled off and the sake has reduced by half, about 5 minutes.

3. Remove the container of dashi from the refrigerator, give it a vigorous shake, and add it to the saucepan. Heat the mixture until small bubbles start to form on the surface (140° to 150°F/60° to 65°C), then remove the kombu; save for another use or discard. Continue heating the mixture until small bubbles form around the edges of the pan (about 185°F/85°C), about 1 minute. Remove the shiitake.

4. Bring the mixture to a boil, then shut off the heat. Transfer the mixture to a countertop blender and blend on high for 1 minute. Pass the mixture through a fine-mesh strainer set over a medium metal bowl, pressing firmly on the solids to extract as much liquid as possible; discard the solids.

5. Add the remaining ⅔ cup (180 ml) soy sauce, tamari, mirin, and salt to the bowl and stir to combine. Let the tare cool to room temperature, then transfer to a sealable container and refrigerate.

STIR-FRIED SHIMEJI MUSHROOMS

YIELD: 4 to 6 servings as a ramen topping, 2 to 3 servings as a side dish

TOTAL COOK TIME: 8 minutes

ACTIVE TIME: 8 minutes

1 teaspoon (5 ml) koikuchi soy sauce

1 teaspoon (5 ml) tamari

1 teaspoon (5 ml) mirin

1 tablespoon (15 ml) neutral oil

7 ounces (200 g) bun shimeji mushrooms, separated into individual mushrooms

½ teaspoon (1.5 g) Diamond Crystal kosher salt

2 garlic cloves, peeled and minced

1 teaspoon (5 ml) rice vinegar

1. Combine the soy sauce, tamari, and mirin in a small ramekin. Set aside.

2. Heat the oil in a carbon steel wok over high heat until smoking. Add the mushrooms and salt and toss to coat the mushrooms in oil. Cook, tossing every minute, for about 5 minutes, until the mushrooms are fully tender and charred in spots.

3. Add the garlic, toss the mushrooms, and cook until the garlic is very fragrant, about 30 seconds. Pour the liquid in the ramekin around the edges of the wok, toss the mushrooms to coat them, and cook until most of the liquid has evaporated, about 20 seconds. Shut off the heat.

4. Add the vinegar and toss and stir the mushrooms. Remove to a plate and set aside until ready to serve.

38%-HYDRATION NOODLES

COOK TIME: 1 minute 30 seconds
THICKNESS: 1 mm (setting #8 on KitchenAid, #7 on Marcato Atlas pasta machine)

Ingredients	*Baker's percentages*	*1 serving (grams)*	*8 servings (grams)*
Bread flour	100.0%	90	720
Tapioca starch	11.1%	10	80
Salt	1.1%	1	8
Sodium carbonate	0.8%	0.75	6
Potassium carbonate	0.3%	0.25	2
Water	42.2%	38	304

thick noodles
assorted toppings
gyofun, naga negi,
radish sprouts
tonkotsu gyokai stock,
shoyu tare, amazu

PORK RIB TONKOTSU GYOKAI TSUKEMEN

FOR REASONS RELATED TO the sheer quantity of pig bones and meat required, and the types of pig bones, making an emulsified tonkotsu stock is impractical for most home cooks (for more on why, see pages 92–93). Here I cheat by using pork ribs to make a concentrated emulsified pork stock in a pressure cooker in about 2 hours, which I then infuse with a relatively large amount of dried fish. The amount of stock this recipe produces is sufficient for 6 servings of tsukemen.

While it is common for tsukemen to feature thick ramen noodles, that is by no means a requirement. For home cooks who make their own noodles, any type can be used for tsukemen, so long as you cook them properly.

Thick noodles will pair better with broth that's very thick, since more of the broth will stick to the noodles as they're lifted, and thick noodles need a lot of seasoning. But if you use a thin chintan to make a broth intended for dipping, a thin noodle will work far better, since the greater surface area of the noodles means more broth will be transferred from the bowl to your mouth.

These noodles are meant for dipping in thick broths like the stock in this recipe. They include tapioca and egg white to create a firm gel when the noodles are shocked and cooled thoroughly. The combination of the thickness of the noodles and the firmness of the starch gel yields a pleasantly chewy noodle. I like to serve about 50 percent more noodles for tsukemen than soup ramen, so while this noodle recipe would make 8 portions of noodle for soup ramen, it only yields 5 portions (about 195g) of thicker noodles for tsukemen.

Ohitashi is a technique in which cooked vegetables are marinated in a seasoned dashi. It works with greens of all kinds, like spinach or, in this case, choy sum. It's also an excellent way to prepare spring greens, like snap peas and asparagus. It imparts a little savory depth to the greens. When served as an accompaniment to tsukemen, the dashi adds just enough oomph for the vegetables to stand up to the aggressively seasoned bites of broth and noodles.

RECIPE CONTINUES →

PORK RIB TONKOTSU GYOKAI TSUKEMEN

continued

For each bowl of tsukemen, you need:

200 ml (¾ cup plus 1 tablespoon plus 1 teaspoon) Pork Rib Paitan Stock (page 261)

1½ servings 40%-Hydration Tapioca/Egg White Noodles (page 263)

2 tablespoons shoyu tare (any will do), or more to taste

2 teaspoons (10 ml) Amazu (page 298)

Pinch of white pepper, or to taste

2 teaspoons Gyofun (page 299)

Sliced scallions or naga negi for serving

Ohitashi Choy Sum (page 262)

Other toppings as desired

Kizami shoga for serving

A wedge of lime for serving

⅔ cup (150 ml) dashi, Niban Dashi (page 269), or chintan stock (optional)

A word of warning about thick emulsified stocks: If you bring them to a boil, they will *boil over*. This is because the emulsion is thick enough that it will trap large bubbles of gas, and it will consequently expand significantly in volume. After many, many spills, I suggest heating this stock over low heat unless you can devote 100 percent of your attention to boiling it.

1. Bring the noodle cooking water to a boil. Bring the soup stock to a simmer over low heat, stirring frequently to prevent scorching.

2. Add the noodles to the cooking water and set a timer for 4 minutes. Fill a large bowl with cold water and place it in the sink.

3. Once the noodles are cooked, drain, shaking off excess water, and dump them into the bowl of cold water. Using tongs or chopsticks, swish the noodles in the water until they're cool enough to handle, about 30 seconds. Turn on the faucet and, with the water running into the bowl, use your hands to swish the noodles through the water until all the surface starches have been rinsed off, about 2 minutes. Pull the noodles out of the water and fold them into a serving bowl.

4. Add the tare, amazu, and white pepper to a warmed serving bowl. Bring the stock to a boil over high heat, stirring constantly, and pour it into the bowl. Taste and add more tare if necessary. Top with the gyofun and scallions or naga negi.

5. Arrange the ohitashi choy sum and any other toppings on a serving plate, along with the kizami shoga and the wedge(s) of lime. Serve.

6. Once the noodles have been eaten, you have the option of adding boiling dashi, niban dashi, or chintan stock to the soup remaining in the bowl, which will temper its salinity and allow you to drink it.

PORK RIB PAITAN STOCK

YIELD: 2 quarts (2 liters)

TOTAL COOK TIME (PRESSURE COOKER): 3 hours, plus time for coming to pressure/depressurizing

TOTAL COOK TIME (STOVETOP): 9 hours

ACTIVE TIME: 30 minutes

A rack of pork ribs (2½ pounds; 1.1 kg), cut into 3-rib sections

2½ quarts (2.4 liters) water

1 large white onion, peeled and diced

1 russet potato, diced

1 head garlic, separated into cloves, peeled, and smashed

A 3-inch piece of ginger, peeled and sliced into coins, divided

2 teaspoons (10 ml) fish sauce

0.5 ounce (15 g) katsuobushi

0.5 ounce (15 g) niboshi

1. Combine the pork, water, onion, potato, garlic, half the ginger, and the fish sauce in a pressure cooker or stockpot; it is fine if bits of ribs are sticking up above the surface of the water.

2. **If using a pressure cooker:** Seal the pressure cooker. If using an electric pressure cooker, bring the pressure to high. If using a stovetop pressure cooker, heat the pressure cooker over medium-high heat until it comes up to pressure, then adjust the heat to medium-low to maintain steady pressure without excessive venting. Cook for 2 hours. Allow the pressure to release naturally, then open the lid of the pressure cooker so the steam escapes away from you; set the lid aside.

3. **If using a stockpot:** Add 2 cups (480 ml) more water to the pot. Bring the water to a boil over medium-high heat. Cover, reduce the heat to medium-low to maintain a steady simmer, and cook for 8 hours, checking the water level periodically and topping it off as needed.

4. Using tongs, remove the pork ribs and discard. Insert an immersion blender into the pot and blend the stock to pulverize the ingredients, about 1 minute.

5. Working in batches, pass the mixture through a fine-mesh sieve into a large metal mixing bowl, pressing firmly on the solids to express as much liquid as possible; discard the solids.

6. Transfer the strained stock to a 3-quart saucepan and bring to a boil over medium-high heat, stirring frequently (any solid material and starches remaining in the stock will sink to the bottom of the pot and may scorch). Reduce the heat to maintain a steady simmer, add the katsuobushi, niboshi, and the remaining ginger, and simmer, stirring occasionally to prevent scorching, for 1 hour.

7. Set a half sheet pan on a wire cooling rack and set a medium metal mixing bowl on top of the sheet pan. Strain the stock through a fine-mesh sieve into the bowl. Let cool to room temperature, then transfer to sealable containers and refrigerate.

OHITASHI CHOY SUM

YIELD: 8 servings

TOTAL COOK TIME: 10 minutes

ACTIVE TIME: 5 minutes

1 bunch choy sum

1½ cups (350 ml) dashi or Niban Dashi (page 269)

1 teaspoon (5 ml) soy sauce, plus more to taste

1 teaspoon (5 ml) mirin

1. Bring a large pot of salted water—about 1 tablespoon (9 g) of salt per quart (0.9 l)—to a boil over high heat. Fill a large bowl with cold water. Add the choy sum to the boiling water and cook until the leaves are bright green and a knife inserted into a stem slides in with little resistance, about 3 minutes. Using tongs, transfer the choy sum to the bowl of cold water and swish it around. Let cool for 5 minutes.

2. Pick up a handful of choy sum at a time, align the stems and leaves, and squeeze out the excess water to form a tight log of greens; transfer to a plate.

3. Combine the dashi, soy sauce, and mirin in a sealable container that can accommodate the cooked choy sum and stir to blend. Taste for seasoning and add more soy sauce as needed.

4. Submerge the choy sum in the liquid. Cover and refrigerate until ready to use.

40%-HYDRATION TAPIOCA/EGG WHITE NOODLES

COOK TIME: 4 minutes
THICKNESS: 2 mm (setting #4 on KitchenAid, #5 on Marcato Atlas pasta machine)

Ingredients	*Baker's percentages*	*1 serving (grams)*	*8 servings (grams)*
Bread flour	100.0%	85	680
Tapioca starch	15.3%	13	104
Egg white powder	2.4%	2	16
Salt	1.2%	1	8
Sodium carbonate	0.9%	0.75	6
Potassium carbonate	0.3%	0.25	2
Water	44.7%	38	304

onsen egg
naga negi
blanched
yu choy
nibo shoyu tare, aromatic
lard, dirty paste, rice vinegar,
thick hand-cut noodles

DIRTY MAZEMEN

MAZEMEN IS SIMPLY RAMEN without soup stock: that's it. The noodles, and the noodle portions, are the same. Every bowl gets the same amount of tare you'd use for soup ramen, and the same amount of fat. And you don't generally need to adjust the seasoning with added sugar or vinegar.

Mazemen have more in common with pasta dishes with uncooked sauces than anything else. The cooked noodles are mixed vigorously with the sauce, and the starches coating the noodles combine with the sauce and fat to create an emulsion, which slicks each noodle strand.

You might think that all that seasoning with no soup at all would yield an incredibly salty dish, and you're right. In part, that's mazemen's defining element: it's superdelicious, but you wouldn't want to eat it all the time.

Since the noodles are so heavily seasoned, it helps to include an egg with a liquid yolk in mazemen. Egg yolks are primarily fat, and that fat, along with giving a luscious richness to the noodles, tempers the salinity. An Onsen Egg (page 285) is perfect for this application, but a raw egg yolk is convenient and equally effective.

The heavy seasoning also means you can top mazemen with blanched vegetables, chashu, soboro—really anything—and once you mix it all up, everything will taste great. "Maze" means "mix" in Japanese, and when you sit down to eat the noodles, you're meant to mix everything in the bowl thoroughly before digging in, which distributes the heavy seasoning among the toppings as well.

Rather than giving you a general formula, here is a recipe for a bowl of "dirty" mazemen, which uses niboshi shoyu tare, "dirty paste," and lard to form the sauce. This bowl doesn't need anything more than a lot of sliced scallions to be superlative. The vinegar here is to take the edge off the dirty paste, but that amount can be added to any bowl of mazemen and it will taste good.

RECIPE CONTINUES →

DIRTY MAZEMEN

continued

For each bowl of mazemen, you need:

2 tablespoons (30 ml) Nibo Tare (page 190)

2 tablespoons (30 ml) lard or Aromatic Lard (page 274)

1 tablespoon (15 ml) Dirty Paste (page 287)

1 teaspoon (5 ml) rice vinegar

Pinch of white pepper, or more to taste

1 serving cooked noodles (any kind)

Other toppings if you like

1 Onsen Egg (page 285) or raw egg yolk

Sliced scallions or naga negi for topping

1. Combine the tare, lard, dirty paste, rice vinegar, and white pepper in a medium metal mixing bowl.

2. Add the cooked noodles and, using tongs or chopsticks, stir them vigorously in the bowl until the sauce emulsifies, about 1 full minute.

3. Scrape the noodles into a warmed serving bowl and fold them over themselves to form a nest for the egg.

4. Arrange any toppings, if using, around the noodles. Nestle the onsen egg or egg yolk on top of the noodles and scatter sliced scallions or naga negi over the top. Serve.

COMPONENT RECIPES

ICHIBAN DASHI

MAKES ABOUT 2 QUARTS (2 LITERS)

SOAKING TIME: 6 to 12 hours

TOTAL COOK TIME: 10 minutes

ACTIVE TIME: 15 minutes

2 quarts (2 liters) water, divided

1 ounce (28 g) kombu (about 2 sheets)

1½ ounces (42 g) katsuobushi

1. Combine 1 quart (1 liter) of the water and the kombu in a sealable container. Cover and refrigerate for at least 6 hours, preferably overnight (12 hours).

2. Transfer the kombu and soaking water to a 3-quart saucepan, add the remaining 1 quart (1 liter) water, and place over medium heat. When the first small bubbles begin to appear on the surface of the liquid (140° to 150°F/60° to 65°C), remove the kombu; reserve for Niban Dashi (below) or another use or discard. Continue heating the liquid until many small bubbles begin to accumulate around the edges of the pan, then shut off the heat, add the katsuobushi, and let steep for 3 minutes.

3. Strain the dashi through a cheesecloth-lined fine-mesh sieve into a large bowl and transfer to a sealable container; reserve the katsuobushi for Niban Dashi or another use or discard.

NIBAN DASHI

MAKES ABOUT 3 CUPS (700 ML)

TOTAL COOK TIME: 15 minutes

ACTIVE TIME: 15 minutes

1 quart (1 liter) water

Kombu reserved from Ichiban Dashi (above)

Katsuobushi reserved from Ichiban Dashi (above)

½ ounce (14 g) katsuobushi

1. Combine the water, kombu, and katsuobushi in a 3-quart saucepan and bring to a boil over high heat. Reduce the heat to medium-low and simmer for 10 minutes.

2. Add the fresh katsuobushi, turn off the heat, and let steep for 3 minutes. Strain the niban dashi through a cheesecloth-lined fine-mesh sieve into a bowl and transfer to a sealable container; discard the solids.

TONKOTSU CHINTAN

YIELD: About 3 quarts (3 liters)

SOAKING TIME: 6 to 12 hours

TOTAL COOK TIME (PRESSURE COOKER): 2 hours 30 minutes, plus time for coming to pressure/depressurizing

TOTAL COOK TIME (STOVETOP): 10 hours 30 minutes

ACTIVE TIME: 15 minutes

A 6-by-3-inch rectangle of kombu (8 g)

3¼ quarts (3 liters) water, divided

Bones, skin, and trim reserved from a butchered and trimmed pork shoulder roast (about 4 pounds/1.8 kg)

A 2-inch piece of ginger, peeled and sliced into coins

6 garlic cloves, peeled

THIS RECIPE IS USEFUL for when you've purchased a pork shoulder and have cut it up to yield roasts and ground meat, leaving you with a pile of skin and trim and a large bone. The stock can be used for ramen in a pinch, and will make a perfectly serviceable bowl, but it can also be used to make stews, soups, sauces . . . any preparation that calls for a flavorful gelatin-rich liquid.

1. **For the dashi:** Combine the kombu and 1 cup (240 ml) of the water in a sealable container and refrigerate for at least 6 hours, preferably overnight (12 hours).

2. **If using a pressure cooker:** Combine the pork bones and skin, ginger, garlic, and the remaining 3 quarts (2.9 liters) water in the pressure cooker. Seal the pressure cooker lid and bring it up to pressure. Cook for 2 hours. Let the pressure cooker depressurize naturally.

3. **If using a stockpot:** Combine the pork bones and skin, ginger, garlic, and the remaining 3 quarts (2.9 liters) water in a large stockpot. Bring to a boil over medium-high heat, then reduce the heat to maintain a bare simmer. Cook for 10 hours, topping off the pot with cold water as necessary to ensure the bones remain fully submerged.

4. Remove the dashi from the refrigerator, give the container a vigorous shake, and pour the dashi into the pot. Let steep for 30 minutes.

5. Set a wire cooling rack on a half sheet pan and set a large metal mixing bowl on top of the pan. Strain the stock through a cheesecloth-lined fine-mesh sieve into the bowl. Let cool to room temperature, about 1 hour, then transfer to sealable containers and refrigerate to chill.

6. Once the chintan has chilled, spoon off the fat that has solidified on top; reserve for another use or discard.

BASIC CHICKEN STOCK

YIELD: 2 quarts (1.9 liters)

TOTAL COOK TIME (PRESSURE COOKER): 3 hours, plus time for coming to pressure/depressurizing

TOTAL COOK TIME (STOVETOP): 6 hours 30 minutes

ACTIVE TIME: 10 minutes

2 chicken carcasses, with their necks and any trimmings from butchering (about 2 pounds; 900 g)

1 head garlic

A 3-inch piece of ginger, peeled and sliced into coins

1 large white onion, peeled and halved

2 quarts (1.9 liters) water

1. **If using a pressure cooker:** Combine all the ingredients in a pressure cooker. Seal the pressure cooker lid and bring it up to pressure. Cook for 2 hours. Allow the pressure to release naturally.

2. **If using a stockpot:** Combine all the ingredients in a large stockpot. Bring to a boil over high heat, then reduce the heat to maintain a bare simmer and cook for 6 hours.

3. Set a wire cooling rack on a half sheet pan and set a large metal mixing bowl on top of the pan. Strain the stock through a cheesecloth-lined fine-mesh sieve into the bowl. Let cool to room temperature, about 1 hour, then transfer to sealable containers and refrigerate to chill.

4. Once the stock has chilled, spoon off the fat that has solidified on top; reserve for another use or discard.

LEFTOVER ROASTED PORK SHOULDER TONKOTSU GYOKAI

YIELD: About 2 quarts (2 liters)

TOTAL COOK TIME (PRESSURE COOKER): 4 hours, plus time for coming to pressure/depressurizing

TOTAL COOK TIME (STOVETOP): 10 hours

ACTIVE TIME: 1 hour

- Leftover bones, meat, and skin from Slow-Roasted Pork Shoulder (page 281)
- 1 white onion, peeled and roughly chopped
- 1 russet potato, peeled and roughly chopped
- 1 head garlic
- A 3-inch piece of ginger, washed and sliced into coins
- 0.35 ounce (10 g) katsuobushi
- 0.35 ounce (10 g) niboshi

BECAUSE THIS RECIPE IS designed to use up the leftovers from a slow-roasted pork shoulder, it's difficult to provide exact quantities. However, that doesn't really matter, as the method is straightforward: the leftovers—skin, bones, flesh, and all—are placed in a pressure cooker or stockpot and covered with water. Garlic, ginger, potato, and onion are added to provide flavor, mask some of the meaty funk, and increase the amount of starch in the liquid (which will help it emulsify), then it's all cooked until the pork basically disintegrates. Then the stock is boiled vigorously until it reduces by about half, after which you steep dried fish in it and then strain it once again. The result is a gelatinous, thick, fishy stock that, seasoned with tare and amazu, is perfect for use in tsukemen.

If you saved the roasted pork shoulder leftovers submerged in water in the refrigerator (and you should have, as that reduces the amount of off flavors that would be produced by oxidation of the cooked meat—see page 98), you can simply transfer that liquid along with the pork to the pot.

1. **If using a pressure cooker:** Combine the pork shoulder leftovers, onion, potato, garlic, and ginger in a pressure cooker and cover with an inch of water, taking care not to exceed the maximum fill line. Seal the pressure cooker and bring up to pressure over medium-high heat, then reduce the heat to medium-low to maintain pressure without excessive venting. Cook for 2 hours. Allow the pressure cooker to depressurize naturally. Open the lid of the pressure cooker so the steam escapes away from you and strain the stock through a fine-mesh sieve set over a large metal mixing bowl.

2. **If using a stockpot:** Combine the pork shoulder leftovers, onion, potato, garlic, and ginger in a large stockpot and cover with several inches of water. Bring to a boil over medium-high heat, then reduce the heat to medium-low and cook, stirring occasionally and topping off the water as needed to keep the pork submerged, for 8 hours. Strain the stock through a fine-mesh sieve set over a large metal mixing bowl.

3. Transfer the stock to a clean stockpot and bring to a boil over high heat. Boil, stirring frequently with a wooden spoon and making sure to reach the bottom of the pot to prevent scorching, until the bubbles rising to the top of the stock begin to look like foam, an indication that the gelatin is quite concentrated, about 30 minutes.

4. Reduce the heat to maintain a simmer and add the katsuobushi and niboshi. Cook, scraping the bottom of the pot frequently, for 30 minutes.

5. Set a wire cooling rack on a half sheet pan and set a large metal mixing bowl on top of the pan. Strain the stock through a fine-mesh sieve into the bowl. Let cool to room temperature, about 1 hour, then transfer to sealable containers and refrigerate until ready to use.

AROMATIC LARD

MAKES 1 CUP (240 ML)

TOTAL COOK TIME: 15 minutes

ACTIVE TIME: 10 minutes

1 cup (240 ml) rendered lard (see pages 59 and 111–12)

1 head garlic, separated into cloves, peeled, smashed, and roughly chopped

A 3-inch piece of ginger, peeled and minced

1. Combine the ingredients in a 2-quart saucepan and heat over medium-high heat, stirring occasionally, until the garlic and ginger begin to sizzle. Then cook, stirring constantly, until the garlic and ginger start to take on color, about 5 minutes.

2. Strain the lard through a fine-mesh strainer set over a small mixing bowl. (The fried garlic and ginger can be reserved for another use or discarded.) Let cool to room temperature, then transfer to a sealable container and refrigerate until ready to use.

RENDERED CHICKEN FAT

YIELD: About 1 cup (240 ml)

TOTAL COOK TIME: 3 hours 15 minutes

Fat and skin from 2 whole chickens, cut into 1-inch-square pieces

1 cup (240 ml) water

YOU CAN RENDER CHICKEN fat from chicken skin on the stovetop or in a microwave oven. Both methods benefit from chopping the skin into smaller bits; 1-inch strips should suffice. The yield can vary wildly depending on the kind of chicken you use. For the effort involved, it's best to save up skin and fat from at least a couple of chickens. (If you want to make cracklings from the skin after rendering the fat, see page 276.)

1. Combine the fat and skin and water in a saucepan and bring to a a boil over high heat. Cook until the skin pieces begin to fry and the water has mostly evaporated, about 12 minutes. Reduce the heat to low; the fat should be at around 210°F (98°C). Cook until most of the fat has been rendered from the skin, about 3 hours.

2. Strain the fat through a fine-mesh sieve set over a medium metal mixing bowl; reserve the solids for another use or discard. Allow the fat to cool slightly, then transfer to a sealable container, let cool to room temperature, and refrigerate.

Microwave Method

TOTAL COOK TIME: 45 minutes

1. Place the fat and skin in a microwave-safe bowl (there's no need to add any water) and microwave at 30% power for 30 minutes.

2. Using a fork, stir the fat and skin; if it has formed a relatively solid mass, flip the mass over. Microwave at 30% power for another 15 minutes. Strain and cool as directed above.

CHICKEN CRACKLINGS

TOTAL COOK TIME: 30 minutes

Skin pieces left from rendering chicken fat (see page 275)

2 teaspoons vegetable oil or chicken fat

Salt to taste

1. Adjust a rack to the middle position and preheat the oven to 400°F (200°C). Grease a half sheet pan lightly with the oil or fat, using your hands to spread it out evenly across the surface. Spread out the chicken skin pieces on the pan and transfer to the oven. Cook until the skin bits are very crispy and golden, about 30 minutes, scraping and turning the pieces over once halfway through.

2. Season the cracklings immediately with salt and transfer to a plate lined with paper towels.

BRAISED BELLY CHASHU

YIELD: 8 to 10 servings

CURING TIME: 5 days

TOTAL COOK TIME: 3 hours

ACTIVE TIME: 15 minutes

*To cure the belly:**

1 tablespoon (9 g) Diamond Crystal kosher salt

1 tablespoon (9 g) sugar

One 2-pound (900 g) skin-off slab of pork belly, cut into 2 equal slabs

To braise the belly:

1½ cups (360 ml) water

1 cup (240 ml) soy sauce

½ cup (120 ml) mirin

½ cup (120 ml) sake

½ large white onion

6 garlic cloves, peeled and smashed

A 2-inch piece of ginger, peeled and sliced into thick coins

4 scallions, cut into 2-inch lengths

8 to 10 black peppercorns

THIS RECIPE ALSO WORKS for a pork shoulder roast, with a few adjustments. Instead of using 1% of the weight of the shoulder as the weight of the salt and sugar in the cure, as for the belly, use 0.75% of its weight. This is because pork belly is much fattier than pork shoulder and so requires more salt to taste sufficiently seasoned. You also need to use a slightly smaller cooking vessel or turn the shoulder more frequently, as a 2-pound (900 g) roast will have a larger diameter than a pork belly roast and will not be as fully submerged in the braising liquid, which will affect the cooking time. Finally, the target cooking temperature for pork shoulder is 190° to 195°F (87° to 90°C), which will yield a better texture.

The braising liquid can be strained, chilled, defatted, and reserved for another use. You can season fried rice or stews with it, or dilute it with water and use to braise other meats, including more chashu. You can also use it as a base liquid for a tare, or even as a tare itself—in which case, it will need more salt.

1. Combine the salt and sugar in a small bowl and mix thoroughly. Place the pork belly on a quarter sheet pan or large cutting board. Sprinkle half the salt/ sugar cure evenly over the top of the pork belly and gently press the cure into it. Flip each slab over, sprinkle the remaining cure evenly over the slabs, and gently press the cure into the belly. Gather up any excess cure on the work surface and gently press it onto the sides of the pork belly.

2. Transfer the pork belly to a zip-top bag. Scrape any excess cure on the work surface into the bag. Work most of the air out of the bag and seal it. Place the bag in the fridge and let cure for 5 days, turning it over every other day.

RECIPE CONTINUES →

* 9 g is 1% of the total weight of a 2-pound pork belly (about 900g). If you are using a pork belly that is more or less than that by ¼ pound (100 g), weigh the belly in grams and use 1% of that weight in both salt and sugar to cure it. For example, if it is 2¼ pounds (1020 g), use 10 g each salt and sugar for the cure.

BRAISED BELLY CHASHU

continued

3. Take the belly slabs out of the bag and pat them dry. Adjust a rack to the middle position and preheat the oven to 300°F (148°C). If you like, you can roll and tie the belly slabs into cylinders (see pages 128–29).

4. Combine the water, soy sauce, mirin, and sake in a 5-quart Dutch oven or other heavy ovenproof pot with a lid and add the pork belly. Add the onion, garlic, ginger, and scallions and bring the contents of the pot to a boil over high heat, then cover partially and place in the oven.

5. Cook for about 3 hours (rolled pork belly will take about 15 minutes longer), taking the pot out of the oven and turning the belly over once every hour, until it is fully tender throughout and an instant-read thermometer inserted into the center reads between 195° and 200°F (90° and 93°C). Transfer the pork belly to a plate and let cool to room temperature.

6. Wrap the belly tightly in plastic wrap, place in a zip-top bag, and refrigerate until completely chilled, at least 6 hours or overnight.

7. To serve: Slice the belly as thick or thin as you like (I like it thin) to add to ramen. Alternatively, you can warm the slices and brown them using a broiler or a kitchen torch: Arrange the slices in a single layer on a half sheet pan. If using a broiler, place the pan under a preheated broiler set on high and cook until the chashu is warm and slightly charred, 2 to 3 minutes. If using a kitchen torch, place the sheet pan on a heatproof surface and run a kitchen torch over the chashu until it is warmed through and charred in spots, 1 to 2 minutes.

ROASTED FENNEL POLLEN BELLY CHASHU

YIELD: 8 to 10 servings

CURING TIME: 5 days

TOTAL COOK TIME: 5 hours

ACTIVE TIME: 15 minutes

*To cure the belly:**

1 tablespoon plus 1 teaspoon (11 g) Diamond Crystal kosher salt

1 tablespoon plus 1 teaspoon (11g) sugar

2 tablespoons (8 g) fennel pollen

One 2-pound (900 g) skin-off slab of pork belly

THIS MAKES A VERY big rolled belly chashu. It looks impressive and tastes great, but its physical dimensions mean it takes a while to cook. Instead of splitting the belly slab in half, you just roll it up from a short side to produce a much larger roll.

Fennel pollen is admittedly pricey, but it has an inimitable flavor. It's often used for porchetta, and the combination of pork and fennel pollen in a bowl of ramen is oddly delicious.

1. Combine the salt, sugar, and fennel pollen in a small bowl and stir with a fork to thoroughly combine.

2. Lay the pork belly on a quarter sheet pan or cutting board. Sprinkle half the cure evenly over the belly and gently press it into the belly. Flip the belly over and sprinkle evenly with the remaining cure, pressing gently on it again. Gather up any cure on the work surface and press it into the sides of the pork belly.

3. Fold the belly in half and place in a zip-top bag. Scrape any remaining cure into the bag as well. Remove as much air as you can and seal the bag.

4. Place the bag in the refrigerator for 5 days, flipping it over every other day to redistribute the cure.

5. Adjust a rack to the middle position and preheat the oven to 300°F (150°C). Roll up the pork belly from a short side to form a large roll and tie tightly using whatever method is easiest for you (see pages 128–29).

6. Set a wire cooling rack on a half sheet pan and place a square of parchment paper just large enough to accommodate the pork belly on top. Set the belly on top of the parchment paper and place the sheet pan in the oven. Cook, turning the belly over every hour, until it is

RECIPE CONTINUES →

* 11 g is 1.25% of the total weight of a 2-pound (900 g) pork belly. If you are using a pork belly that is more or less than that by ¼ pound (100 g), weigh the belly in grams and use 1.25% of that weight in both salt and sugar for the cure.

ROASTED FENNEL POLLEN BELLY CHASHU

continued

browned on the exterior and tender all the way through and an instant-read thermometer inserted in the center reads 195° to 200°F (90° to 93°C), about 5 hours. Remove the pork belly from the oven and let cool to room temperature.

7. Wrap the pork belly tightly in plastic wrap, place in a zip-top plastic bag, seal, and refrigerate until thoroughly chilled, at least 6 hours, preferably overnight (12 hours).

8. To serve, slice the belly into thin rounds to place atop ramen. Alternatively, you can warm the slices and add some browning by using a broiler or a kitchen torch: Place the slices in a single layer on a half sheet pan. If using a broiler, place the pan under the preheated broiler set on high and cook until the chashu is warm and slightly charred, 2 to 3 minutes. If using a kitchen torch, place the sheet pan on a heatproof surface and run a kitchen torch over the chashu until it is warmed through and charred in spots, 1 to 2 minutes.

SLOW-ROASTED PORK SHOULDER

YIELD: 10 to 12 servings

CURING TIME: 8 hours

TOTAL COOK TIME: 9 hours 30 minutes

ACTIVE TIME: 1 hour

One 8- to 10-pound (3.6 to 4.5 kg) whole boneless pork shoulder with skin (minus a pork shoulder roast if you cut one out)

Salt

THIS RECIPE TRANSFORMS A whole pork shoulder into a roast to serve a crowd. You can also use it for a pork shoulder that you've already cut a roast out of for use in ramen (see page 94). Slow-roasted shoulder makes an incredible meal when paired with rice or potatoes, particularly if you serve it along with a chimichurri to give the roasted meat a little character. You can turn any leftovers into a cheaty tonkotsu gyokai (page 272), which is one of the best uses for leftover pork shoulder I've ever devised. If you plan on using the leftovers for making tonkotsu, place them in a large sealable container and cover them with cold water (see page 98); you can refrigerate them for up to 2 days before making the stock.

1. Place the pork shoulder on a half sheet pan. Using a sharp knife, score the skin at 1-inch intervals to form a crosshatch pattern. Sprinkle salt generously over every exposed surface (including the area where you cut out a roast, if you did so). Refrigerate the pork, uncovered, for at least 6 hours, preferably overnight (12 hours).

2. Adjust a rack to the middle position and preheat the oven to 250°F (120°C). Set a wire cooling rack on a half sheet pan and place a square of parchment just large enough to accommodate the pork shoulder on the rack. Place the pork skin side up on the parchment paper and transfer to the oven.

3. Cook the pork until a fork inserted into the flesh down to the bone encounters little resistance and can be twisted easily, about 8 hours. An instant-read thermometer inserted close to but not touching the bone in the thickest part should read 200°F (93°C).

4. Remove the pork from the oven and set aside. Turn the oven up to 500°F (260°C) and let it preheat for at least 30 minutes. Return the pork to the oven and cook, rotating the pan every 5 minutes, until the skin is blistered and puffy all over, about 20 minutes. Remove the pork from the oven and let it rest for at least 30 minutes before slicing and serving.

SOUS-VIDE PORK SHOULDER CHASHU

YIELD: 8 to 10 servings

TOTAL COOK TIME: 21 hours

ACTIVE TIME: 10 minutes

One 2-pound (900 g) boneless pork shoulder roast, tied at 1½-inch intervals with kitchen twine to form an even cylinder

1 garlic clove, peeled and crushed

1½ teaspoons (4.5 g) Diamond Crystal kosher salt

1½ teaspoons (4.5 g) sugar

1 tablespoon (15 ml) soy sauce

2 teaspoons (10 ml) mirin

SOUS VIDE GIVES YOU the ability to cook pork to temperatures that would be impossible with conventional methods. If you cooked a pork shoulder in the oven to 150°F (65°C), it would be incredibly tough, as the collagen it contains would be effectively unchanged. But if you can hold that pork shoulder at 150°F (65°C) for about 20 hours, the collagen will convert to gelatin, and you can carve off attractive slices that are tender and juicy.

This is the only sous-vide recipe in this book that calls for a lengthy cook time. To ensure that the water bath stays at temperature, and that the water level remains high enough for your immersion circulator to continue functioning, you must cover the water bath, either with a lid designed for that purpose or the judicious application of plastic wrap. Covering it prevents the water from evaporating. For more on sous-vide cooking, see page 132.

1. Set up a hot water bath with an immersion circulator and set the temperature to 150°F (65°C).

2. Place the roast on a plate or sheet pan. Stir the salt and sugar together in a small bowl to thoroughly combine, then sprinkle the mixture evenly over the roast on both sides. Place the roast and the garlic in a zip-top bag or vacuum-sealable bag and add the soy sauce and mirin. Seal the bag using the water displacement method or a vacuum sealer.

3. Place the bag in the water bath, making sure that the roast is completely submerged and there's ample room for the water to circulate around it. Cook for 20 hours.

4. Prepare an ice water bath. Transfer the bag of pork to the ice bath and let it cool to room temperature, about 1 hour.

5. Remove the pork from the bag, blot it dry, and refrigerate until ready to slice and serve.

SOUS-VIDE CHICKEN BREAST

YIELD: 8 servings

TOTAL COOK TIME: 2 hours

ACTIVE TIME: 10 minutes

2 boneless chicken breast halves (about 1 pound; 450 g), skin removed

1 tablespoon (3 g) Diamond Crystal kosher salt

Black pepper

SOUS-VIDE WILL PROVIDE YOU with the most consistent and delicious chicken breasts, superior to all but the fussiest poached chicken recipe.

You can also use skin-on breasts rather than the skinless breasts called for in this recipe, and then sear the skin side after the breasts have cooked to give them textural complexity. Alternatively, if you'd like crispyish skin for a chicken breast topping for ramen, you can pan-roast the breasts (see page 217). When I sous-vide chicken breasts for ramen, I usually remove the skin and throw it into the stockpot or reserve it to render its fat (see page 275).

I give a cooking temperature of 150°F (65°C), as that yields firm but juicy chicken breasts. If you cook them at a lower temperature (145°F/62°C) for the same amount of time, the breasts will be juicier and less firm. If you cook them to 160°F (71°C), they will be less juicy and firmer (it will be very easy to use your fingers to tear the meat into large shreds perfect for chicken salads).

1. Set up a hot water bath with an immersion circulator and set the temperature to 150°F (65°C).

2. Sprinkle the salt evenly all over both breast halves. Place in a zip-top bag or vacuum sealable bag and seal using the water displacement method or a vacuum sealer.

3. Place the bag in the hot water bath, making sure the chicken is completely submerged and there is ample room for water to circulate around it. Cook for 2 hours.

4. Prepare an ice water bath. Transfer the bag of chicken breasts to the ice bath and let cool completely.

5. Remove the breasts from the bag, pat dry with a kitchen towel, and refrigerate until ready to use.

6. To serve, remove the breasts from the bag and rub off any gelled juices. Slice into ¼-inch to ½-inch-thick slices to place atop ramen.

SUPER SIMPLE AJITAMA

YIELD: 6 marinated eggs

SOAKING TIME: 12 to 72 hours

TOTAL COOK TIME: 8 minutes

ACTIVE TIME: 15 minutes

1¾ cups (400 ml) water

¼ cup (60 ml) soy sauce

1 tablespoon plus 1 teaspoon (20 ml) mirin

2 teaspoons (10 ml) fish sauce

6 large eggs, straight from the fridge

THIS RECIPE PRODUCES A lightly marinated soft-boiled egg in 12 hours of soaking time. Keep in mind that because the marinating liquid is highly seasoned, the eggs will become saltier the longer they are kept in the liquid. The marination time will also affect the texture of the white and yolk: The white of a soft-cooked egg, which I prefer, will take on a firmer texture the longer it sits in the liquid, and the liquid yolk will become jammier. Soaking the eggs for less than 12 hours will yield relatively bland eggs, while soaking them for longer than 3 days will yield very salty eggs with yolks that are stained a dark yellow bordering on red and totally jammy.

1. Combine the water, soy sauce, mirin, and fish sauce in a sealable 1-quart container and stir to thoroughly blend.

2. Fill a medium mixing bowl with cold water and add 8 ice cubes. Fill a 3-quart saucepan with enough water to fully submerge the eggs and bring to a boil over high heat.

3. Using a slotted spoon or spider strainer, carefully and slowly lower the eggs into boiling water. Using a spoon, stir the eggs slowly but constantly for 1 full minute (this is to center the yolks).

4. Cook the eggs for an additional 6 minutes and 10 seconds. Transfer the eggs to the ice bath, gently stir them for 1 minute, and let cool completely, about 10 minutes. Drain.

5. Carefully peel the eggs and place them in the marinade. Refrigerate for at least 12 hours, and up to 72 hours.

ONSEN EGG

YIELD: As many eggs as you like

TOTAL COOK TIME: 13 minutes

ACTIVE TIME: 2 minutes

Large eggs

A LOW-TEMPERATURE SOFT-BOILED EGG that has a jelly-like set white and a liquid yolk, an onsen egg is particularly good when paired with mazemen, or soupless ramen (page 265). As long as the eggs lie in a single layer in the water bath, you can make as many eggs simultaneously as you want.

1. Set up a hot water bath with an immersion circulator and set the temperature to 167°F (75°C). Fill a large mixing bowl with cold water and ice.

2. Add the eggs to the hot water bath and cook for exactly 13 minutes.

3. Transfer the eggs to the ice bath and gently stir them for 1 minute to cool slightly. Let cool completely, then remove the eggs and pat them dry.

4. To serve, crack an egg as you would a raw egg and plop onto a small plate. Pour off any loose liquid and slide the egg onto your bowl of ramen. Refrigerate if not using immediately.

NAGA NEGI OIL, WITH FRIED NAGA NEGI

YIELD: About 1½ cups (360 ml) oil and about 1 cup fried naga negi

TOTAL COOK TIME: 15 minutes

ACTIVE TIME: 20 minutes

1¾ cups (410 ml) neutral oil

10½ ounces (300 g) naga negi (about 2 large), diced

THIS AROMATIC OIL, which produces crispy fried bits of onion as a by-product, is one of the most efficient ways to use naga negi (Welsh onions). Excellent as toppings for ramen, both the oil and fried onions are also delicious in other preparations, like fried rice or braises.

You can use the same process to make flavored oils (and crispy fried bits) with other alliums, like spring onions, scallions, and shallots.

1. Line a half sheet pan with a layer of paper towels.

2. Heat the oil in a 3-quart saucepan over high heat until it registers 350°F (176°C) on an instant-read thermometer.

3. Carefully add the naga negi a handful at a time to the hot oil, pausing if the oil foams and seems in danger of boiling over, and cook, stirring frequently, until the naga negi take on a golden color and start to brown, about 15 minutes.

4. Strain the oil through a fine-mesh strainer into a medium metal mixing bowl, tapping the strainer to drain the oil thoroughly. Transfer the fried onions to the lined sheet pan and let cool to room temperature, about 30 minutes, then transfer to a sealable container lined with paper towels. Set the oil aside to cool completely, about 1 hour, then transfer to a sealable container and refrigerate.

DIRTY PASTE

YIELD: A little less than ½ cup (120 ml)

ACTIVE TIME: 3 minutes

Fried niboshi and scallions from making Nibo Oil (see Naga Negi Oil, page 286)

6 tablespoons (90 ml) hot Nibo Oil

CREATED BY KEIZO SHIMAMOTO, dirty paste is a quintessential example of how creative cooks can take by-products from different elements of ramen and miraculously transform them. At his Ramen Shack restaurant in Queens, New York, which was open from 2016 to 2019, Shimamoto served some of the best ramen I've ever had in the United States. His Dirty Shoyu stood out for its sheer originality. The broth was incredibly murky, so greenish brown as to seem black, covered with a slick of greenish oil that smelled powerfully of niboshi.

When Shimamoto closed the Ramen Shack, I asked him for the recipe for the paste he used to make his dirty shoyu. This is a version of that recipe, tailored for a home kitchen. And, yes, it's really that simple.

1. Combine the niboshi, scallions, and hot oil in the canister of a high-speed blender. Blend on high until the fish and scallions are completely pulverized, about 3 minutes.

2. Transfer the contents of the blender to a sealable container. Let cool to room temperature, then refrigerate until ready to use.

PORK WONTONS

YIELD: About 70 wontons

TOTAL COOK TIME: 3 to 5 minutes

ACTIVE TIME: 1 to 2 hours (depends on proficiency)

For the filling:

8 ounces (230 g) ground pork

8 scallions (about 60 g), thinly sliced

A 2-inch piece of ginger, peeled and grated

2 garlic cloves, peeled and grated

2 teaspoons (10 ml) koikuchi soy sauce

1 teaspoon (5 ml) mirin

1 teaspoon (3 g) sugar

1 teaspoon (3 g) Diamond Crystal kosher salt, or to taste

About 70 wonton wrappers (store-bought)

Cornstarch for dusting

I LIKE WONTONS MOSTLY for their skins, so I use only a small amount of filling. If you add a lot, you will have to adjust the cooking time significantly upward (and the yield will be lower). If you're in doubt about whether they're cooked or not, split one open, or check the temperature with an instant-read thermometer; it should be above 150°F (65°C). If you want thinner wonton skins, liberally apply starch to the surface of the skins, stack three on top of each other, and run them through progressively thinner settings on a pasta machine to thin them out. (See page 135 for more on wontons.)

If you substitute ground chicken for the pork, I strongly recommend coarsely grinding the chicken (thighs and leg meat) yourself or finely chopping it rather than using store-bought ground chicken.

1. **For the filling:** Combine the ground pork, scallions, ginger, garlic, soy sauce, mirin, sugar, and salt in a medium mixing bowl and, using clean hands, mix thoroughly for about 3 minutes.

2. Place a grape-sized ball of the ground meat mixture on a plate and microwave for 15 seconds on high, or fry in a nonstick pan over medium heat, turning once, until cooked through, about 2 minutes. Taste for seasoning; it should be a little saltier than you'd like.

3. Cover the mixture and refrigerate for at least 6 hours, preferably overnight (12 hours). Alternatively, you can immediately proceed to step 4.

4. Set up your wonton wrapping station: Dust two half sheet pans with a layer of cornstarch. Fill a small ramekin with cold water. Set out the wonton skins and filling. If you refrigerated the filling, using a spoon, give it a good stir.

5. Place a heaping teaspoon of filling in the center of a wonton skin, wet its edges with water, and fold over into a rectangle, or fold it on the diagonal to make a triangle, and press the edges together to seal, making sure to avoid incorporating air pockets. Place the wonton on one of the prepared sheet pans and repeat with the remaining wonton skins and filling.

6. Place the sheet pans in the freezer until the wontons are frozen solid, about 4 hours. Transfer the wontons to zip-top freezer bags and freeze until ready to use.

7. To cook the wontons, bring a large pot of water to a boil over high heat. Add the wontons and cook until the skins are tender and the filling is cooked through, 3 to 5 minutes. Drain.

BLANCHED SPINACH

YIELD: 8 to 10 servings

TOTAL COOK TIME: 1 minute

ACTIVE TIME: 10 minutes

Salt

1 bunch leaf spinach, washed thoroughly and spun or blotted dry

THERE ARE FOUR KEYS to making tasty blanched spinach: Use leaf spinach, not baby spinach; wash it thoroughly to remove all dirt and grit; salt the blanching water; and don't overcook it.

Once it's been blanched, you can use the spinach as is for topping ramen, or you can toss it with a light dressing and use it as a topping or serve it as a side dish for another meal.

1. Bring a large (at least 3-quart) pot of water to a boil over high heat and season the water generously with salt. Fill a large bowl with cold water.

2. Add the spinach to the boiling water and cook just until bright green, about 1 minute; do not overcook. Using tongs, transfer the spinach to the bowl of cold water and swish it around, then let cool completely.

3. Lift about half of the spinach out of the water and, using your hands, squeeze it firmly to make a log; you want to remove as much water as possible. Repeat with the remaining spinach.

4. Wrap the logs tightly in plastic wrap and refrigerate until ready to use.

5. When ready to use, slice the logs of spinach into 2-inch lengths and add to bowls of ramen, or dress as desired.

CHARRED SCALLION WHITES

COOK TIME: Depends on how many scallions you are using

Scallion whites (as many as you like), cut into 2-inch pieces, preferably from thick scallions

Neutral oil for coating the scallions

THE WHITE PARTS OF scallions and naga negi take on a delicious sweet-bitterness when their exterior is charred; and when cut into even 2-inch segments, the charred whites are also pretty. The combination of charred negi and poultry is a classic one in Japanese cuisine, and you'll encounter it at yakitori and soba restaurants. While the charred scallion whites could be added to almost any bowl of ramen, I like them for those with chicken or duck, a nod to yakitori and kamo negi soba (duck and scallion soba).

You can char the whites using a cast-iron skillet, a grill, or a broiler. If you use a cast-iron pan, the process takes only a few minutes. Using a pan also means that the strip of char on the vegetable will be only where it makes contact with the the pan, so it gives it a more attractive look.

The scallion (or naga negi) greens can be reserved to slice up for a ramen topping, or used in stir-fries.

1. Preheat a cast-iron skillet over medium heat until it begins to smoke, about 5 minutes.

2. Pour a little oil into the palm of one hand and rub your hands together, and then pick up the sections of scallion and smear their exteriors with a thin coating of oil.

3. Place the scallion lengths in the hot pan in a single layer (do not overcrowd the pan) and cook, without disturbing them, until lightly charred on the first side, 1 to 2 minutes. Using tongs or chopsticks, flip the scallions over and cook, again without disturbing them, until lightly charred on the second side, 1 to 2 minutes. Remove to a plate.

PIG'S FOOT TERRINE

YIELD: 4 to 6 servings

CHILLING TIME: 12 hours

ACTIVE TIME: 20 minutes

One 1¼-pound (560 g) pig's foot, simmered in stock for about 7 hours or pressure-cooked for 2 hours, picked clean of bones while still warm, and remaining tendons, skin, fat, and connective tissue chopped (a little over 8 ounces/270 g)

3 medium shallots (70 g), peeled and minced

A large handful of parsley including tender stems (25 g), minced

3 garlic cloves (15 g), peeled and minced

Grated zest of 2 lemons (2 g)

1¼ teaspoons (4 g) Diamond Crystal kosher salt, or more to taste

Black pepper to taste

THIS RECIPE TRANSFORMS a pig's foot that has been used to make ramen into golden fried pucks of herby, lip-smacking terrine with a crispy exterior and a meltingly soft interior. A pig's foot is made up mostly of tendon, connective tissue, skin, and fat, with a little meat. Even after it's been simmered for 6 hours or so or pressure-cooked for 2 hours, it still holds on to a lot of gelatin, which means that after it is deboned, pressed, and chilled, it will form a relatively solid log of flavorless pig Jell-O. Adding minced aromatic vegetables, herbs, and salt can make that log tasty, particularly if you coat it in flour, egg wash, and panko and deep-fry it.

I serve the sliced fried pig's foot pucks with a salad with an acidic dressing, like ribbons of carrot, celery, and fennel dressed in a tart, mustardy vinaigrette. They're also a good sandwich filling; you'll want balance with acidic pickles or mustard, or, ideally, both. If you submerge the disks of terrine in noodle soups, they will dissolve completely, adding a hit of salt, herbs, and aromatic freshness, as well as unctuous bits and gelatin.

It is easiest to pick through the pig's foot to remove the bones when it is still warm. Gloves help. Take your time removing the bones—there are a lot of small bones—and if a bone is left in the terrine, it can mess with the way it gels, can get in the way of making neat slices, and will result in an awful surprise while eating.

How finely you chop the pig's foot is up to you. Some people like the texture that larger pieces give the terrine. If you are unsure, chop it finely. Be sure to wash your knife immediately after chopping, as the gelatin will stick to the knife and harden if it dries.

While the recipe below lists specific quantities, the way I usually do this is to weigh the picked meat, then add about half that weight in aromatic vegetables/herbs, and season the mixture using around 1% of its total weight in salt. If approximating, round up, as a pig's foot really needs the seasoning.

1. Combine the picked pig's foot meat, shallots, parsley, garlic, lemon zest, salt, and pepper in a large mixing bowl and, using a clean spoon, mix thoroughly. Taste and adjust the seasoning with salt (it should be very herby/aromatic and well seasoned—like gyoza or wonton filling, it should be saltier than you'd like).

2. Lay out a large sheet of plastic wrap on a work surface, with a short end facing you. Spoon the terrine mixture onto the plastic wrap in the rough shape of a rectangle, leaving about a 2-inch margin along both sides and the bottom.

3. Using the bottom and edges of the plastic wrap to aid you, roll and form the terrine mixture into a loose, thick log. Once the log is entirely encased in plastic, twist the excess plastic at either end of the log to tighten the ends (the log will become more densely packed). Holding the twisted ends firmly with your fingers, roll the log forward on your work surface several times to tighten it further.

4. Place the wrapped log in a loaf pan or similar container and wedge an object, like a can of vegetables, into one end of the pan to keep the ends of the log from unraveling. Refrigerate until completely chilled, at least 12 hours.

5. When ready to serve the terrine, slice into ½-inch-thick coins directly through the plastic wrap (this will help create clean slices). Remove the plastic wrap and use the coins for Fried Pig's Foot Terrine (page 294), or as you like.

FRIED PIG'S FOOT TERRINE

YIELD: 4 to 6 servings

TOTAL COOK TIME: 20 minutes

ACTIVE TIME: 30 minutes

THESE ARE BEST SERVED immediately after they are fried, either with a zesty salad or stuffed into a sandwich with pickled vegetables and mayo.

1 Pig's Foot Terrine (page 292), sliced into ½-inch-thick coins

½ cup all-purpose flour

2 large eggs

1 cup panko breadcrumbs

Pinch of salt

Neutral oil for deep-frying

Flaky salt, such as Maldon, for sprinkling

1. Set up a breading station by putting the flour, eggs, and breadcrumbs in three separate shallow bowls or quarter sheet pans. Add a pinch of salt to the eggs and beat with a fork until homogenous.

2. Place a wire cooling rack on a half sheet pan. Heat 2 inches of oil in a wok or a Dutch oven until an instant-read thermometer inserted into the oil registers 350°F (176°C).

3. Dip one coin of terrine into the flour and turn to coat, gently shake off any excess flour, transfer to the beaten eggs, and turn to coat. Lift the coin out of the beaten eggs, allowing the excess egg to drip back into the bowl, transfer to the panko, and turn to coat completely, gently pressing on the breadcrumbs on each side so they adhere.

4. Drop the breaded coin into the hot oil and fry until the exterior is golden, 2 to 3 minutes, flipping once. Remove to the prepared rack and immediately season with a light sprinkling of flaky salt. Repeat with the remaining coins. Serve immediately.

DUCK HEARTS AND LIVERS ON TOAST

YIELD: 1 serving

TOTAL COOK TIME: 7 minutes

ACTIVE TIME: 7 minutes

1 duck heart, trimmed of excess fat

1 duck liver, trimmed of any obvious veiny membranous stuff

Salt

¼ cup all-purpose flour

2 tablespoons butter

Sherry vinegar or red wine vinegar

A slice of good bread (from a bakery), toasted

Flaky salt

Hot sauce (optional)

HERE'S A DELICIOUS, QUICK way to serve duck (or chicken!) hearts and livers that will not be used for ramen. Don't waste them!

1. Season the heart and liver (or liver pieces, if you've cut it up) aggressively with salt on all sides, then dredge in the flour. Tap off excess flour.

2. Melt the butter in a small skillet over medium-high heat. When the butter stops foaming, add the heart and liver and cook, flipping them several times, until well browned on the exterior and cooked through, about 5 minutes total.

3. Add a glug or two of vinegar to the pan, enough to form a small amount of "sauce" in the bottom of the pan, and toss the heart and liver in this sauce until coated.

4. Transfer the contents of the pan, duck and sauce and all, to the slice of toast. Sprinkle with flaky salt and with hot sauce, if desired.

WAKAME

YIELD: 2 to 3 servings

SOAKING TIME: 10 to 15 minutes

3 tablespoons dried wakame or a handful of salt-packed wakame

WAKAME IS A THIN, soft, edible kelp often used in soups and salads. You can find it in both dried and fresh/cured form, where the leaves are packed in salt. Dried wakame can simply be reconstituted in hot water; salt-packed wakame should be rinsed thoroughly to remove exterior salt, then chopped. I then soak it in hot water, much as you would reconstitute dried seaweed, to remove more of the salt.

Dried wakame expands *a lot* when reconstituted; you don't need more than a tablespoon or so for two people.

1. **If using dried wakame:** Place the wakame in a medium mixing bowl, fill the bowl with cold water, and let sit until the wakame is completely reconstituted, about 15 minutes. Drain thoroughly.

2. **If using salt-packed wakame:** Rinse away all the salt on the wakame under running water. Place in a medium mixing bowl, cover with cold water, and let sit for 10 minutes. Drain thoroughly.

3. Transfer the wakame to a sealable container and refrigerate until ready to use.

BRAISED FISH (SAKANA NO NITSUKE)

YIELD: 4 servings as part of a larger meal with rice

TOTAL COOK TIME: 20 minutes

ACTIVE TIME: 5 minutes

¾ cup (180 ml) water

½ cup (120 ml) sake

¼ cup (60 ml) koikuchi soy sauce

2 tablespoons (30 ml) mirin

2 teaspoons (6 g) sugar

A ½-inch piece of ginger, peeled and sliced into thin coins

4 skin-on fillets black sea bass or red snapper (1 pound; 450 g)

Several strips of julienned fresh ginger or pickled kizami ginger for garnish

IF YOU PURCHASED TWO whole fish to make Fresh Fish Shoyu (page 205) and don't want to use the fillets in the ways described there, you can braise the fillets and eat them with rice. You can also plunk a braised fillet on top of a bowl of ramen.

Braising is a common cooking technique for fish in Japan, particularly for white-fleshed fish. The fish is often served cold, although I prefer to eat it warm. Since the fish is left submerged in the flavorful braising liquid for storing, it keeps well in the fridge for several days.

This is the way my aunt Nori makes nitsuke. According to her, she makes "very good nitsuke." I agree!

1. Combine all the ingredients except the fish and garnish in a skillet that can comfortably hold the fish in a single layer and stir to dissolve the sugar.

2. Nestle the fish skin side down in the liquid; the fillets should be completely covered by the liquid. Make a parchment paper "lid" that fits within the pan and place a small pot lid on it so the fish is gently weighed down to keep it submerged. (Alternatively, you can use a Japanese drop lid, or otoshi buta.)

3. Bring the liquid to a simmer over high heat, then turn the heat to medium-low to maintain a bare simmer and cook until the fish is completely cooked through, about 15 minutes. Let the fish cool to room temperature in the liquid, then cover and refrigerate until ready to serve.

4. To serve, rewarm the fish in its liquid, then arrange skin side up on serving plates, with several spoonfuls of the braising liquid spooned over the top. Garnish with the ginger strips or pickled ginger.

AMAZU

YIELD: 1 cup (240 ml)

TOTAL COOK TIME: 3 minutes

ACTIVE TIME: 2 minutes

1 cup (240 ml) rice vinegar

½ cup (100 g) packed light brown sugar

THE WORD "AMAZU" MEANS "sweetened vinegar," and in classical Japanese cuisine, you can simply add sugar to vinegar, which is what I use to adjust the seasoning for ramen dishes. There are alternative versions of amazu where the mixture is diluted with water or dashi, or steeped with kombu to add umami depth.

While rice vinegar is traditional, other vinegars can be sweetened and used to great effect. I deviate from the traditional recipe by using light brown sugar, which adds complexity.

1. Combine the vinegar and brown sugar in a small saucepan and bring to a simmer over medium-high heat. Shut off the heat and stir to fully dissolve the sugar.

2. Let the vinegar cool to room temperature, then transfer to a sealable container.

GYOFUN

YIELD: Scant ½ cup

ACTIVE TIME: 5 minutes

1 ounce (30 g) katsuobushi

0.35 ounce (10 g) niboshi

GYOFUN IS POWDERED DRIED fish, used as a topping or seasoning/souring agent for soup. This gyofun is a mix of katsuobushi and niboshi, toasted briefly to dehydrate the dried fish and make it easier to grind. If you like, add a small amount of dried chilies before grinding for a spicy gyofun.

1. Toast the katsuobushi and niboshi in a cast-iron skillet or a carbon steel wok over medium heat, stirring frequently, until fragrant and slightly dried, about 4 minutes. Transfer to a bowl and let cool to room temperature.

2. Working in batches, transfer the toasted fish to a spice grinder and grind to a fine powder. Transfer to a sealable container and refrigerate until ready to use.

GYOZA

YIELD: About 50 dumplings

TOTAL COOK TIME: 15 minutes

ACTIVE TIME: 1 hour (if you can fold dumplings fast)

For the filling:

1 pound (450 g) Napa cabbage, cored and finely chopped

1 tablespoon plus ¼ teaspoon (10 g) Diamond Crystal kosher salt

8 ounces (230 g) ground pork

1 small carrot (70 g), peeled and grated

1 bunch scallions (5 to 9; 80g), finely sliced

A 2-inch piece of ginger (30 g), peeled and grated

6 garlic cloves, peeled and minced

1 tablespoon (15 ml) soy sauce

2 teaspoons (10 ml) mirin

1 teaspoon (5 ml) fish sauce

1 teaspoon (5 ml) toasted sesame oil

Large pinch of white pepper

½ teaspoon (1.5 g) sugar

For folding and cooking the gyoza:

Cornstarch or potato starch (optional)

About 50 gyoza skins

1 tablespoon (15 ml) neutral oil

GYOZA, PANFRIED JAPANESE PORK and vegetable dumplings, are often served at ramen restaurants as a side dish, and many ramen restaurants and chains, like Korakkuen, are (justifiably) famous for the quality of their gyoza. Just as ramen derives from Chinese cuisine, gyoza are a Japanese riff on jiao zi (and, in fact, they are denoted using identical Chinese characters). The main distinction between jiao zi and gyoza is that the latter usually have thinner skins.

This gyoza recipe approximates the gyoza served at Korakkuen. The vegetables account for more than half of the filling, yielding an interior that is soft, aromatic, and juicy, with no trace of rubberiness. While gyoza need a dipping sauce, it's customary for diners to make their own using soy sauce, rice vinegar, and sesame oil dispensers that are placed on the table; here I offer my preferred ratio of soy sauce to rice vinegar and sesame oil.

The filling benefits from a rest in the fridge after mixing; the salt in the filling works its way with proteins in the meat, making the mixture stickier, and the flavors of the different vegetables have a chance to mingle and redistribute; let the filling rest for at least 6 hours, preferably overnight, or up to 48 hours. While Japanese gyoza skins are preferable because of their thinness, Chinese dumpling skins will work. Once you open the package, wrap the skins in a damp cloth or paper towel so they don't dry out while you fold the dumplings.

To cook gyoza, it's helpful to use a nonstick pan. The next best option is a preheated well-seasoned cast-iron pan with an ample amount of oil. Give yourself room in the pan so you can maneuver a spatula underneath the gyoza, should you need to pry the skins loose.

One of the main problems I've encountered with cooking gyoza is that the tops of the dumpling skins fail to fully gelatinize. To address this, I spray the tops with a spritzer of water. If you don't have a spritzer, pour the water you're adding to the pan over the tops of the gyoza to wet them thoroughly before they steam.

1. For the filling: Combine the cabbage and salt in a medium mixing bowl and, using clean hands, toss and compress the cabbage to distribute the salt, about 1 minute. Let the cabbage macerate for at least 30 minutes, and up to 1 hour.

2. Using clean hands, squeeze the excess water from the cabbage and place it in a large mixing bowl. Add the remaining ingredients and mix thoroughly, about 2 minutes.

3. Place a teaspoon of gyoza filling on a microwave-safe plate and microwave on high for 15 seconds. Alternatively, heat a small nonstick skillet over medium heat until hot, add a teaspoon of the filling, and cook, turning once, for 1 to 2 minutes, until cooked through. Taste the filling for seasoning; it should be quite savory and delicious and a hair saltier than you think it should be, to account for the wrappers being bland. If necessary, to adjust the seasoning, add more salt ½ teaspoon at a time, mixing thoroughly, and repeat the tasting process. Although you can proceed directly to wrapping the gyoza, the filling can be refrigerated, covered tightly with plastic wrap or in a sealable container, for up to 48 hours. If you refrigerate the filling, stir it thoroughly before making the gyoza.

4. Set up a gyoza-wrapping station: Dust two half sheet pans with a fine coating of cornstach or potato starch; alternatively, line the pans with parchment paper. Set out a small ramekin or bowl of cold water, the filling, and the gyoza wrappers; keep the wrappers covered as you work to prevent them from drying out.

5. Place 2 to 3 teaspoons of the filling in the center of one wrapper. Dip the tip of a finger into the water and lightly wet the edges of the wrapper. Fold the wrapper in half, creating a half-moon shape. Starting from opposite ends of the half-moon shape, press the edges together to seal, taking care to squeeze out any excess air that could be trapped in the dumpling. Place the gyoza on one of the prepared sheet pans, pressing down slightly on it to create a flat base. Repeat with the remaining filling and wrappers.

6. The gyoza can be cooked immediately or frozen. To freeze, place the sheet pans in the freezer until the gyoza are frozen solid, about 3 hours, then transfer to zip-top freezer bags; cook them directly from frozen.

RECIPE CONTINUES →

GYOZA
continued

7. Heat the oil in a medium or large nonstick (see headnote) skillet (depending on how many gyoza you are cooking) over medium-high heat. Arrange the gyoza snugly in the pan, flat bottoms down, so that they are in contact with one another, either in straight rows or in a circular arrangement, and cook until the bottoms are lightly browned, about 2 minutes. Spray the tops of the gyoza thoroughly with water (or moisten them with the water when you add it to the pan). Add 3 tablespoons (45 ml) cold water into the pan, cover, reduce the heat to medium-low, and cook until the filling is cooked through and the skins are soft, about 8 minutes. Remove the lid, increase the heat to medium, and cook until all the water has evaporated, the gyoza are sizzling, and the bottoms are browned, about 5 minutes.

8. Using a spatula, remove the gyoza to a plate, bottom side up. Alternatively, shake the pan to loosen the gyoza (use a spatula if you need it), invert a large serving plate over the top of the pan, and, using an oven mitt, place one hand firmly on the bottom of the plate and, with the other hand, quickly turn the pan over. Serve with the dipping sauce alongside.

Gyoza Dipping Sauce

YIELD: 1 serving

1 tablespoon (15ml) soy sauce

2 teaspoons (10ml) rice vinegar

1 teaspoon (5ml) toasted sesame oil

Combine soy sauce, vinegar, and sesame oil in a small ramekin and stir. Serve.

BAKED BAKING SODA (SODIUM CARBONATE)

YIELD: Makes about 7 ounces (200 g)

TOTAL COOK TIME: 15 minutes

ACTIVE TIME: 5 minutes

1 cup (267 g) baking soda

SODIUM CARBONATE IS ONE of two alkaline salts often used to make alkaline noodles. While you can purchase sodium carbonate, you can easily heat baking soda (sodium bicarbonate) in a pan on your stovetop to make sodium carbonate.

This recipe will make about 200 grams (7 ounces) of sodium carbonate, which is two-thirds of the starting weight of the baking soda. You can use any amount of baking soda and the process is identical; simply heat until it loses at least one-third of its weight and maintains a steady weight to ensure that the chemical reaction is complete. Another indication that the reaction is complete is that you'll no longer see fissures of gas forming in the powder. (If you use baking soda from a box that's been open for some time, the loss in weight will be bigger, as it will have absorbed moisture from the surrounding environment.)

Do not touch the powder with your bare hands—sodium carbonate is a caustic substance. If you do get it on your hands (or bare skin), flush thoroughly with running water.

Sodium carbonate can be stored in a sealable container at room temperature indefinitely.

1. Weigh an 8-inch sauté pan on a scale, note the weight, and tare the scale.

2. Add the baking soda to the pan and place over medium-high heat. Cook, swirling the pan occasionally to distribute the heat evenly, until you can no longer see gas escaping from the powder and the weight of the baked baking soda is two-thirds of the starting weight (178 g), about 15 minutes.

3. Let cool to room temperature, then transfer to a sealable container.

MAKE-AHEAD AND STORAGE INSTRUCTIONS

HERE ARE SOME GENERAL GUIDELINES for storing cooked food. "Up to 6 months" translates as "It will probably keep indefinitely but I feel uncomfortable saying, 'Sure, eat those noodles that have been frozen for 2 years.'"

Dashi and Stock

Ichiban dashi is best used immediately. However, it can be refrigerated in a sealable container for up to a week. The same is true of niban dashi.

Defatted stocks made from beef and other animals or vegetables can be refrigerated in a sealable container for up to a week or frozen for up to 6 months.

Stock made from fresh fish is best used within a few days of preparation (although it can be refrigerated or frozen like other stocks, the flavor will be inferior).

Noodles

Noodles made entirely from wheat flour can be refrigerated in a sealed zip-top bag for up to 1 week, but they are at their peak for 2 to 3 days after they've been made, and their quality will decline thereafter.

Noodles made with wheat flour and added starch can be refrigerated in a sealed zip-top bag for up to a week and a half. They are at their peak 3 to 4 days after they've been made.

Noodles made with wheat flour, added starch, and egg white powder can be refrigerated in a sealed zip-top bag for up to 2 weeks. They are at their peak 5 to 7 days after they've been made.

All noodles can be frozen in zip-top freezer bags with as much air expressed out of the bags as possible. Noodles will keep frozen for up to 6 months with little to no diminishment in quality; in some cases, frozen noodles take on a better texture. For best results, noodles should be frozen as close to their peak as possible. Frozen noodles should be cooked straight from frozen, but slight adjustments to the cooking time may be necessary, depending on your preferences.

Fats

Properly rendered fat can be refrigerated in a sealable container for at least a month. For longer storage times, I suggest freezing the fat; it will keep for up to 6 months.

Rendered fat that has been flavored with aromatics will also keep for a very long time, but because of the possibility that a not-insignificant amount of water may be present in the fat, it's best to use it quickly. Aromatic fats can be refrigerated in a sealable container for up to 2 weeks or frozen for up to 6 months; the same is true for seabura.

Tare/Pastes/Vinegars/Powders

Tare with no added fat can be refrigerated in a sealable container for up to 6 months, with only slight changes in flavor and aroma. Tare with added fat can be refrigerated in a sealable container for up to 1 month.

Tare can also be frozen for up to 6 months.

Nibo paste can be refrigerated in a sealable container for up to 2 months, provided the paste is entirely covered with oil.

Amazu can be refrigerated indefinitely in a sealable container.

Gyofun powder can be refrigerated in a sealable container indefinitely, although it will start to decline in quality within a week.

Toppings

Depending on how various meat toppings have been cooked, they will keep in the refrigerator for anywhere from 3 to 10 days. (See the discussion of "Warmed-Over Flavor" on page 131.) When storing meat toppings, wrap them tightly in plastic wrap or submerge them in liquid to prevent oxidation reactions that would contribute to off flavors.

Meats that have been cured and then braised can be refrigerated in a sealable container for up to 10 days, provided they are fully submerged in the braising liquid. Wrapped in plastic and placed in a zip-top bag, they can be frozen for up to 3 months.

Cured and roasted meats can be refrigerated, well wrapped in plastic, for up to 1 week. Wrapped in plastic and placed in a zip-top bag, they can be frozen for up to 2 months.

I suggest slicing braised or roasted meats into serving portions before freezing, so you won't need to defrost a whole roast when all you want is three slices of chashu. Stack as many slices you want per portion (I usually do two) on top of one another to limit the amount of exposed surface area, then wrap tightly in plastic wrap. Multiple portions can be placed in a single zip-top freezer bag after wrapping; express as much air as possible before sealing the bag.

Uncured meat toppings, like pan-roasted chicken breasts or thighs, are best eaten within 1 to 2 days.

Ground meat preparations, like meatballs, are best consumed immediately, although they can be refrigerated in a sealable container, covered with their poaching liquid, for several days in the refrigerator.

Dumplings (wontons/gyoza) are best frozen for storage. Freeze in a single layer, taking care not to let their skins overlap, on a sheet pan lined with parchment paper or dusted with cornstarch. Once they're frozen solid, transfer to a zip-top freezer bag, express as much air as possible, and seal the bag. Dumplings can be frozen for up to 6 months.

Cooked vegetables can be refrigerated in a sealable container for up to a week, but they are best used within 3 days.

Raw vegetable toppings, like sliced scallions, should be used immediately.

Charred scallion whites are best used immediately, but they can be refrigerated in a sealable container for 2 days.

Reconstituted wakame is best used immediately, but it can be refrigerated in a sealable container for 2 days.

Fried scallions or long onions and chicken or duck cracklings can be refrigerated in paper towel-lined sealable containers for up to 1 week.

Marinated soft-boiled eggs can be refrigerated in a sealable container, submerged in their marinade, for up to 1 week, but they will become progressively saltier and will take on a very cured texture. Removed from their marinade, they can be refrigerated in a sealable container for up to 2 days.

Onsen eggs in their shell can be refrigerated for up to 3 days.

REFERENCES

BOOKS IN ENGLISH

Cwiertka, Katarzyna J., *Modern Japanese Cuisine: Food, Power, and National Identity* (Reaktion Books, 2006).

The Japanese Culinary Academy, *Flavor and Seasonings: Dashi, Umami, and Fermented Foods* (Shuhari Initiative, 2017).

——, *Introduction to Japanese Cuisine: Nature, History, and Culture* (Shuhari Initiative, 2017).

——, *Mukoita 1: Cutting Techniques: Fish* (Shuhari Initiative, 2017).

——, *Mukoita 2: Cutting Technique: Seafood, Poultry, and Vegetables* (Shuhari Initiative, 2017).

Kushner, Barak, *Slurp! A Social and Culinary History of Ramen—Japan's Favorite Noodle Soup* (Global Oriental, 2012).

LaFrieda, Pat, and Carolyn Carreño, *Meat: Everything You Need to Know* (Atria Books, 2014).

McGee, Harold, *On Food and Cooking: The Science and Lore of the Kitchen* (Collier Books, 1988).

Orkin, Ivan, *Ivan Ramen: Love, Obsession, and Recipes from Tokyo's Most Unlikely Noodle Joint* (Ten Speed Press, 2013).

Pépin, Jacques, *The Art of Cooking*, volume 1 (Knopf, 1987).

Singleton, Nancy Hachisu, *Food Artisans of Japan: Recipes and Stories* (Hardie Grant, 2019).

——, *Japan: The Cookbook* (Phaidon, 2018).

Tsuji, Shizuo, *Japanese Cooking: A Simple Art* (Kodansha USA, 2011).

BOOKS IN JAPANESE

黒木直人, 上質を追求した旬のラーメン 「饗 くろ㐂」の春夏秋冬 (旭屋出版, 2018).

Nishio, Ryoichi, *The Complete Ramen* (Asahiya, 2021).

ONLINE RESOURCES

Satinover, Mike, *The Ramen Lord Book of Ramen* (2020), https://docs.google.com/document/d/1qLPoLxek3WLQJDtU6i3300_OnNioqeYXi7vESrtNvjQ/edit.

Yung, Elvin, "Basic Menma," https://elvinyung.notion.site/Basic-Menma-3851a7eba9284ccb8216749684f4d5c8.

% HYDRATION NOODLES

COOK TIME:
THICKNESS:

Ingredients	*Baker's percentages*	*1 serving (grams)*	*6 servings (grams)*

% HYDRATION NOODLES

COOK TIME:
THICKNESS:

Ingredients	*Baker's percentages*	*1 serving (grams)*	*6 servings (grams)*

% HYDRATION NOODLES

COOK TIME:
THICKNESS:

Ingredients	*Baker's percentages*	*1 serving (grams)*	*6 servings (grams)*

% HYDRATION NOODLES

COOK TIME:
THICKNESS:

Ingredients	*Baker's percentages*	*1 serving (grams)*	*6 servings (grams)*

ACKNOWLEDGMENTS

This book owes its existence to a long list of family, friends, and colleagues, without whom the odd idea of writing a tome about making ramen at home—dreamed up during the eternity of the coronavirus pandemic—would have never come alive.

MY ETERNAL THANKS TO:
Catherine, my sine qua non, for everything. Aya, for being my brutally honest taste-tester. My brother, Ryu, for believing in my ramen, and me. And, of course, my father, Anthony, for the dubious gift of writerly ambition, and my mother, Ritsu, who would have been equal parts mystified and proud at this expression of Japanese identity—I wish you could've seen it, if only for the laughs. And my aunt, Nori, for helping me translate from Japanese the very first ramen recipe I made at home in 2006.

My agent, Rica Allanic, who seeded the idea of writing a cookbook, and who supported this project from the very beginning. My editor, Melanie Tortoroli, for buying the damn thing, but also for "getting it," as they say; also to Lauren Abbate, Annabel Brazaitis, Allison Chi, Susan Sanfrey, Huneeya Siddiqui, and all the staff at W. W. Norton & Company for their work in making it a reality. And Judith Sutton, for copyediting and saving me more times than I can count from embarrassing myself.

THE PHOTOGRAPHY TEAM:
Linda Xiao, for the beautiful photos; her assistant, Christina Zang; Emma Rowe, for the stellar food styling; Maeve Sheridan, for all the beautiful bowls and props, and her assistant, Ashleigh Sarbone, for all the help on set.

THE FEXY-ERA SERIOUS EATS CREW:
Niki Achitoff-Gray, for taking a huge risk and hiring me at Serious Eats, and giving me opportunity after opportunity to grow, including encouraging me to produce ramen recipes, which is where this all started. Ed Levine, for his support both during and after my tenure at Serious Eats. Also, Paul Cline, Vicky Wasik, Daniel Gritzer, Ariel Kanter, Vivian Kong, Tim Aikens, Roxy Lane, Joel Russo, Maggie Lee, Grace Chen, Elazar Sontag—I apologize for making many bad bowls of ramen in the test kitchen all the time, and I'm sorry for charging 50 cents for rice.

SOME OF THE SERIOUS EATS CREW I'D LIKE TO SINGLE OUT:
J. Kenji López-Alt, for inspiration, encouragement, and a lot of help over the years. Stella Parks and Sohla El-Wayly, for commiserating with me about the absurdity of writing a cookbook. Sasha Marx, for teaching me how to develop and write recipes. Kristina Bornholtz, who is single-handedly responsible for my Instagram following. ("No one wants to see you butcher fish badly, just post overhead shots of noodle soup," she said, and she was right!)

THE RAMEN-MAKING COMMUNITY:
From the best community on the internet, I'd like to thank two people in particular. The first is Keizo Shimamoto, the best ramen chef in the country, for showing that truly great ramen can be made in the United States, and for his advice and encouragement over the years. (And for graciously allowing me to publish his Dirty Paste recipe!) The other is Mike Satinover, who "unlocked" making noodles at home for me. If ramen-making is having a renaissance right now, I firmly believe it's because of these two men.

FINALLY, THANK YOU TO THE RECIPE CROSS-TESTERS, ALL VOLUNTEERS:
The recipes in this book would be markedly inferior were it not for your generosity. Alia Ali; Richelle Amponin; Giordano Bermudez; Robin Blythe, PhD; Leonardo M. Borges; Chesa Cox; David Conison; Lauren Ann Davies; Alex Green; Matthew Guinn; Lindsie Hartman; Lucien Hickman; Jack Holden; Alberto Kujan; Laurance Lee; Al Lochiatto; Kyle Manfredo; Alex Manisier; Kyle Maxey; @nofishgiven; Connor O'Brien; John Oh; Octavio Peña; Deesha Singh; Will Yarinsky; and Quyen Weng.

INDEX

Note: Page references in *italics* indicate photographs.

T

U

Prop stylists: Maeve Sheridan and Ashleigh Sarbone
Food stylist: Emma Rowe

Printed in Malaysia
First Edition

Manufacturing by Imago
Book design by Toni Tajima Design
Art director: Allison Chi
Production manager: Lauren Abbate

ISBN: 978-1-324-02099-8

W. W. Norton & Company, Inc.
500 Fifth Avenue, New York, NY 10110
www.wwnorton.com

W. W. Norton & Company Ltd.
15 Carlisle Street, London W1D 3BS

1 2 3 4 5 6 7 8 9 0